Be Fruitful and Multiply

BE FRUITFUL AND MULTIPLY

HOW FERTILITY AND INNOVATION HAVE CHANGED HUMANKIND AND THE EARTH

• • •

DONALD WORSTER

Yale
UNIVERSITY PRESS
New Haven and London

Published with assistance from the foundation established in memory of James Wesley Cooper of the Class of 1865, Yale College, and from the Kingsley Trust Association Publication Fund established by the Scroll and Key Society of Yale College.

Copyright © 2025 by Donald Worster.
All rights reserved.
This book may not be reproduced, in whole or in part, including illustrations, in any form (beyond that copying permitted by Sections 107 and 108 of the U.S. Copyright Law and except by reviewers for the public press), without written permission from the publishers.

Yale University Press books may be purchased in quantity for educational, business, or promotional use. For information, please e-mail sales.press@yale.edu (U.S. office) or sales@yaleup.co.uk (U.K. office).

Set in Adobe Garamond type by Newgen.
Printed in the United States of America.

ISBN 978-0-300-27897-2 (hardcover)
Library of Congress Control Number: 2025931743
A catalogue record for this book is available from the British Library.

Authorized Representative in the EU: Easy Access System Europe, Mustamäe tee 50, 10621 Tallinn, Estonia, gpsr.requests@easproject.com

10 9 8 7 6 5 4 3 2 1

For Shen Hou

Contents

	Preface	ix
	Introduction: Human Nature	1
1	Out of Africa	15
2	The Agrarian Whip	41
3	Humpty Dumpty and the Fate of Power	74
4	The Discovery of Second Earth	113
5	Dreams of Infinite Wealth	142
6	The Good Muck	164
7	The Empty Cradle of Hope	209
8	Building the Ecological Civilization	238
	Epilogue: This Fertile Earth	260
	Notes	267
	Acknowledgments	297
	Index	299

Preface

Historians, if they would only admit it, always write autobiography. They see the past through their personal nature and experience. This historian and this book are no exception; the book reflects events, opportunities, and some major changes in perception that the author has gone through over a period of eight decades. How could it be otherwise?

Here, briefly, is what has shaped and reshaped me from the beginning, all of which I wish to acknowledge with gratitude. I was born to working-class parents who settled briefly as Dust Bowl refugees in a California railroad town. Later, after growing up in a Protestant-dominated community on the Kansas prairie, I was fortunate to be awarded a college scholarship funded by a local car dealer—all praise to such unseen benefactors and low-tuition public universities! My postgraduate studies came during the unsettled 1960s, when I joined fellow students at Yale University to protest war and injustice. My writing still reflects those student days, although, being what one of my professors called an underprivileged outsider, I was critical of dogmas on the left as well as the right. That has not changed.

How, after such varied experiences, could I ever have remained fixed in mind about anything? Ralph Waldo Emerson called fear of inconsistency the "hobgoblin of little minds." I have never been afraid of seeming inconsistent. However, I see this book's shift to a planetary history not as an inconsistency but as broadly consistent with my evolution as a scholar, although it reflects some big changes that have gone on in me as well as the world.

PREFACE

China appears in this book again and again, though it is not a book about Chinese history. In 1998 I traveled for the first time to that country and have been back many times since. Nobody ever told me that China could be so beautiful and thrilling. I was especially enchanted by a voyage down the Yangzi from the city of Chongqing through the famed Three Gorges, passing a construction project that would, a short time later, be dedicated as the largest hydroelectric dam in the world. That massive intrusion into the environment both impressed and appalled me. Over the next two decades I repeatedly went back to China, holding for almost ten years the position of visiting professor of world history at Renmin University. To its faculty, administrators, and students—above all, to my colleague and translator Professor Shen Hou to whom this book is dedicated—I owe more than I can say. Through my travels across China, I have known not only professors and students but also farmers, janitors, agency heads, publishers, drivers, and museum guides. I have walked along some of the world's most densely populated streets, and they impressed me with the significance of human fertility. Through those journeys, I have come to love both China and its people, although I wish them more moderate numbers.

My years abroad have helped me understand that all people share a common nature, even though we have biological and cultural differences that should be respected. This book is based on that perspective. It is a very large perspective, nothing less than a planetary history. From the title the reader knows this is not a conventional monograph, with every fact or source exhaustively noted, but rather an essay on the nature of history. As Emerson also said, "it is not instruction, but provocation, that I can receive from another soul." Consider this book then as a provocation and speculation, based not only on my reading but also on my childhood, formal education, and travels to all the continents.

Historians who hunker down in one place, who remain committed to only one question or theme their entire career, have my deep respect. But for me it has seemed necessary to explore what lies beyond my own country,

PREFACE

to go beyond disciplinary boundaries, and to try to integrate culture and nature. Now in my eighties, I can say that through a broadening of perspective I have become surprisingly more hopeful than ever before. Here in these pages, I offer neither gloom nor despair, but rather the hope that comes from an experienced, science-based, and transnational perspective.

A note about this book's title: it comes from the King James Bible (Genesis 1:28), which reads in full, "And God blessed them, and God said unto them, Be fruitful, and multiply, and replenish the earth, and subdue it: and have dominion over the fish of the sea, and over the fowl of the air, and over every living thing that moveth upon the earth." The words are a divine command to all males and females, but nowadays they should be taken as outmoded, unreasonable, and tribalistic; certainly, this book does not endorse them. Quite the contrary, my purpose is to subvert those words. I believe that such subversion is possible, that in fact it is already happening, and that therefore we have reason to hope.

Be Fruitful and Multiply

INTRODUCTION
Human Nature

In the *Book of Mencius,* one finds this simple rhyme: *shi se xing ye.* It can be translated as "food and sex are the basis of human desire and human nature."[1] The words suggest that humans, for all their differences, share some inborn appetites, instincts, tendencies, and inclinations and that those commonalities are intrinsic to our being. Particularly, we feel an urge to eat and most of us feel also an urge to reproduce ourselves, two core desires that are closely intertwined. They are not fixed, absolute, or universal. However, they are strong and compelling because they determine whether the species survives and flourishes or not, and that desire unites and drives us humans as it does all other species. All forms of life want to eat, find mates, and promote their kind.

The rhyme came not from Mencius, but from a fellow philosopher named Gaozi. Although Mencius did not refute its message, he did caution his followers against oversimplifying human nature. We are not born, he emphasized, exactly like one another. Our wants and needs vary from person to person, for we are not clones. We differ because we reproduce sexually, leading to an almost unlimited set of outcomes: big feet or little feet, round eyes or almond eyes, light or dark skin, low or high sexual hunger.

Mencius added that there are more than two desires that make up our nature. But he did not dispute Gaozi's main point: strong desires exist within us that we share with one another and with the rest of nature. That conclusion, though it did not explain why such commonalities exist, is in danger today among many intellectuals and philosophers. The Harvard psychologist Steve Pinker has criticized their "blank slate" theory, which holds that people are made purely and simply by their cultural environment, that we do not follow any inherited tendencies, and therefore we can be radically improved or redeemed.

One word of caution: Gaozi's belief in an inborn human nature did not make him a conservative rather than a liberal. He also does not say that humans cannot change, reform, or become better than they are. Take Mencius, for example: he was a moral reformer who nonetheless accepted the observation that human nature is real and powerful. Although he was not a modern scientist, he was a wise, shrewd, and balanced observer. At heart he was a moralist, but even his moralizing he regarded as part of human nature.

Our species, Mencius argued, is naturally inclined to nurture a few "moral sprouts" within us that interact with our desires for food and sex. Springing up like cabbages in a garden, those sprouts help determine who we are. We should cultivate our sprouts, Mencius said, but never "pull" too hard on them—that is, never turn them into absolute, overpowering imperatives. We should see those sprouts as part of an inborn system of checks and balances and respect their moral influence, as we respect all nature.[2]

A search for balance lay at the core of Confucianism, and Mencius was a founding figure of that social philosophy. He followed a pragmatic view of right and wrong, not insisting on his own special brilliance or on tribalistic tendencies that would fracture our humanity. Confucianists were not opposed to seeking good food and good sex, though they thought there was more to life than those desires or the survival of the species.

Neither did Mencius maintain that some people are superior to others because they are born with greater intelligence, charisma, or physical attractiveness. If our inner appetites are natural and good, if they can be found across the human spectrum, then why should some people assume they are born superior to others? We should not assume that any philosopher or other kind of authority, no matter how elevated in thought he or she might be, is somehow better than anyone else.

Jump ahead twenty-some centuries to the eighteenth and nineteenth centuries in the West. A similar egalitarian, pragmatic, balanced understanding of the relation between our inner nature and our moral ideas was expressed by the British naturalist Charles Darwin (1809–1882). It was Darwin who founded the scientific study of humans as part of the study of nature. Out of his observations have come evolutionary psychology, neuroscience, ethnology, and other formal inquiries to objectify and explain human behavior as it has evolved over time.

Darwin followed the scientific method of hypothesizing and then seeking proof to establish or disprove the reality of those powerful desires within us. He wrote about the desire for food in his classic work *On the Origin of Species* (1859), and he took up the equally strong desire for sexual reproduction in *The Descent of Man* (1871). Like Gaozi, he singled out those two urges as central to human nature, but like Mencius he understood that humans have evolved a moral capacity too, which functions as a check on our appetites to prevent their undermining our survival.

Thus, ancient Chinese philosophy and modern Darwinian science agree that all people have a nature within us just as there is a nature without. The two desires and the two natures interact constantly. Each has been a powerful determinant of behavior throughout history, and each deserves to be acknowledged, respected, and understood.[3]

Standing in contrast to both Mencius and Darwin have been many leaders of organized religion, who for a long time and in various parts of the world have tried to shape and reshape ordinary people to fit some transcendental moral standard. They have insisted that while the two natures may indeed exist, we should be highly critical of our human nature and struggle against its influence. We have been put on earth, many religion-based believers have argued, to rise above our appetites, not merely check them. Reformers on the left and right have come out of that anti-nature tradition. At times their reproving views have even led them to deny altogether any inner nature, to withdraw into a cold, stark, monkish cell and to mortify the flesh. They are the would-be authoritarians of the world. And if a desire for freedom is also one of those inborn desires, as one can argue, then our nature may at times cause humans to rise in rebellion against our oppressors. From this desire for personal freedom comes the self-determination that manifests itself across the planet.

On the other hand, if our inner self is really and truly bad, as some maintain, then so also must the nature of the earth be bad. So too must be our communities, institutions, politics, even our musical pleasures—all of them must be deplorable, justifying the improvers. If we pursue that attitude, then we will end up with teachers who, unlike Mencius, are ideologues rather than tolerant thinkers. They will write books peopled by self-righteous heroes who go out to subdue nature and tame the wild, outside and inside us. Their disapproving spirit, though it promises hope, can lead to a deep pessimism about our own nature and that of our fellow humans, about the earth, humanity, and those two natures that have given birth to us. It can teach us to wage war against the "evil" we see within or around us and to denounce all the natures we find.

Darwin was not altogether free of such dogmatism. In the fall of 1838, not long after he returned from a round-the-world scientific voyage during which he got his first important glimpse of evolution at work, he turned to the popular discussion of the history of humans and the earth going on in Victorian England. Among the books he picked up was Reverend Thomas Malthus's *Essay on Population,* first published in 1798. Though seeming objective, Malthus was in fact a radical idealist, a firm Christian preaching the subduing of the flesh. He opposed the Poor Laws of Great Britain for undermining people's self-discipline, and in opposition to social idealists he preached individual responsibility. Why did Darwin read him? Here is his own recollection: "I happened to read for amusement Malthus on *Population,* and being well prepared to appreciate the struggle for existence which everywhere goes on from long-continued observance of the habits of animals and plants, it at once struck me that under these circumstances favorable variations would tend to be preserved and unfavorable ones to be destroyed. The result of this would be the formation of new species."[4] Malthus did not teach Darwin the scientific theory of the evolution of species. Rather, he reinforced Darwin's own readiness to believe in a fierce struggle for existence going on everywhere with no end.

We can dismiss Darwin's explanation that he read Malthus for "amusement." Reverend Malthus, who had been an ordained minister in the Anglican church before turning to economics and demography, was perhaps the least amusing writer in modern British history, for he believed that a very large number of humans are doomed by God to a miserable existence. They should not, he argued, blame their fate on the Creator, for their suffering was due to their inner reproductive desires overshooting the earth's fixed capacity to produce food. They were improvident and irresponsible, and they deserved their fate.

Malthus was not a scientific thinker. His negative view of human nature was based on Judeo-Christian theology. Humans, he assumed, always tended to produce more babies than any habitat could support. For a religious man like Malthus, that tendency had to come from God, who he believed had designed humans and their environment, creating a world that was deliberately imbalanced. He had instilled in his children a tendency to produce too many offspring, yet he had limited the land's capacity to produce as much food as their offspring needed. Such was the famous formula that Malthus offered, and it made no sense scientifically. The only reason Malthus offered for such a devilish imbalance was that God wanted humans to work hard and achieve more. God had acted on certain ideas swimming in his head, even if they did not result in a happy world for his children. Theologically, it was quite a dilemma. Scientifically, it was poppycock—not merely the fixed "arithmetic" rate of agricultural change that supposedly God had decreed in the production of food but also the "geometric" rate of reproduction that he had designed for humans. There were no data, observations, or science behind those conflicting rates—there was only creed.

Darwin generally did not follow such dogmatism in explaining the origins of humans or nature. Although he agreed that the poor were losers in the struggle for existence, he did not believe that a Great Designer had made some individuals into losers and others into winners. Elsewhere in his research, Darwin the scientist argued that we live in an undesigned world that has only natural limits, like the qualities of soil or the quantity of rainfall, but there are no iron laws governing outcomes among the land or people.

Malthus and Darwin represented quite different approaches to nature and human nature. The first was a dogmatic idealist, the other an open-minded scientist.[5] Yet it was Darwin who, in a moment of weakness, succumbed to Malthusian dogma. Ever since that encounter, Malthusians and Neo-Malthusians have ignored the science of evolution, even though their famous "laws" have been disproved again and again.

Why did Darwin agree so quickly that there must be a fixed imbalance between fertility and resources as Malthus posited? "A force like a hundred thousand wedges," Darwin wrote, is constantly "trying [to] force every adapted structure into the gaps in the economy of nature, or rather forming gaps by thrusting out weaker ones."[6] That was a culture-based interpretation of the dismal, ruthless side of nature, popular among Victorians living in a ruthless economic culture. Darwin had done no research that supported it. It certainly did not describe the evolution of the planet.

During his travels along the South American coasts and among the Galápagos Islands, Darwin kept finding new species and trying to understand how they came to be where they were, but he brought home no data on their natural desires, their rates of fertility, or their fixed limits of food supply. What then prepared him to accept Malthus's views? Nothing other than his own cultural background—his social upbringing, his newspaper reading, his impressions of class warfare in Victorian England.

Darwin in general maintained that human nature was not designed by God. It came from laws of matter over which humans had only limited control. Why would those laws include a permanent imbalance between human desire and food supply? Evolution taught, after all, that human appetites evolve and adapt to their material circumstances. And so does the production of food. There are no fixed arithmetic or geometric laws governing people or the land.

A female Pacific oyster releases once a year some one million to two hundred million eggs—so large and yet so variable a fertility in response to other species preying on her eggs. In a sense, her egg laying is an evolved, flexible response to external pressures. Similarly, a queen leaf-cutter ant in Brazil gives birth to 150 million daughters during her life span of about a dozen years. She has so many babies because so many die quickly. High fertility became necessary to assure species survival. Why, in contrast, does a human produce only three hundred to four hundred eggs in her lifetime and yet also produce on average merely two, five, or ten babies, and why does that number vary over time? Is that a case of waste in nature? Of poor design? The evolutionist's answer must be that reproduction is always evolving. No species is so fixed in nature that it stubbornly, regularly overproduces, for that would be a fatal drain on the birth mother. Like an eye or a set of horns or a prehensile tail, sex and reproduction adapt to their environment. That is how matter works—following laws but not laws that have been rigged by a higher intelligence.

Tellingly, the statistical data Darwin gathered on human reproduction mainly came from Malthus, including observations Malthus took from Benjamin Franklin on the North American colonies. There, Franklin wrote, "the population has been found to double itself" under the unusual circumstances of a new land, new soils, new forests. Human fertility, in other words, adjusted up or down in response to environmental conditions. Humans, like all species, reproduce more progeny when their circumstances permit; they reproduce less when circumstances do not. Malthus turned that responsiveness to environment into a decree of God, warning that one day Americans might cover every square yard of the earth with four inhabitants—a day that was never going to happen.

How could the science-minded Darwin have been so misled by Malthus's theologically based reasoning? How could anyone say what is "normal" in nature without collecting facts or making deductions from them? How could a scientific theory of evolution start from the assumption that human nature is rigidly determined by God, when in fact it varies according to natural conditions?

Only once in *Descent of Man* did Darwin note that reproduction might be a more complicated behavior than Malthus supposed, but here again the scientist drew on popular culture and again he erred. We might, he wrote, "expect that civilized men, who in one sense are highly domesticated, would be more prolific than wild men. It is also probable that the increased fertility of civilized nations would become, as with our domestic animals, an inherited character."[7] Quite the opposite was true. The birthrate in civilized Britain was falling, not rising. It was falling so fast that "civilized" people began worrying that they were being outbred by "wild men." Darwin did not foresee that women and men in every country might one day be able to control their reproduction through science-based contraception, as they were beginning to do in Victorian England. When that possibility appeared, the innate desire for reproduction would change, becoming radically detached from the desire for sex, and the average fertility rate among women would plunge downward.

We must allow that Darwin, like other scientists, was not always a scrupulous observer. Sometimes his musings were clouded by the ideas and prejudices of his day. After all, he was not only a naturalist but also an upper-class gentleman, schooled in the attitudes, values, and sensibilities of his culture. He departed from the common mores when he married his first cousin, Emma Wedgewood. The two produced no fewer than ten children, far higher than average. Ten was not unheard of among the gentry of the day, but it was more than what was standard among less affluent people. Three of Darwin's children, it should be added, died before the age of eleven.[8]

Malthus the clergyman led Darwin to assume that what was a temporary historical pattern of intense fertility was the unchanging law of nature. Without judging him harshly for that lapse, we should acknowledge that not all of Darwin's ideas, observations, and conclusions were carefully verified or deserve to be called science. The superiority of science to religion lies in its appeal to fact checking and verification, which allows us to build on, challenge, reject, or accept old mythologies or tales as true or false. Darwin on this occasion did not follow scientific evidence or logic.[9]

Evolutionary theory is based on the hypothesis that all behaviors and instincts, all ideologies and tales, exist as adaptation or maladaptation. They change to fit conditions. Thus, they lie beyond the moral categories of good and evil. Human nature does not show such categories, and our reproductive behavior has not been determined once and for all by a Creator, or for that matter by a former clergyman like Malthus.

Cultural beliefs, like instincts and desires, should be understood as dependent on nature, products of some past interaction between inner and outer nature. Darwin followed that principle when he asked why religion existed in the first place, how a belief in God or other divinity might have been useful for survival under certain circumstances. Like one's legs and arms, eyes and sex organs, one's moral or religious sensibilities and cultural values evolve over time. They are in that way instrumental, like the horns of a rhinoceros or feathers on a bird, but they cannot offer any transcendental truth to guide our behavior. They are not mandates from heaven or absolute principles, nor are they material outcomes of evolution. They are secondary, proximate effects of evolution, not fundamental causes.

The closest Darwin ever came to a less Victorian, more thoroughly scientific approach to sex, reproduction, and fertility were the insights he offered in *Descent of Man,* but there he backed away from any claims to verified truth. That book's subject was the nature of human nature. His method was not laboratory practice but the comparative analysis of species and cultures, which he realized was not always reliable. At the same time, his guiding rule was to reject the notion that "man is the work of a separate act of creation." He started from the hypothesis that we humans have evolved from "a hairy tailed quadruped, probably arboreal in its habits." Go back far enough, he argued, and we will find that even the invertebrates, perhaps even the slime mold, have left their mark on our nature.

"Sexual Selection," the explicit theme of the second part of *The Descent of Man,* deals with how sexual partners choose each other as mates. Here Darwin hypothesized that the male-female gender divides among humans and other animals emerged through natural selection, but he stopped short of reducing gender to a set of fixed behaviors, confining himself to what he called the "secondary" sexual characteristics, such as the evolution of bird songs and dances, gaudy plumage and body sizes.

How could Darwin have done better? He could not have known about such material forces as hormones (such as progesterone, testosterone) for they were not discovered until the early twentieth century when scientists learned of their production in the endocrine glands and began to understand their role as internal regulators of the body. After that, scientists would trace those chemical compounds to internal communication methods among multicellular organisms dating back some five hundred million years ago. Darwin did not know why such chemical substances existed or how they ruled the human brain and body. Consequently, a better understanding of male-female sexuality lay beyond his day.[10]

He also could not have known in his lifetime that organisms, according to animal behaviorists, begin to feel a diminished desire to reproduce as their numbers increase, a change called "density dependence."[11] Fertility adjusts to the density of our own kind, a completely instinctive and natural form of adaptation. With *Homo sapiens,* however, density dependence gets more complicated, as culture and genetics interact with one another. The drive to reproduce, strong though it is, has like all things naturally evolved within a context, and as the context changes so does human nature. As the earth has filled up with people, density has influenced our desires, sexual appetites, and feelings about babies.

Humans, like all organisms, interact with the rest of nature but also with cultures, values, and institutions that go through their own evolution. So complex is the interaction that we may never know completely why this or that behavior occurs or find any grand purpose or plan in the whole. That is why we cannot follow even Gaozi's little rhyme, *shi se xing ye*. The study of human nature is still in its beginnings, and there is no quick way to define or explain what that nature is. We are even now standing before a partially closed door that science is slowly opening, and until that door is as wide open as the doorway to knowledge of the rest of nature, we must proceed tentatively, carefully, and with a great deal of speculation.

Darwin wrote when such topics were considered immoral merely because they compared humans to other animals. Since then, science has succeeded in cracking apart what had been a monopoly exercised by the Church over the nature within us. Once a scientific approach to all nature became possible, scientists began to ask what Darwin himself could not: How do natural drives like sex evolve in the first place, and how do they change? What behaviors do humans share with other species? If checks and balances have not been designed by God, what explains them? We still lack complete answers to those questions, but someday we will be able to know and apply a much better knowledge to the study of human history.

Meanwhile, we should try to understand why evolution has been such a persistent force over billions of years and why it has been so successful in turning this earth into the living planet we see today—a rambunctious community of living organisms all possessing impressive survival skills. It starts with sex. Sexual desire has not been the rotten apple that Eve induced Adam to eat, leading straight to the fall of humanity. Above all, we should understand that evolution is a deeper kind of history and that its outcomes are not all that bad.

A post-Darwin explanation for human sexuality starts with the core material deoxyribonucleic acid (DNA), the molecule that carries genetic information for the development and functioning of an organism. In human reproduction, like that of many other species, there are two sets of DNA involved because two are better than one in generating variability. Mixing genes leads to more diversity in one's children, and diversification improves survival chances. Because of sexual reproduction, over generations organisms become better at enduring floods and droughts, parasitic or microbial invasions, fiery asteroids, volcanic eruptions, or climate change. That is why, about two billion years ago, reproduction came to be the norm among organisms. Since then, it has added immensely to the variety and success of life and the several ways of producing and living. DNA has made sex and reproduction the biggest show on earth.

Without the breakthrough to more than one form of sexuality, would we have acquired so much knowledge of this earth or become so adept at survival? Would we have aspired, dreamed, invented, explored, and experimented as we have? The material nature of sex belongs at the heart of human nature and of history.[12]

Those are the major themes and arguments of this book. The following chapters are organized by the two great transformations that occurred in the human past, both of which were driven, I will argue, by the intertwined drives of human sexuality and hunger for food. It has been human gonads, along with hormone-producing glands, brains, and bellies, that have made those great transformations happen, far more than moral values or big ideas. This book does not, therefore, focus on the usual chronicle of great civilizations shaping the past, the old saga of human cleverness. On the contrary, it will—while keeping humans central to the story—suggest that we are not the godlike center of everything.

The first big transformation in the age of humans was the shift from foraging, a way of life or mode of production we have shared with many species. Foraging gave way to the agrarian mode, which we shared with relatively few other species, mainly the ants and termites. Then came a second transformation, from the agrarian to the industrial capitalist mode of production, which made humans unique among species. Those two transformations are familiar subjects for historians, anthropologists, geographers, and others, but too often they have been interpreted as the result merely of cultural change, which is to say, of taught beliefs and values.[13]

The idealists who generally have been our guides to history want to give all credit to the uniqueness of the human brain and organism, to ideas and philosophies or ethics. An example is the historian-anthropologist Karl Polanyi, whose book *The Great Transformation* (1944) attempted to explain the ideas behind the new form of civilization, industrial capitalism, that became well established in Darwin's time. It started, Polanyi declared, as a moral ideal: "The fount and matrix of the system was the self-regulating market. It was this innovation which gave rise to a specific civilization." Polanyi disagreed with that idea and instead promoted his own alternative, a utopian form of socialism.[14]

Polanyi's target was Karl Marx, who likewise tried to explain the transformation to industrial capitalism by emphasizing the significance of markets. Marx, however, was a materialist who strenuously rejected the many idealisms of his day, urging that the biggest change had come through a war among economic classes. That war, he said, had led to changes in the "modes of production." But on one occasion he admitted that beneath the shifting modes of production was something far more basic, what he called "the increase of population."[15] That observation has been steadily ignored by his followers and almost everyone else. As human numbers grew, Marx was saying, new ways or modes followed. He was right in that thesis, though he avoided the population factor in his later writings. Here we will allow that Marx was right, adding that both an increase and a decrease in population can be driving forces for material change and that both factors derive from human nature.

Sex has been the most powerful and pleasurable of our desires, but that does not make sexuality a villain, seeking to destroy us. On the contrary, sex is neither good nor evil, but merely a desire we share with other species.

This book asks, how has our sexual nature—a nature that is separate from culturally generated gender ideas or roles—remade us and the earth? When did the desire for libidinal satisfaction and the act of reproduction become separated? And what have been the consequences of their union or their separation? These are questions that no historian alone can answer, but by following the example of natural history we might succeed better than we have.

This book provides a new overview of human history. It does not pretend to be a work of science, but it is a work *about* science. It asks how science might help us understand our own nature as a determinant over time. To provide complete answers would take a huge team of experts, and they would need several lifetimes to complete their work—and then it would be out of date. Better knowledge is accumulating at this moment. Ecology, evolutionary biology, psychology, and the neurosciences will provide more and more evidence from which we can write a new and better history of humanity and the earth.

The aim of this book is nothing less than to put human history into a more multifactorial, planetary, and material determinist perspective. We might call it making humans part of natural history. Success will lead to a more complex, comprehensive understanding of why we have become what we are. This book concludes that over all evolution has turned out to have been good for us, at least measured by our numbers and material success. We have succeeded not because we were designed by divine intelligence or by some political theory but because we are the children of a planet alive with fertility.

What follows may seem at times to be overly speculative, offering hypotheses that often require much testing and debate. Some of the arguments or interpretations offered may turn out to be flatly wrong. But out of deep respect for the natural sciences, out of a sense that we need a new, more inclusive natural history, this book (really an extended essay) asks readers to think about the shaping role and power of both nature and human nature.

CHAPTER 1

Out of Africa

How little we know about the history of the planet on which we live—its elemental chthonian forces, its intricately braided flow of matter and energy, its irrepressible fertility. Until recent decades and the data from radiocarbon dating, we had little knowledge of the pace, scale, and frequency of changes the earth has gone through—its cycles of birth and rebirth, its evolution through many stages, all of that inscribed in the lithosphere.[1]

Among the most startling discoveries is that the solid-seeming continents have regularly wandered this way and that, forcing massive historical changes in the earth's climates, rainfall, and biota. That wandering has not been without cause; it has been driven largely by heat rising to the surface from the earth's mantle and core, dissipating into space but not before forcing landmasses to shift their location. Such shifting will continue until the day when all the inner heat of the earth will have dissipated and the planet will have become a cold, lifeless rock.

More than three hundred million years ago the earth's continents drifted together, forming a single supercontinent temporarily encircled by a single ocean. Previously, they had been floating independently; now they became a single unified landmass. Species could mix more easily and spread into new territory. But 175 million years later that supercontinent broke apart, as narrow fissures widened into new seas and oceans, resembling the earth we see today. It was not the first time such integration and disintegration had occurred, and it will not be the last.

Almost all such planetary change has been steady, relentless, and slow—except for occasional abrupt punctuations caused by an asteroid slamming into the planet, by flip-flopping atmospheres, or by eruptions of red-hot magma. One such eruption caused the most severe extinction crisis in earth history—the Permian-Triassic Extinction event, which occurred 250 million years ago and killed almost all plant and animal species. Extinction has been a regular part of nature before and after that event, and yet some life managed to survive and proliferate, producing us.

According to scientific theory, the same natural laws and processes that operate today have always operated on earth and everywhere else in the universe. At a slow, gradual, and steady rate water vapor in the atmosphere had condensed as rain a long time ago, forming the great oceans. Slow or fast in time, all earth changes were part of the unstoppable flow of fertility. In terms of biology, all change has been progressive—more complex life forms appearing over time, offering more complexity of interaction. Humans have exemplified that progress, gaining a more permanent hold on the land and becoming the dominant species. That complexification is all we can mean by progress. Everything else is wrapped in ambiguity.

In the early twentieth century the German meteorologist Alfred Wegener drew out of that ancient past a new theory he called continental drift, which has now become the science of plate tectonics.[2] Wegener's theory was not at all progressive, for his continents never arrived at some higher state; they just kept drifting. For the latest merger of continents, he suggested the name Pangea, a term derived from the Greek word *pangaia,* meaning all the land. Surrounding the supercontinent was Panthalassa, or all the oceans, a single sea covering most of the earth's surface. Somewhere in that watery expanse, life originated and then crawled onto dry land. All of that happened as quietly as the moon moved through space, but no one can say whether the continents were progressing or not.[3]

Origin stories are like stars shining above the desert at night: brilliant, poetic, and perhaps useful for personal navigation. Most origin stories, however, are not like Wegener's. They are not based on scientific hypotheses and data. For example, the Chumash people of Southern California tell an origin story that claims they have always lived in the same place, a small part of the Pacific coastal zone. The story tells them that their birthplace was a nearly perfect zone surmounted by the heavens and protected from a monstrous underworld by giant serpents whose movements caused many earthquakes.[4] A human-created myth, it had a childlike charm but has become less credible with the light of science.

Another famous origin story was recorded in the Hebrew Bible, in the first chapter of Genesis where God is said to have created the first man and first woman, Adam and Eve, and placed them in a glorious natural garden where they could easily satisfy their needs, until the devil appeared in the form of a serpent and tempted Eve to act on her desires and persuade Adam to do the same. After giving in to their bodily urges, the couple's days in paradise abruptly came to an end. God kicked them out of the garden and forced them to live among weeds and brambles, to bear children with pain, and to raise their food as sweaty farmers. The only thing that did not change for Adam and Eve was God's original mandate, "Be fruitful, and multiply, and replenish the earth" (Genesis 1:28). That instruction they faithfully obeyed, with the result that humans subsequently migrated over much of the earth. In fact, that instruction became a license for aggressive expansion, as the migrants displaced other species and other humans to gain support for their own progeny.

Both the Chumash and Judaic stories have not withstood Charles Darwin's evolutionary biology or the science of plate tectonics. Now we know that all peoples, including those who still maintain they were first created by some god or gods in the Americas or the Middle East, in fact emerged on the continent of Africa. Their first home probably was a rift valley, a place created by tectonic plate movements. It was not designed to be easy or harmonious for people, or to be a hell on earth. Human reproduction in that place did not follow God's decree. Sexual reproduction evolved naturally within humans as it did in other species: a hormonal, not a divine, mandate that both men and women have long obeyed. Sexual desire led to reproduction, and reproduction was long considered a positive good among all peoples.

Africa had once been located at the very heart of Pangea, with the Americas joining on one side and Antarctica, Australia, India, and Eurasia on other sides. Like the other continents, Africa had been patched together from a cluster of cratons, which are large, stable masses of basement rock. One of those cratons became southern Africa, a chunk of land that would someday be profitably mined for iron, chrome, diamonds, cobalt, nickel, and copper.[5] The other cratons were not so well endowed with mineral wealth. In fact, much of the continent of Africa was not well endowed with natural resources, lacking good soils and ample rainfall in particular; nonetheless, it developed a stunning diversity of plant and animal species. After Pangea broke apart, Africa's location on the planet shifted slightly southward until it straddled the equator, giving Africa a mostly dry climate that was prone to extreme droughts. Yet as habitat, it proved suitable enough for organisms to proliferate and diversify. Variant after variant appeared in all the gene pools, and some of those variants became naturally selected by the environment.

Today Africa occupies more than 30.3 million square kilometers, enough land to cover all of China and the United States, with enough room left over for India and several European nations. Almost half of Africa's terrain became desert or near-desert. Less than 10 percent was covered with steamy rainforest, although that part often would become identified as the true Africa. More than half of the ground cover evolved into savannah, steppe, or grassland—forming a vast green and brown expanse where there was just enough rain to sustain ecosystems rich in grasses and their seeds. Even though most African soils are unglaciated and therefore poor in nutrients, and even though the temperatures are on the warm side, Africa long ago gave birth not only to humans but also to a wide spectrum of other species. Many of them were grass eaters, while others lived by eating those who ate the seeds. Perhaps no continent has surpassed Africa for diversity and resilience.

Humans first emerged as an integral part of the African equilibrium. They were small, dark, intelligent, but highly vulnerable creatures, constantly threatened by the hungry predators around them and by the many droughts that killed the vegetation on which people depended. Yet the first humans became well-adapted foragers, sustaining themselves for more than eight thousand generations. No people have ever been as sustainable as the Africans.

Most scientists have agreed that humans first appeared in the Great Rift Valley located in eastern and southern Africa. The rift had opened between twenty-four million and thirty million years ago, a geological fault zone running along the eastern side of the continent.[6] Pulling away on one side of the fault was the Arabian Plate, and on the western side the Nubian and Somalian plates. The fault was a great rent in the earth, filling with eroding soils and fresh water. It is still quite visible, extending from what is now Tanzania northward through Ethiopia, Sudan, and Egypt, all the way to modern-day Palestine and Israel.

As the African Great Rift's cliffsides pushed higher and higher, they captured moisture blowing in from the sea. In addition to grasses heavy with seeds, the rain brought sedges, wildflowers, tubers, and trees like the acacia and baobab, which provided food for species as large as elephants, which can subsist on low-energy food such as grasses if the quantities are abundant. Here too was sufficient food for many primate species—chimpanzees, bonobos, baboons, and gorillas, all predominately seed and fruit eaters that ventured down to the valley floor where they found plenty of sustenance. Co-evolving species included zebra, kudu, giraffes, white and black rhinos, hippos, wildebeest, eland, impala, and the African buffalo, along with many superb predators—lions, leopards, cheetahs, wild dogs, and hyenas—forming not an Edenic harmony exactly but an ever shifting ecosystem based on checks and balances. For all of those species, the Great Rift Valley offered the right conditions—what some call Goldilocks conditions, which are neither too hot nor too cold, but just right for life to feed on and reproduce.

Twenty-five million years ago in this place a tiny branch of hominids began splitting from the others, until around five million years ago, a small creature named *Australopithecus africanus* appeared, walking upright on hind legs, its small brainy head held erect against the sky. In 1924, Raymond Dart of South Africa discovered remains of this species and declared it was the ancestor of humans. He described it as carnivorous, warlike, and violent, crafting hideous weapons from old bones to use in the hunt. It carved out a special niche, he concluded, by learning to kill other animals. From their beginning, in short, humans were supposed to have a propensity for hunting and killing, for making deadly weapons, and for marking off and defending their own territories. Later research challenged Dart's characterization of *Australopithecus:* dental studies have shown that its diet consisted mainly of fruits, nuts, seeds, roots, insects, and eggs, not meat. Humans did not begin as simply a killer species.[7]

It is hard to say when the first humans appeared, for it is not easy to say what a human is or is not. There never was any first couple, created by divine intervention and set up to exercise dominion over all the other species. The first humans and their offspring could not claim that they were chosen to rule. Instead, individuals and variations competed for success, and much mixing and mating occurred all over Africa. Early humans merged their DNA regularly with that of their near relatives, making the task of identifying a single ancestral father or mother quite arbitrary. So many kinds of humans, hominids, hominins, and proto humans lie in our past that evolutionists now speak not of a single, branching tree but of an interlacing trellis of speciation.[8]

Yet all the new hominins shared certain traits. They were grassland creatures that added meat to their diet, although mainly they were vegetarians. Although they were territorially aggressive toward outsiders, they could also be, within their territories, quite communistic, sharing what they hunted and gathered. They also shared an upright posture, were able to see far and run fast to find protection, and, thanks to opposable thumbs, were adept at climbing trees. All those traits helped them survive in what was an intensely competitive environment.

The most important trait uniting the hominins was their comparatively large brains, well protected inside rigid skull cases. Environmental conditions did not *design* that brain—it emerged from the roll of genetic dice—but the Rift Valley and its mountains, the many lakes and rivers, proved supportive. Scientists say that after the appearance of *Australopithecus* came *Homo habilis,* showing up in the Pleistocene epoch about 2.3 million years ago. Around two million years ago, another hominin called *H. erectus* (or *H. ergaster)* followed; then came *H. heidelbergensis,* seven hundred thousand years ago, followed by *H. neanderthalensis,* four hundred thousand years ago. And there may have been other competing hominins that have not yet been discovered.

Then along came *H. sapiens* and then *H. sapiens sapiens,* emerging several million years after *Australopithecus.* This last organism in the line appeared as a distinct subspecies about two or three hundred thousand years ago.[9] They shared more than 99 percent of their DNA with other hominins, but it was the Twice Wise *sapiens* whom scientists have identified as anatomically modern humans. All of the *Homo* species were more intelligent than the rest of the animal kingdom, but the Twice Wise were a little more so. Their brains were nearly three times larger than those of chimps or gorillas. More important than size, their brains were more intricately wired than those of any other creature on the continent of Africa.[10]

The *sapiens* brain varied considerably from individual to individual, as did other features—their intelligence, body size, musculature, speed, grace, ability to sing or calculate, and susceptibility to disease. On average, the human brain constituted less than 2 percent of overall body mass, although it required 20 percent of the energy that humans consumed. It was a very hungry organ, demanding to be fed all the time, especially with high-protein meat. By way of compensation for its weight and other drawbacks, the brain organ gave its possessors the ability to find food where other creatures failed. It facilitated the expansion of their niche and the ability to secure mates and reproduce; it helped keep their babies alive and safe. However weak humans were, they were formidably endowed with intelligence to succeed in the struggle for survival.

All of the other hominin relatives eventually disappeared. *Homo sapiens sapiens* survived to become the dominant animal across Africa and other continents, and a powerful force on the planet. Not only did its close relatives vanish, but so did many other animals—tigers and rhinos once found all over Asia and Africa were forced into extinction by the intense interspecies competition. Humans were able to prevail over other species, even over their close kin, because their complex brains gave them a formidable advantage in food procurement and sexual reproduction. Those brains succeeded precisely because they were not blank slates, waiting to be taught how to behave or react. They were not unusually wired for aggression; they outcompeted the others because they managed better to satisfy their inner desires. In satiating those natural hungers, they increased their numbers and became masters of Africa. Puny though they were compared to giraffes or gorillas, they were gifted with a formidable alliance between their brains and other body organs. It was those partnerships that would bring them so successfully through long cycles of climate change and microbial threats that otherwise might have destroyed them.

Was theirs, as the historian John Brooke writes, "a rough life"?[11] Yes, it was, but not only because the climate kept changing. They could adapt to climate cycles, to floods or droughts, to volcanoes erupting, or microbes invading their bodies. More powerful than any of those environmental threats was the pressure of their own numbers, which forced them continuously to move, innovate, and scrounge for food. A memorable description of their predicament comes from the seventeenth-century English philosopher Thomas Hobbes, though he too failed to see the cause of their predicament in their inner urges to eat and have sex. Human life, wrote Hobbes, was "a Warre of everyone against everyone; in which case everyone is governed by his own Reason; and there is nothing he can make use of, that may not be a help unto him, in preserving his life against his enemyes."[12]

But conditions in Africa and within the human body were never so rough that the Twice Wise were overcome and vanquished. On the contrary, they prospered in the survival game, not because they were the most rational or intellectual species, able to write books or think big thoughts, but because they proved skillful at hiding, evading, and avoiding being caught or eaten, at finding a sufficiency of food, and above all at locating mates and securing the lives of their children. Along the way they suffered many tragic losses; nonetheless, they gained a lasting foothold in Africa and elsewhere.

Over their first hundred millennia, however, the Twice Wise managed little more than to eke out a modest living within their niches, sometimes a barely adequate subsistence. Their brains proved able to store information efficiently and take advantage of whatever came along. They inherited from other species a propensity for culture, which more and more allowed them to produce innovations and develop socially. *Sapiens'* relatives had plenty of neurons too, allowing them to create tools and invent new behaviors; they were hardly robots. But the Twice Wise surpassed all others in their capacity for learning, resilience, and transmission of skills. Henceforth the planet would more and more feel their presence.

For a long while, humans made rather little impact on their environment. Their priority was to gather wild food. Males of the early forging bands took on the work of bringing home meat, while females became skilled in gathering most of the carbohydrates, fruits, and vegetables on which their subsistence mainly depended.[13]

We should not forget that our earliest ancestors lived during the Pleistocene epoch, when global climates were quite unsettled as a result of a periodic tilting of the earth's axis. During the 2.6 million years of that epoch, massive ice sheets formed in the higher latitudes and elevations and advanced across the terrain, grinding down rocks, plowing up soils, driving plant and animal species toward warmer climes. Through all of the extreme ups and downs of the Pleistocene epoch *sapiens* managed to survive and even flourish—so much for climate's fatal impact! Of course, it may have helped that during their years in Africa they did not experience, except where there were mountain glaciers, the full effects of the big freeze.

After the Pleistocene gave way to warmer conditions, the Twice Wise found more and more to eat, until their numbers became substantially larger, and it was then that their foraging way of life became unsustainable. Before that, about seventy thousand years ago, *sapiens* may have gone through a nearly fatal setback, when an extreme drought may have occurred across southern Africa, forcing their numbers down to a few thousand. That drought would have been caused by the eruption of the Toba volcano in far-off Sumatra, which spread ash across the planet, cutting short the growing season of plants and devastating the foragers' meat supplies. Sumatra straddles another rift zone that now and again explodes, sending magma and ash into the atmosphere. The Toba volcano may have affected the planetary environment for as long as ten years, though its impact remains disputed. Paleobotanists can find no traces of vegetational change in African lake sediments during or after the Toba eruption, so they have questioned whether that event had much of an impact on early humans.[14] Whatever the facts turn out to be, we should not put too much weight on a single climatic event or jump to the conclusion that the early millennia in Africa were full of catastrophes. Somehow, humans endured and even increased their population, despite the ups and downs they experienced.

The biggest threat to human survival came not from climate change or volcanic ash clouding the sky but from other, competing hominins. And there the outcome was indisputably positive for the Twice Wise, who turned all threats into lopsided victories for their side. First, the competing cousins were forced to migrate out of Africa to other continents—and then they died out everywhere on earth. They did so wherever the Twice Wise entered the scene. They were killed directly, captured as sex slaves, or lost their foraging grounds, leaving them to starve. More difficult to defeat were myriad other enemies large and small that forced coexistence on humans remaining in Africa.

The total number of human beings who died before written records were invented fluctuated from time to time, although we have no sure way of determining what their numbers were. Currently, the standard view is that early humans experienced a lot more direct, interpersonal violence than people do today and that struggles within and outside their bands reduced their life spans and those of their offspring. We know that early humans died at what seem to moderns very early ages—generally before the age of thirty. Many died in childbirth or infancy. Those who lived beyond infancy reached puberty a little later than people do today, giving them a short fertility span—only a decade or so—and others were cut down in the prime of their lives.

Still, those who survived the dangers of tribal warfare, fierce animal attacks, microbial infections, and all the other threats around them did manage to reproduce well enough to replace their numbers and even increase. Ever so slowly, decade by decade, century by century, millennium by millennium, their numbers kept increasing, even though they did so at the rate of a mere fraction of 1 percent per annum. The demographer Ansley Coale has written, "Whatever the size of the initial human population, the rate of growth . . . was exceedingly small."[15] But small as it was, they still managed to add at least one new person to their bands every three, four, or five generations, although each generation might not have noticed any increase at all. Such a slow, incremental increase would not have been a source of worry for tribes. Yet even such a slow rate of increase, if it continued for one hundred thousand or two hundred thousand years or more, could and did lead to overpopulation and environmental stress. That is a commonsense conclusion. Adding just one or two mouths per century could strain a band's food supplies, could adversely impact its environment, and, where it led to an increasing number of childbearing women, could raise populations over time.

All animal species are restrained in numbers and gain slowly over a long period of time, if at all, but there comes a point when they may begin to grow exponentially. Instead of leveling off at some stable plateau, their rate of increase may explode from one half of 1 percent to 1, 2, or 3 percent per annum, at least for a while. In the foraging lives of early humans, there were no population explosions like those we know today, but there was always the potential of demographic pressure.[16]

A growth rate of one half of 1 percent per year has been observed today among the !Kung foragers of the Kalahari Desert in southern Africa. Keep up that rate for a long enough time, and a band of one hundred people could eventually double to two hundred, then four hundred, then sixteen hundred. Over the span of thousands of years, even a very low rate of population growth could become unsustainable.[17] No dramatic jump in numbers ever happened in the early years, as couples either restrained their reproductive behavior or were restrained by their environment. But over the course of nearly two hundred thousand years, fertility rates must have been high enough to begin to exceed replacement levels. When that occurred, people were forced to migrate—or innovate.

By 10,000 BCE, just before agriculture, the Twice Wise may have numbered worldwide as many as five million to fifteen million individuals.[18] That estimate comes from demographers. If their estimates prove too low and the totals turn out to be *thirty* million individuals, then the argument that long-term gain is possible among foragers is made only stronger. If, however, the estimate proves too high, if we conclude that a mere *two* million or *three* million humans were alive on earth ten millennia ago, that will still represent a substantial increase over time.

What do those estimates suggest about the vaunted African equilibrium? It must have broken down now and then, here or there, at least for a while. But eventually it was preserved because a door opened for emigration of the human surplus. *H. sapiens* discovered that there were vast new lands or underexploited habitats on other continents that were not impossibly far away. We can know rather precisely, from archaeological evidence, when human foragers began leaving Africa and exploring those other continents. The reason for that exodus had to be that their way of life was proving unsustainable for themselves and their offspring.

A way of life based on foraging for wild food comes, to be sure, with a natural check on female fertility. Foraging requires regular movement, which discourages surplus childbearing. Today's remnant hunters and gatherers tend to move camp every few months to avoid overharvesting local foods, moving ten to twenty kilometers away to where there are greener pastures. Even though they are burdened with few material possessions, they must carry in their arms everything they own—and the heaviest load would have been the babies and young children. The ones who carried the babies were usually adult females, strong in frame but perhaps in some cases undernourished. Lugging a five- to twenty-five-pound baby on a search for new territory must have been hard work, but carrying more than one would have been an intolerable burden.

Fortunately, it was unusual for migrating women to carry more than one child in their arms or on their backs. The physical act of breastfeeding the babies, if prolonged for several years, naturally inhibits female egg production, thus ensuring that women do not get pregnant so often. This inherited biological response, a genetically based form of birth control, assured that populations would remain lower than they would become under a post-foraging, sedentary way of life. Here was a material adaptation involving a hormonal release affecting the hypothalamus, one of the oldest parts of the brain, and it was so powerful that it could even stop ovulation for four or five years, if mothers could breastfeed a child that long. This trait allowed foraging women to achieve more space between births and reduce the number of infants needing their care and transportation. Even so, with that natural check, the numbers increased over millennia.[19]

Foragers could not dare to overestimate the carrying capacity of the land or depend on a relief package arriving from elsewhere. They must carefully preserve the surrounding plant and animal life and be careful not to extract too much for their use. This too is a behavior that shows up in many species: eat and move, eat and move, hoping that mobility will minimize impact. Africa could have been, in this way, a sustainable home for humans over a very long time. But no matter how much they learned about their bodies or how skillfully they practiced breastfeeding to inhibit reproduction, they still must obey their inner imperatives. In due course, it seems obvious, there was enough reproduction going on to mean that millions were competing for survival, and the African horn of plenty began to seem empty.

Africa was no Eden in the biblical sense, but it was the true point of human origin—Africa, not Asia—yet living there required holding to very low human reproductive rates. If women and men succeeded in keeping those rates low, Africa's ecosystems could be sustaining—not forever, perhaps, but for a very long stretch of time. The continent could offer beauty and delight along with ample nutrition. But always humans were required, like every other species, to stay in balance with their food supply. The body's inner urges had to be adjusted to the outer environment. Once they achieved that adjustment, they must have found it difficult to shift to any less familiar terrain or a new way of life. In their success lay also their confinement, restraint, and vulnerability.[20]

This simple ecological truth seems to have eluded many great scholars. Take the famous anthropologist Marshall Sahlins, for example, who described ancient foragers as the "original affluent people." He extolled them for being rich in ways that we moderns have forgotten. "Wants," he pointed out, "may be 'easily satisfied' either by producing much or desiring little."[21] Did foraging people desire little? Yes, if we ignore the number of children they desired—even three might have put a strain on the environment. Babies were their biggest desire, their chief possessions, their future security, and their deepest pleasure. Assiduously, they gathered food to feed their offspring whenever it was abundant, and when food became scarce, they may have fed the children first, before themselves. We cannot, in the absence of written evidence, say how many babies they wanted or how many they had or how much food they thought they needed. We must reason in this instance from extremely limited evidence.

What we can say with utter assurance is that *H. sapiens* managed to survive as foragers for two hundred millennia. According to Sahlins, their survival required only a few hours of work per week—perhaps fifteen hours in all, a mere two or three hours each day. The rest of the time, he argues, they slept, lay about their camps, made up songs and stories, or played with their children. Although they may have been affluent in nonmaterial terms, they were not so in material goods, but was that by choice or by necessity? It is reasonable to conclude that their principal desires were to find food and raise children. Perhaps that was enough to make them different from us, but few today would give up our consumer society for their fragile, vulnerable way of life.

Foraging, to be sure, still goes on around the planet, including in a small part of Africa's Great Rift Valley where the Hazda people still live in the old way. The Hazda, however, are under intense pressure to stop foraging for food and accept modern employment. The pressure comes not only from their farming and urban-minded neighbors. They themselves desire more material wealth than their ancestral way can yield. Once human desires become sharpened by hardship, the old ways become more and more difficult to maintain, until the last surviving foragers must seek sanctuary in the most marginal, undesirable environments on the planet.

We modern humans still feel within us the urges of our hunting ancestors, including their sexual desire. But there are far too many of us now to satisfy that desire and live by foraging. How could today's Lagos (Nigeria) or Kinshasa (Democratic Republic of the Congo), each numbering more than 15 million people, manage to live and reproduce as foragers did? We now are in a different age, not because we have been corrupted by modernity but because we want much longer life spans than a mere thirty years.

Sahlins rightly complains that we moderns have constructed "a shrine to the Unattainable: *Infinite Needs.*"[22] We have come to want a lot of things—including a smaller population. It would not, however, be easy for us to go back in time, no matter how much guilt we might feel or how effective our methods of birth control might be. Thousands of years of biological and cultural evolution have made us what we are. But just as we have created, through following our desires, an astonishing new life, so we have created many profound changes in the earth. It is because of our own evolving nature that we have made those changes, and now we cannot extricate ourselves from them easily.

Perhaps the foraging life offered a better kind of existence than today's consumer society, but which of our modern wants should we reject? Should we give up automobiles, houses, supermarkets, or sexual freedom? Should we have fewer or even no children? It is unrealistic to say that we are now corrupt because we seek more than the foragers did or to say that the poor of the world do not want what the middle class has. No species has ever voluntarily devolved to a lower rank in the ecosphere.

Our ancestors were forced out of their African Eden and set on the road to modernity not because they disobeyed God or because they had become corrupt, but because they had too many babies. Should they have had fewer? How could they have done so? Their lives were probably determined more by natural necessity than by moral choices.

The determinant of carrying capacity ultimately sets limits to the number of people who can eat at nature's table. Those who cannot eat must walk long distances to find new territory. Those who stay in place must practice geronticide or infanticide if they have no condoms. Among early foragers, one out of three children may have died at or soon after birth, deliberately killed by parental neglect or lack of food. That was the dark side of the first human way of life, the truth embedded in ecological "harmony" as it was experienced during the heyday of foraging.

If by Eden we mean a place that offers easy goods, free sex, and a perfect equilibrium between humans and the rest of nature, we have not found it anywhere. Always there have been difficult challenges that require intelligence, knowledge, and self-discipline to overcome. To survive humans have had to acquire more knowledge, more control over nature and their own nature, and more protection from their competitors.

Besides the gruesome practice of getting rid of excess children or grandparents in times of crises, the Twice Wise have had two methods to sustain their way of life. First came innovation—that is, the development of new tools and strategies for securing food and fighting for territory. Second, they could migrate to a more bountiful environment. Both strategies appear to have been followed in ancient times. Innovation in place, archaeologists have shown, was always active—new tools made of stone or bone, new hunting techniques, new social relationships. And so also migration happened repeatedly. In many cases the latter must have been the only choice that people had.

Among the most important of the foragers' innovations was the intentional burning of the land. Long before humans emerged, earlier hominins had discovered how to set fire to their surroundings. *Homo erectus* was doing that some eight hundred thousand years ago, long before the Twice Wise had evolved. Burning changes the composition of the atmosphere—it is not very different in principle from burning fossilized fuels. Oxygen constituted, then as now, about 20 percent of atmospheric gases, with the natural result that spontaneous fire became common among the earth's ecosystems.[23] Africa's savannahs, which had long been set ablaze by natural lightning igniting dry brush or dead grass, became fire-adapted over time. Early humans as they grew hungrier tried to catch and use fire as they might catch a lion by its tail. After burning of any sort, a fresh burst of vegetation might improve the land's output. Holding a lion by the tail, however, can get a man bitten. Human-set fire had many unintended consequences; it might suddenly change its course, turn around and burn down one's camp, even destroy all of its inhabitants. And even when the trick was well managed, it might make only a small improvement in the food supply.[24]

Other innovations occurred in the form of new tools, including the bow and arrow, fishhooks, harpoons, or sharpened sticks used for digging up tubers. When invention failed, migration was the only alternative. Surplus people must go out looking for another homeland.

The migratory routes taken by early humans are not easy to discover from the few traces left in the soil, yet we know that they managed over many millennia to spread across nearly the whole planet. First they went looking for new African-like savannahs beyond the horizon, and then they ventured into dark and mysterious forests or turned to the ocean shores and tried to subsist on marine food. Almost all of Africa, even its most difficult environments, eventually became homes for humans—new sources of food and energy—from the southern African coasts to the Mediterranean shores. Whenever the Pleistocene went through one of its warming phases, bringing more rainfall and better growing conditions, humans could expand their range. Yet when cold, dry conditions returned, they had to be ready to retreat and alter their diet. They might find themselves eating birds, snakes, and other small animals whenever the larger game failed. Once they reached a point of diminishing returns, if no innovation was available, they were forced to start walking to find lands that might better accommodate their numbers.

More than once, it appears, early humans reached the limits of Africa and were forced to migrate beyond that continent into the adjoining lands of Eurasia. Doing so relieved the pressures on those who stayed behind, restoring some of the old equilibrium, at least for a while. Possessing no reliable maps of Eurasia or the continent they were leaving, the migrants could not imagine the size of the planet we know today. Nonetheless, they managed to find and occupy all the shifting tectonic plates on earth except those of Antarctica. Again and again, they gathered up their children, clothing, tools, and weapons and searched for something better. In doing so, they were in effect pulling back together the drifting continents, creating a new kind of human-made supercontinent, a single interconnected land base that covered much of the planet. Their urge to migrate, to uproot and start walking, was part of the legacy that foragers handed down to later generations.

Determining exactly when the first migrants left Africa and when they arrived somewhere else depends on tracing scattered bones and stone chippings. New evidence appears regularly and still more will come to light. We know that people began exiting Africa during the late Pleistocene, as long as a hundred thousand years ago. They moved northward and eastward, spreading over the Eurasian continent at a time when much of it was still in the grip of glacial cold. As they migrated into unfamiliar northern climes where there was less sunshine and more ice, they acquired new knowledge, new energy, new foods, new clothing, and even new, lighter shades of skin pigmentation. We lack a detailed knowledge of their exact routes out of Africa or the ecological consequences of their movements, but we know they got as far as today's Great Britain and Russia, Southeast Asia, Australia, the islands of the Pacific, even the Americas. Their travels, if we could only know them better, would yield many incredible stories of heroic risk and courage.

Human migration, it is clear from later examples, selects according to people's willingness to tolerate risk. Migrants rank high for risk and daring. At the same time, the desires pushing them to leave home must have been powerful enough to overcome any inborn resistance to change. Emotions must have run high, expectations must have soared, disappointments must have followed whenever people ended up in worse places than they left. Those most willing to abandon their hearth land were not necessarily the smartest or strongest; on the contrary, they may have been losers at home but still confident enough to seek a new landscape. All migrants typically leave home with the idea of replicating their ways somewhere else: that too is a trait embedded in human nature. First they head for the places that look most like home in terms of food, work, and security, and only after that do they venture into the completely unknown.

Paul Mellars, an archaeologist at the University of Cambridge, used a combination of DNA data, fossilized bones, and stone artifacts to trace the early phases of the great diaspora that, he believed, originated in the southern part of the African continent. He argues that around one hundred thousand years ago *sapiens,* after they first exhausted the possibilities of Africa, migrated into Eurasia. Those who found the coasts crowded ended up in what we now call the Middle East. They were relatively few; nonetheless, they managed to take possession of the land, just as Europeans would do thousands of years later when they "discovered" the Americas and the Antipodes.

A second wave of emigration, which was bigger in size and even more deadly to anyone standing in the way, began around sixty thousand years ago. "Rapid population growth" was occurring around that time in southern Africa, according to Mellars, providing the strong push that migrants needed.[25] That growth came from innovations in catching fish and seabirds. When the marine environment became overfished, humans were forced to trek northward along Africa's eastern shores, until they reached the Gulf of Aden, a narrow expanse of saltwater separating Africa from Arabian shores. Once across the Gulf, they entered a brave new world, just as Spanish ships did when they first sailed from Europe to the Americas.

Whether Mellars is right about his dates or not, Africa's early pioneers kept proliferating and migrating, bands following other bands across mountains and rivers and along shorelines, some of them trudging all the way to the South Asian coast where they discovered the submerged subcontinent of Sahul, a landmass that had flooded as oceans warmed, creating the archipelago of Indonesia. When they reached that point, they may have seen smoke from wildfires in what we now call Australia and, with the aid of rafts, managed to cross the saltwater to that land of marsupials and eucalypts. The first *sapiens* arrived in Australia about forty thousand to fifty thousand years ago, and within another ten thousand years they had managed to spread across the entire island continent.

OUT OF AFRICA

Meanwhile, an even more impressive migration was going on across the vast interior of Eurasia, the largest landmass on the planet. Bands of migrants flowed northward into Africa's Nile River region and then trudged eastward across the sands of the Sinai Peninsula, fetching up in what would one day become known as the Fertile Crescent. That migration went on from sixty thousand to thirty thousand years ago.

At first those migrations into Eurasia led to some happy outcomes—the hilly lands around the Dead Sea, the Jordan River, the Sea of Galilee, the Tigris and Euphrates rivers, the grass-covered and forested uplands and valleys of Turkey's Anatolia, and the shorelines of the Mediterranean. Thousands of kilometers to the east, beyond tall mountain chains and stark deserts, some forty thousand years ago other migrants arrived at another kind of happiness: the big river valleys of China, especially the Huang He and Changjiang, where elephants and tigers still roamed as they did in Africa.[26] Later humans, finding no room in those favored places, fanned out across the colder north. With the aid of animal pelts for clothing, they learned to survive even at extreme latitudes. An abundance of large, meaty animals attracted them into those bitterly cold, inhospitable regions. In contrast to Africa's more human-wary wildlife, the native species of Eurasia would prove to be easy pickings for skilled hunters.[27]

Hairy mammoths and other Ice Age animals were for a while common across the northern latitudes, but at first their large size intimidated human hunters much as the big game of Africa had done. It would take several millennia before the newly arrived humans could devise weapons that could kill such monsters, and when that happened, they went after their prey with wild, unleashed desire, slaughtering many species to the point of extinction.

In their eager quest for meat, the immigrants had to compete again and again with their Neanderthal relatives, who had been there a much longer time and acted as though the new continent was theirs and theirs alone. But rather quickly the Twice Wise dispatched or absorbed them, until they alone were left standing triumphant. They took possession of the new territories, at last claiming all of Eurasia for themselves. Wherever they went the invading foragers may have instigated genocidal cleansing. Like their future counterparts, they were not evil—they were merely following their inherited nature, the urgencies of their loins and appetites.

The full conquest of the Eurasian landmass took a long while to complete, and it is not quite finished today. Three thousand years after the first *sapiens* reached China, another demographic wave was washing over eastern Europe. Eventually, migrating humans figured out how to survive in that region too, spreading across its broad grasslands, occupying the game-rich valleys of the Danube River and the Carpathian Basin.

The Eurasian continent was both highly appealing and highly resistant. It took humans a long time to explore all of it, carve it into new hunting territories, and figure out how to stay warm there. Eurasia covered fifty million square kilometers, twice as large as Africa, though much of that new frontier had an inhospitable climate. Thanks to plate tectonics, it had become one single landmass as the Indian subcontinent pushed northward, creating the Himalayan chain and the Tibetan Plateau, while the Alps had bumped into Europe, creating the European subcontinent we see today, a patched together mosaic of countries with incomparable but scattered riches. Much later, during the warming Holocene epoch that followed the Pleistocene, Eurasia would become the most densely populated of all the continents. That outcome required many thousands of years to accomplish through the densification of human numbers, resulting in a fiercely competitive assortment of farms, cities, states, and empires.

Today, five billion people live in Eurasia, or 70 percent of all humans, an achievement that has taken tens of thousands of years to realize. For a long time, Eurasia had been a nonhuman place, a wilderness, but then it became populated by rugged bands of human hunters and seed gatherers. Those people were healthier because they had escaped many of the disease organisms that had plagued them in Africa. Consequently, they may have become more prolific reproducers than ever before. Quickly they learned the daily movements of the local game, figuring out which species they could hunt down or harvest most easily. The newcomers, however, remained prone to many mishaps, and perhaps some waxed nostalgic over what had been left behind in their quest for more food and more reproduction.

The dispersal and growth of human numbers did not end with those big waves flowing out of Africa. The migrations continued and may even have intensified as the Pleistocene epoch waned and warmer temperatures ensued. Climate change did not cause the migrations, but undoubtedly it materially affected their routes and rates of success. As humans settled into new environments, from the Mekong Delta to the still frozen north, new cultures emerged, based on and derived from local ecological conditions—cultures of the Danube and Volga, of the Carpathians and Alps.

As the glaciers continued to retreat, yet before ocean levels rose and flooded the coastal zones, a land bridge known as Beringia connected Eurasia to North America. Once again, humans showed up throbbing with unsatisfied desires. Perhaps they admired the tundra grandeur spread before them, as they crossed the land bridge before it disappeared under a rising sea. Perhaps they stood admiring the herds of caribou, bison, horses, and camels migrating into Eurasia. They proceeded on, nonetheless, trekking all the way down the length of what we call the Americas, past the Isthmus of Panama to Tierra Del Fuego, the archipelago located at the very tip of South America. They spread laterally too, walking from the Pacific to the Atlantic Ocean, settling most of the Caribbean islands, which proved paradisical and yet violent places to hold on to.

Archaeological evidence reveals that this earlier American frontier took more than ten, perhaps fifteen, millennia to be overpopulated by humans, a process that kept unfolding right down to the nineteenth century, when it became a site of clash between Asian and European migrants. Some of the early Eurasians may have explored Pacific coastal waters as others were exploring the Atlantic shores. All of them had to walk a lot as they had always done, carrying their worldly goods and their children with them. No humans, however, crossed the open Pacific until 400 CE, when the Polynesians, who had originated in Southeast Asia and were driven by the familiar human desires and pressures, bravely set sail in their catamarans and reached Hawai'i, one of the remotest places on earth, located at the very center of the Pacific Ocean, one of the last habitable places that humans came to occupy. Only a few volcanic islands like Iceland, New Zealand, and Jamaica were settled later than the Hawai'ian Islands.

A diaspora that had begun in Africa ended, after more than a hundred thousand years, with *H. sapiens* in possession of most of the planet. Their swarming and the resistance they encountered from other species, including fellow primates, would continue right down to the present. Yet no migrants before the modern era were able to conceive of the planet as a whole or recall how their ancestors first got to all the new places or how long they had been there. Such knowledge came much later, after centuries of discoveries made by mapmakers, seamen, governments, naturalists, and homesteaders.

Assigning guilt only to the latest of those migrants while celebrating the human occupation in general is untenable. Who among those leaving Africa or Asia, entering today's Australia or the Americas, should we call guilty—which plants, herbivores, carnivores, hominins, or humans? By modern moral ideals, there was guilt, to be sure, and yet there was innocence and ignorance too. Those who migrated before written languages existed were no more or less evil than those who came later and wrote down their stories. From a planetary perspective, assessing the past according to today's values is provincial and meaningless. We humans have committed everywhere a great deal of violence, acted selfishly again and again, and thought ethnocentrically and anthropocentrically. The many species that preyed on us were no better. All of us earthlings acted as we did because of natural, inborn desires, not because of an innately evil nature. Evil is a concept that belongs to the religious past, not to modern science and its moral pragmatism.

Remember that many other species, including rats, mosquitoes, head lice, redwood trees, and dandelions, migrated too, invading the same landmasses, following the same coastlines and rivers. Often they killed or were killed by other migrants. What we call history has been, most essentially, a continuous diaspora, lasting two hundred thousand years and more, displacing thousands of competing species and human-like competitors. The last and the most intelligent set of invaders, *Homo sapiens,* has been fighting for millennia to assert primacy, waging war and seizing resources from other creatures.

In retrospect, all those migrations may seem quite slow compared with our modern pace of travel and invasion. Mobility and adaptation have speeded up considerably as humans have adapted culturally as well as genetically. But make no mistake: early *sapiens* spread faster and farther than other hominins did because they felt a greater urgency to migrate, because they wanted more babies, and because their brains allowed them to satisfy that want. Even so, the great planetary migrations occurred at a tedious pace. In contrast, our kind has managed since those early migrations to fly at hundreds or thousands of kilometers per hour. We have spread and multiplied like no other species before us. Our ancestors went out to replenish the earth, and they were not to be denied. In almost every kind of habitat they found sustenance for their progeny. They left a devastating impact on the earth's wild plants and animals as well as their hominin relatives, though it is nearly impossible today to measure that impact. Always, they practiced aggression, no matter how pacific they appeared at times. They conquered and killed, subdued and possessed, advanced their self-interest, and always privileged the security of their own progeny above all others. Yet at the end of the trail, they also commonly settled down to a more communitarian life, at least within their own tribe. We moderns may seem insatiably greedy for material gain, but at the same time we have also been quite peaceful, cautious, scrupulous, cooperative, and nonviolent.

Such is the story of the first great migrations according to modern science. Our history starts in Africa and then follows the same paths that other species have blazed and followed. Humans have trekked to the very ends of the earth, and they have only recently discovered that the planet is a globe, with no ends at all and yet with real limits. We are left with the question of what it means to be a human being now facing the limits of a round earth. Are we a species that must, by our nature, migrate—instinctively go out to discover and occupy the earth—or are we a species that just as instinctively accepts limits, given the right circumstances, and, deep within, desires to stay home?

CHAPTER 2

The Agrarian Whip

Who was the first farmer on Planet Earth? Was it the Olympian goddess Demeter, or was it China's mythical emperor Shennong, who lived twenty-eight centuries ago and is still celebrated as the divine farmer? Neither can claim to be first. No emperors or goddesses, no brilliant human entrepreneurs or geniuses, no woman or man invented agriculture. It was not even, strictly speaking, an invention, but more a complex, long-drawn-out, interactive process whereby humans tried to enhance their food production through many small and big experiments. And that process did not occur first among humans.[1]

Long before *Homo sapiens sapiens* evolved, there were the lowly Formicidae, belonging to the order Hymenoptera, which includes bees, wasps, termites, and ants. Those small fellow creatures were the first farmers. For a long time, we have been watching them swarm out of their nests to attack their enemies or march across the kitchen table or the forest floor, seeking something to eat in the most inaccessible places. Tiny though they are, we love, admire, fear, and despise them. And now we historians should know more about them, for they were pioneers in a new way of life that we humans too have pursued.[2]

Ants first appeared on earth 170 million years ago when the supercontinent Pangea was breaking up and dinosaurs were lumbering over the land. The ants diversified into some twelve thousand species—most of them highly social organisms, all finding security in rigidly programmed, collective, and obedient behavior. Among them it was the more collectivized species that first introduced farming. The outcome was that their numbers grew extraordinarily large, until today they total an estimated one quadrillion individuals, compared with only eight billion humans. The sheer weight of their numbers may equal the combined weight of all humans alive.

"Go to the ant, thou sluggard. Consider her ways and be wise." Proverbs 6:6 thus urges us to stoop down to ground level and admire. Although ants may work harder than we humans, it is not their virtue we should seek. No form of agriculture has required any special virtue, ethic, or philosophy. All the same, there is much to be learned from the ants, especially from their turn to agriculture. For ants as for humans, agriculture grew out of species insecurity caused by food shortages. The ant's response to such insecurity can help illuminate the first great transformation that we humans went through in our history.

Fifty million to sixty-five million years ago the ants first took up farming, as variants in their genes appeared that favored domestication and spread through sexual reproduction among the ants. Eventually, those variants pushed some ants into closely packed nests that were ruled by hierarchies of power. The result was agriculture, a crowning achievement of instinctive, unconscious adaptation, mixed with an inherited propensity to bow to authority. The leaf-cutting ants of the American tropics, which constitute some sixty species, evolved into farmers about eight million to twelve million years ago.[3] They are still farming throughout the tropics. Selected individuals of a typical nest go out to cut leaves from the rainforest and bring them home, where smaller-sized workers chew them into green pulp, and then a cadre of even smaller ants feed that pulp to captive aphids, which are tiny soft-bodied insects that suck sap out of plants, a behavior for which they were exploited like tiny cattle in a protected space. The results were not as sophisticated as the agricultural civilization that humans would create much later, for leaf-cutter farming was limited to a single captive species. Even so, this behavior, though it produced only a limited kind of agriculture, may seem like a lot to derive from instinct. So far ants have not had the necessary variants to go further, to develop larger bodies and bigger brains or undertake a general war on the wild. Their reproduction has remained severely checked not only by a paucity of genetic variants but also by a voracious circle of predators—beetles, spiders, snakes, snails, lizards, fish, birds, bears, and anteaters (Vermilingua, whose long tongues can lap up thirty-five thousand ants a day). Other checks have come from torrential rain showers that can drown multitudes in their underground nests. Their transition to agriculture, albeit wonderfully successful in meeting the demands of food and sex, did not make them completely secure or transform them into hierarchs of the planet.[4]

Edward O. Wilson attributes ant success to eusociality, meaning an inherited capacity for advanced social life that far surpasses the togetherness seen in a flock of birds or a school of fish. "Members of a eusocial animal group," writes Wilson, "such as a colony of ants, belong to multiple generations. They divide labor in what outwardly at least appears to be an altruistic manner. Some take labor roles that shorten their life spans or reduce the number of their personal offspring, or both. Their sacrifice allows others who fill reproductive roles to live longer and produce proportionately more offspring." Eusociality is not conscious or purposeful. It evolves from variants that survive and are passed on to later generations. And it is not what we usually think of as altruistic—a conscious elevation of the welfare of others over self—even though it resembles altruism in leading to self-sacrificing behavior. Ultimately, there is selfish purpose in the ants, giving them more success, as Wilson puts it, in producing "more offspring."[5]

Wilson credits eusociality with "the social conquest of Earth," but there he goes too far. No ant armies ever really conquered the rest of nature or waved their antennae and chomped their mandibles as they proclaimed themselves masters of the planet. Agriculture did not lead the ants to any general conquest, for they remained tiny, subordinate parts of larger ecosystems, subject to many checks and balances. All that the first farmers achieved was to overcome some checks on their numbers; they never posed a threat to local ecosystems or planetary ecology. Eusociality among the first farmers did not depend on overcoming instinct. Rather, it came from tiny brains that played a subordinate role as helpmate to tiny desires.

Farming began among ants, as I said, about fifty million years ago, whereas among humans it began a mere ten thousand years ago. But what drove them both were similar interactions between reproductive instincts and environments. An ant has only 250,000 brain cells packed in its minuscule head, compared with one hundred billion cells in the human brain. Yet that minuscule organ, multiplied through sex, led to an elaborate division of labor including farming and domestication. As ant organization became more complex, ant brains remained small and simple. Ant farming may deserve a sustainability prize, for they are still carrying it on, but they get no prize for possessing high IQs.

Variations occur all the time, perhaps in all forms of matter, most of them providing no advantage to the individual and disappearing quickly. Like typos in a manuscript, they confuse rather than help and usually get corrected quickly. But now and then a variation may survive and get replicated over and over simply because it functions better. It comes along at the right moment and offers a better match between organism and environment, resulting in the successful competition of some individuals with others.

Genetic variations have been appearing among ants for millions of years, with only a few of those variants surviving and passing on body shapes, social relations, and inner desires. It was enough to allow ants to increase in numbers. If we want to understand human agriculture, we would do well to learn why another species began farming long ago and how that behavior unfolded. Of course, it may be impossible ever to answer why, for much of ant farming developed so far back that the process is hard to trace. We know that other insect species like butterflies, spiders, and flies did not go through the same set of changes or become farmers. Only careful research may reveal why it was that some kinds of ants changed and thrived, while others did not.

Climate change has been suggested as a primary cause of the successful rise of human agriculture, which happened after the end of the Pleistocene, when a warmer, wetter climate appeared. More precisely, one might say that climate has been credited with determining the success rate of agriculture-friendly variants in human behavior. This explanation may be plausible in many instances, but we should be cautious about relying on that environmental cause as the key to unlock all historical mysteries. We should remember the forces within organisms as well as without—genomes as well as soils, temperatures, rainfall, ecosystems, the power of inner desires to adapt to external change and create their own success. We should also be careful to specify exactly what "agriculture" is supposed to mean. Does it mean the attempted cultivation of wild plants and animals, or does it refer to a more ambitious program of "domestication," involving the power of farmers to control other organisms' genetic makeup?

A climate-based summation of the origins of human agriculture can be found in John Brooke's *Climate Change and the Course of Global History* (2014). No one has made a more impressive effort than Brooke to identify climate as the great determinant of the ancient world. "The origins of agriculture," he concludes, "lay in the sudden end of the Pleistocene, as the cold, dry glacial world, after some climate oscillations, gave way to the warm, wet Holocene that has sheltered humanity ever since."[6] But does climate change explain all agriculture? The case of ants suggests that it does not: the ants' own inner drive for food security went on over millions of years, leaving climate as at best a secondary or proximate cause, not an ultimate cause, if indeed we can make any correlations between ant husbandry and a changing climate. Agricultural innovations were enabled, most likely, by genetic variations coupled with the ants' desire to reproduce. Climate was regularly changing throughout the insect's history. That change within the gene pool had nothing to do with the temperature or humidity outside the

THE AGRARIAN WHIP

nest. Looking to the ants' own nature, their struggle to survive the volatility of the world, explains better their turn to farming.

Ants began enslaving aphids back in the Cretaceous epoch, when world temperatures were much warmer and more equable than today, and they continued to do so across seven more epochs, from the Paleocene and Pleistocene down to the warmer, wetter Holocene. At no point did any big shifts in the climate make or unmake ant farming. The cold, dry conditions of the Pleistocene were not, of course, ideal for raising aphids, but the ants ignored those conditions and did not even shift to different kinds of livestock. Instead, they sought protection from the cold by digging their nests deeper into the soil or avoiding northern latitudes altogether, always fighting to keep their bodies, their aphids, and their progeny warm. Climate may have influenced them, but it was their own inner nature, not the force of global or regional warming or cooling, that pushed them to become farmers.

The same was likely true of humans. They became farmers in a benign time and stayed that way all through the subsequent cycles of drought and cold. Brooke suggests that human agriculture was a consequence of the Younger Dryas cold period (circa 13,000–11,600 years ago), during which time, he argues, human foragers turned to the domestication of plants and animals. Yet human agriculture did not appear anywhere until more than a thousand years after the Younger Dryas ended, and throughout the subsequent emergence of independent centers of plant domestication there was no significant change in the climate. As the agricultural historian Peter Bellwood declares, "If the Younger Dryas was a trigger, the gun took quite a while to go off."[7] Something besides hot and cold temperatures pushed the first great human transformation. That factor must be a rising population among *sapiens,* turning foragers into farmers. There was no sudden population "explosion" among them, but there was a slow, steady rate of increase that produced more and more mouths needing to be filled.

What was the compelling cause not only among the ants but also among the first half dozen independent sites where human agriculture appeared?

THE AGRARIAN WHIP

There is no better explanation than the pressure of species reproduction on environment. Agriculture appeared whenever and wherever there was a deteriorating food supply. That deterioration was caused not by the outer environment but by progeny overwhelming wild food supplies, making conditions right for new behaviors to emerge that could help provide enough food. To assume otherwise, to insist that each origin of agriculture had an environmental or some different cause, is to violate the logic that all science has followed since William of Ockham: when faced with two possible explanations, the simpler of the two is the one more likely to be true. And in this case, the simpler and the ultimate cause was our common natural urge for food and sex.

We know a lot more about humans than about ants creating agriculture. For example, we know that human farming first appeared in a small corner of Eurasia, a hilly terrain stretching from Turkey to Iraq that we call the "Fertile Crescent." There, hungry migrants had settled tens of thousands of years earlier, for here they found a reliable, abundant source of food and security. Rainfall was ample in the hills, grasses heavy with seeds grew thickly on their slopes, and the grasses were rich enough to support large herds of wild herbivores or human children. Among the hills, an intricate network of rivers, including the Jordan, Euphrates, and Tigris, flowed to the sea, and it was along their banks that migrants found new homes of abundance. Wherever the rivers' flooding watered the vegetation thoroughly one could find good prospects for foraging.

Bruce Smith, an archaeologist at the Smithsonian National Museum of Natural History, explains human agriculture as the outcome of affluence, not of poverty, but what kind of affluence does he mean? Not at all Marshall Sahlins's notion, involving a high level of material consumption. Smith means only an abundance that reduced risks. Foragers were not in any immediate danger, he says, but as far-sighted consumers they sought "ways of increasing the yield and reliability of promising species."[8] In other words, their brains led them to a place of abundant resources and then, through rational planning, they tried to extend that abundance into the future.

Smith points to a human capacity for long-term planning—for deliberate, rational thinking and for a deliberate strategy of sustainability. Through lean and fat years, he argues, our kind learned how to even out shortages by storing up surpluses. That theory comes from the old ant versus grasshopper comparison: some species had foresight (those we admire) while others did not (those we pity). But is it true? Were ants of fifty million years ago or humans of ten thousand years ago thinking about achieving sustainability over millennia to come? More likely both proceeded without any conscious, rational, long-term plan. They were motivated by the growing hunger in their families, as they heard their babies cry loudly in the night for something to eat and realized there were too many of them to feed.

Agriculture in the Fertile Crescent began because the food supply was shrinking. For tens of thousands of years, the Fertile Crescent supported a hunting and gathering life, and people could kill and eat without much forethought. They lived in a kind of paradise. Here in this place, they could avoid migrating and settle down for the foreseeable future. They began arriving in the Fertile Crescent as much as a hundred thousand years before they turned to agriculture. Why did they not become farmers when they first got there? We have plenty of evidence that it took a long time for them to become sedentarized, but as that was happening, they continued living the good life by foraging for only a few hours per week. But then their numbers increased, not explosively, but just enough to lead them instinctively, as it had led the ants, to begin manipulating the gene pools of a few plant species around them.

At both ends of the Great Rift cutting across Africa and western Asia humans were instinctively drawn to well-endowed landscapes that long ago had been created by colliding continental plates, a zone where there was a wide diversity of species to be hunted and gathered. When early humans found their way to the northern end of the Great Rift Valley, they discovered a new, unexploited richness. Here at last, we can almost hear them saying, we have come to "the good place" where we won't have to move so often or compete so fiercely. Not all places on earth were equally productive for the foraging life; each had its own array of species, its unique capacity or incapacity to sustain human appetites. Humans arriving in this place sensed they had found their spot. Compared with much of Africa and Asia, the Fertile Crescent was a veritable Shangri-la, one of the planet's most superbly alive and diversified habitats.

The first people to become farmers, domesticating wild plants and animals, were the Natufians, descendants of the African migrants who first discovered this region. Two anthropologists, Joy McCorriston and Frank Hole, were among those who first studied the Natufians, living in the Jordan River valley where "the critical preconditions for the domestication of Southwest Asian crop plants co-occurred earliest."[9] The scientists describe a long settling-in that took place. They point to the sickles made by the Natufians from sharpened stones to cut the wild grasses and the round stones on which they pounded grass seeds into flour. Through such tools they created the neolithic revolution, another name for the first great transformation.

The Natufians built permanent, year-round, stone-lined houses with food storage pits dug immediately under them. They learned how to store seeds to get them through the ups and downs of cold and heat. More and more they turned to subsisting on the high-protein grains that grew nearby, particularly emmer wheat and hulled barley. They selected other wild plants, removing their weedy competitors, shaping natural evolution. At first their meat supplies had been bountiful, but then they almost died out because of overhunting. For a while they could go on foraging around their houses, eating lower and lower on the food chain, until in the end they were forced to try manipulating plant DNA. In short, early humans changed their environment more than the environment changed them, until they seized on a few annuals as the basis of a new agriculture.

Necessity born of desire lay behind those developments. No longer migrating, free of migration's suppressive effects on female hormone flow, they surely produced more and more children than ever before, and their populations increased steadily. The Natufians were not more inventive or brilliant than people elsewhere, and they were driven by a familiar gonadic imperative. But after a long success of foraging in one of the most abundant habitats anywhere outside Africa, of learning the habits and needs of local plants and animals, and of experiencing the overharvesting of resources, they made the transition to agriculture.

If that had been the only place on earth where abundant natural resources were available, then agriculture might never have become the planetary success it is today. But what the Natufians invented eventually began to show up elsewhere on the planet. That was not because the Natufians publicized their achievement. Other peoples who lived far away and at much later times, who lived in places that had similar rich endowments, began to cultivate and domesticate all on their own, for they had the same human nature and the same reproductive drives. It was thus a common human nature and an insistent need for sex that made humans agricultural.

Peter Bellwood approximates the birth date of agriculture as 11,000 years before the present (BP), or 9000 BCE. The geographer Jared Diamond sets the birth date at 10,500 BP, while others have pushed it back to 12,000 BP.[10] All agree that agriculture's next important breakthrough came in China's Yangzi and Yellow (also the Wei) river valleys, about 9000 BP, a thousand years after the Natufians.[11] Those East Asian river valleys had been settled by humans later than the valleys and hills of the Fertile Crescent, but they offered a similar natural abundance that allowed a similar upward curve in human numbers, to the point of pressing once again on a wild food supply.

The historian Ping-ti Ho (also known as Bingdi He) has argued that the loess plateau, which forms much of the Yellow River's watershed, was the first point of emergence for the Chinese agrarian way of life and agrarian state.[12] Later scholars have challenged that view as too narrow, but it seems obvious that ancient windblown deposits must have offered enormous potential as a food supply. The loess soils, a blanket of nutrients that had been blown in by strong post-Pleistocene winds from Mongolia and Xinjiang, covered much of the north. Over the span of millennia those soils continually washed down from the dry, scantily vegetated hillsides to fill the lower valleys and spilled onto the plains. Everywhere they washed, they brought a fertility that seemingly was inexhaustible.

In the warm, humid years that followed the Pleistocene, hardy grasses and shrubs soon covered the loess region and its river valleys, anchoring the soil and keeping it in place. Then humans arrived, and as their numbers increased they set out to destroy native vegetation that did not produce food. That meant removing the bunch grass and cultivating millet when human numbers grew large enough.

At first, the loess-region farmers raised abundant crops year after year without much labor. Now and then they had to restore depleted nitrogen to their fields, but this they could do by fallowing for a few years or planting a nitrogen-fixing crop like soybeans. For a while they could plant and harvest without needing any fertilizer at all.

In China as in the Middle East, a warming trend may have helped push people into agriculture, but again we must be careful not to exaggerate climate change as the sole or principal cause. Climate is always changing somewhere, but climates over the past ten millennia, during the Holocene epoch, have been remarkably stable and consistent. When humans began abandoning a way of life that had lasted for two hundred thousand years, they were responding to more than warming temperatures or receding glaciers.

China's foragers, like the Natufians, began by domesticating annual grasses. They focused first on wild millet growing in the north across the plains and hills bordering the Yellow River (the Huang He), and then south of there they focused on wild rice, another annual grass that grew abundantly, this time in lakes and marshes along the Yangzi (Changjiang), the most important river in China. As initially favorable environmental conditions vanished, people nonetheless tended to stay put but also stay innovative.

THE AGRARIAN WHIP

As many as four thousand years after the Natufians and the Chinese, and far away from those early agricultural hearths, far off in the western hemisphere, other independent centers began to form.[13] The first non-Asiatic site appeared in the hilly midlands of Mexico, followed closely by the mountains and river valleys of Peru. Both sites of agricultural breakthrough appeared where there was a richness of soils, water, and biodiversity. The first farmers there could not have known that agriculture had already emerged in faraway Eurasia, for they were isolated from circles of knowledge by the broad Pacific Ocean. Their ancestors had arrived in the Americas by foot or coastal canoes around five thousand to ten thousand years earlier, and long after that they began to feel the pinch of overpopulation and to seek to raise food productivity, free of influence from other world regions. That pinch led to plant and animal domestication in the Americas around four thousand to five thousand years BP (according to Bellwood) or 5500 BP (Diamond). Still another independent site was the Mississippi Valley of North America, where humans began to domesticate an array of local plants, including goosefoot (*Chenopodium*), sunflower (*Helianthus*), and squash (*Cucurbita*).[14]

From those five independent centers of innovation—there may have been others—agriculture spread as a human practice in all directions, beginning with crops and herds and then with ideas, cultures, and a way of life. From the Fertile Crescent, agriculture spread into the Nile Valley of Africa, into India, and into Europe. Around 3300 BCE a mix of domesticated livestock and cereals showed up in the British Isles (coming from the Middle East). From China's magnificent river valleys, agriculture diffused into Japan, Korea, Southeast Asia, the Philippines, and Indonesia, until thousands of years later it reached remote islands in the Pacific.

Remarkably, it took the agrarian way of life just a few millennia to replace on all the inhabitable continents a life based on foraging. No matter which dates are used, the transition from one way to another took only a moment in geological time. Roughly speaking, it began around ten millennia ago. Although foraging or pastoral herding would continue on the margins, by the first century CE almost all humans across the planet had become farmers.[15]

The *when* and *where* of agriculture are now well established. *When* was whenever humans settled down to a sedentary life and became densely packed in one place. *Where* was wherever there was a well-favored environment that produced plenty of nutrition that humans needed. The best places were those that other species had settled too, where many forms of life had evolved and proliferated together. Agriculture, it must be emphasized, did not begin on windswept plains or in dense jungles that were hard to settle, inhabit, or clear.

It may be part of a common human nature to look for predictable patterns in all change. But we are also able to think more complexly. Agriculture has never been a highly linear or purposeful enterprise, never a stepping out of darkness into light made possible by the uniqueness of human reason. Instead, we should see its appearance as a change full of contingency, with no overall purpose other than to alleviate growing demographic pressures and to provide for growing numbers.

What was the source of the ecological pressures that came with agriculture? *Homo sapiens* wanted sex as often as possible. Nine months later they got babies, and then those babies had to be fed, perhaps over a life span of three decades. The Twice Wise were the Twice Hungry: driven by food and sex hungers. But there were other influences and determinants, including local variations that appeared at just the right time. Agriculture began, therefore, as part of the natural evolution of the earth. It did not mark a breach with the rest of life; rather it grew out of the drive of all species to multiply and replenish themselves and out of variations in human gene profiles competing for survival.

We have seen how, given enough time, the power of desire could lead a few sex-seeking humans to produce a worldwide population of perhaps ten million. First came desire, uprooting and redistributing people across the face of the earth, always the search for a patch of sunshine that would yield meat, tubers, fruits, and seeds. Everywhere they went, they carried that desire and the resulting children with them. Without much intention they found themselves living in closely settled, fixed villages, where lugging babies in their arms along interminable game trails could come to an end, where women and men would raise their food in fenced-off fields and house their animals in makeshift pens and stockades. In short, where they could become farmers.

The hungers that drove humans varied from person to person. Both women and men had a set of inner desires pushing them on, but how they responded varied over time and circumstances. Generally, their bodies told them they must reproduce, while the mates they found resulted from the contingencies of time and place. Eventually out of that complicated mix came "a social conquest of Earth" that far surpassed that of the ants.

That conquest was never complete. The first farmers never exercised any power over volcanoes, earthquakes, oceans, or climates. And they controlled only a very small subset of their fellow plants and animals. But as human numbers reached a critical threshold, they did manage to disturb the old foragers' equilibrium with the earth. There was no single day or year when that happened, but once a demographic threshold was reached, they could not turn back and recover their old intimate, humble place in a self-balancing natural order. There were too many of them to allow that. Reproduction of the species had been their most compelling desire but also their source of stability, until one day they found themselves destabilized by their own fertility.

The historian Yuval Noah Harari has offered a different, provocative but finally rather perverse interpretation of the new relationships that came out of agriculture. He calls the agricultural way of life a "Faustian bargain," for in it, he says, humans were forced to give up their freedom and the power they had achieved over nature. During a six-thousand-year period, stretching from 9500 to 3500 BCE, he writes, they struck a bargain with other species—a bad bargain for *sapiens,* for it turned out to be lopsidedly against their self-interest. Harari calls agriculture "history's greatest fraud."[16] Although most species proved ill-suited to captivity or refused to enter into any agreements with humans, a few—wheat, rice, maize, potatoes, millet, and barley; cattle, sheep, goats, and dogs—were glad to sign up, for they gained by becoming captives. The wheat plant, says Harari, allowed itself to be captured, for then it could get humans to dig irrigation canals to keep its roots watered in times of drought. Dogs and sheep got an even better deal, forcing their human owners to pamper and take care of them in perpetuity. Paradoxical and amusing as it is, this notion of a contract or "bargain" is, nonetheless, a misleading, inapt metaphor for agriculture.

Ask the aphids whether they were happy to lose their wings, which were bitten off by their ant captors. Ask the wild rice whether it was happier in a rice paddy than along the shores of lakes. Those species may have gained some protection in their struggle for existence, but it did not come without costs. The domesticates became trapped forever in servitude. If it was a bad bargain, it was bad for the aphids more than for the ants. Likewise, the domestication of wheat and dogs did not truly allow those species to set any terms, negotiate their employment, or sign contracts. On the contrary, they were captured, enslaved, and made to perform whatever their masters wanted. Most of the power coming from agriculture accrued to farmers or other humans. Through farming, humans became real, not puppet, masters, and if their mastery at times resembled slavery, it was not wheat or dogs they should blame. It was their own bellies and gonads. They became captives of their inner desires.

Always shaped to some extent by local conditions of biodiversity, soils, and climates, human agriculture managed to gain a lasting foothold on all the major continents. The last important origin site was Africa, where farmers began spreading south of the Sahara about four thousand years ago. Thousands of years passed during which many competing local forms of

THE AGRARIAN WHIP

agriculture flourished until a few standardized versions appeared over most of the continent's land surface.[17]

Why was Africa the last continent to turn to agriculture? Scientists can find no racially based differences separating its peoples from those on other continents, which leaves material differences in outer ecologies and inner drives as the only plausible explanation. In Africa wild species had been defending themselves against hungry humans far longer than anywhere else. As their ecosystems were tapped for nutrition, as any human surplus had migrated to other continents, what was left behind were relatively stable and intact ecosystems that had evolved in balance with the people. As late as 1500 BCE "the whole southern half of the African continent, including the rain forest and all regions below the Equator, still remained the terrain of hunters and gatherers."[18] Africa's foragers, free of the intense reproductive pressures that developed in other regions, continued to find what they needed to survive, that is, until *their* babies also began crying from hunger, and until there was no new space for expanding their hunting and gathering mode.

The Bantu people from Africa's northern latitudes were among the last to become farmers, borrowing crops from the Middle East and Egypt and carrying them southward all the way to the Cape, including some of their own domesticated foods like sorghum, rice, and yams transported from the Sahel, Ethiopia, and tropical West Africa. Until that happened, the only place on the continent where a major agrarian civilization arose early and endured for thousands of years was in the Nile River watershed, another river valley where all things were just right for agriculture. There is a severe paucity of reliable data on early Africa, but it seems plausible that this long-inhabited continent stayed low in numbers until about three thousand to four thousand years BP. A diversity of plants and animals lived there, as everywhere, but perhaps not many of them were easy to tame and manage by a population that had good foraging prospects.[19]

Yet today, in contrast to its more stable past, Africa is becoming one of the most dynamic agricultural regions on the planet—wherever it has good soils and water. It is booming with human babies, so much so that one day it may surpass Asia as the most heavily populated landmass. Following today's unprecedented explosion in population, agriculture has begun expanding rapidly across the continent, leaving many native plant and animal species more endangered than they have been in a long time.

Joseph Ogutu, senior statistician at the University of Hohenheim's Institute of Crop Science, has nicely summarized the changes: "Wildlife numbers are declining sharply across Africa, including migratory populations. In Kenya, wildlife numbers declined by 68% . . . from 1977 to 2016 both outside and inside protected areas. Most wildlife still occurs on private and communal lands outside protected areas, which cover only 10% of Kenya's land surface. As with other parts of Africa, protected areas are too small to meet all the needs of their wildlife populations all year in East Africa. Many wildlife species, therefore, spend part or all the year outside protected areas."[20] We are now witnessing on the African continent a familiar kind of environmental degradation resulting from rapid population growth, exactly like the one that took place earlier across Eurasia and the Americas.

One of the best books on the question of why agriculture has again and again undermined the foragers' world is Mark Nathan Cohen's *The Food Crisis in Prehistory,* a classic in anthropology and archaeology published in 1977. Cohen challenged the popular narrative in which human foresight and progressive intentions explain agriculture. He asked what motivated our ancestors to change. We cannot, of course, be perfectly sure of how the first human farmers thought, for they left no written records or data, forcing us to seek answers in material artifacts, migrant routes, and estimated reproductive rates. "Agriculture will occur," Cohen concluded, "only in situations where greater production per unit of space is required."[21] Required because desired.

Farmers seek to make the earth grow grains or beef or potatoes in greater abundance. But when did humans begin itching to do that? Cohen answers that the itch began whenever reproduction pressed hard on the food supply. Humans did not worry abstractly about some distant, far-off-in-the-future problem. Here, in this place or in this time, they felt the need to produce more through innovation.

Such an argument was not original with Cohen, for earlier it had been broached by such anthropologists as Kent Flannery and Lewis R. Binford.[22] They too found evidence of population growth pressing on food supplies. They too tried to estimate the number of shelters that people had built and inhabited over time, the size of their families, and the frequency of births and burials. Beyond such material evidence, they too sought a coherent, comprehensive hypothesis that did not depend on faith in human exceptionalism. In fact, such an emphasis on human fertility continued to be popular among many social scientists well into the 1970s and 1980s, but then that approach got swamped and forgotten by recent fashions featuring the contending powers of culture or climate.

Many scholars, fearful of the bogey of environmental determinism, have argued that the first transformation must have derived from changes in human worldviews or values. Others, influenced by debates over anthropogenic climate change, have countered with graphs that correlate human change with environmental shifts, mainly shifts in climate. Both parties have ignored the possibility that human nature itself might be a powerful agent. Although Cohen did not directly acknowledge the combined power of human nature and environment, he did accept that human reproductive urges might be more fundamental than cultural values or climatic shifts. "Changes in climate," he wrote, "would be significant only if population was already approaching critical densities."[23]

Cohen was among the few agricultural anthropologists who stayed clear of the shift to cultural or climatic explanations. He kept looking for non-cultural data and drawing deductions from it. In particular, he explored the mountains and shorelines of Peru, one of the original hearths of agriculture, paying little attention to values, worldviews, religions, mythologies, or beliefs. He dug up old ruins, estimated the size of families that had once lived in them, and collected desiccated foods they had left behind. He was not persuaded that ancient societies, based on either foraging or farming, had consciously aimed at the ideal of equilibrium, or what we would now consider the idea of "sustainability."[24]

If foragers ever truly aimed at achieving sustainability, if they ever made balancing with their environment a strong ruling principle or value, their way of life might have gone on even longer, but they did not. They wanted sex more than balance, which resulted in too many pregnancies to sustain. Human sexual desire could be influenced by environmental, genetic, or cultural factors, to be sure, although in most cases the expression of desire led to higher population density, which in turn led to more pressure on the food supply. Achieving a balance with nature was too abstract an ideal to matter as much.[25]

The Ancón coast–Chillón river region just north of Lima, Peru (which today is a megalopolis of more than eleven million inhabitants), seemed to Cohen a good place to study the transformation. Archaeologists had reconstructed a human history for the region, covering twelve thousand years. They had identified a key native ecosystem that offered a vegetation type called *lomas,* a nutritious mix of potato-like tubers and herbaceous annual plants. Humans had eaten from that ecosystem until it was nearly gone. When their appetite exceeded the biomass of *lomas,* they were forced to import from Mexico the corn-beans-squash crop system. Cohen describes the region's early humans as "needing to travel progressively farther afield to obtain food, because [their] population was expanding and because resources closer to home were being exhausted." Over a 750-year period, he calculated, the reproduction rate might in a few decades have doubled the population. Faced with such increases, foragers were compelled to take up agriculture, but they did so only after "the absence of wild resources necessitated cultivation."[26]

THE AGRARIAN WHIP

Cohen's meticulous field studies led him to a revolutionary theory of agricultural emergence: "human population has been growing throughout its history, and . . . such growth is the cause, rather than simply the result of much human 'progress' or technological change, particularly in the subsistence sphere."[27]

Besides field research, Cohen gathered evidence from modern agricultural societies that afforded insights into the dim, unwritten past. From the 1940s on, the Food and Agriculture Organization of the United Nations reported on the urgent problem of malnutrition across the Global South. Development economists showed up to give advice, among them the Danish expert Ester Boserup (1910–1999), who traveled to Senegal and India and drew from her own field studies a powerful argument in favor of greater population increase. And Cohen became her disciple.[28]

Boserup was decidedly not a fan of the controversial English demographer Thomas Malthus, who accused the poor of bringing too many children into the world. Population increases, Boserup countered, were not a curse but a blessing and did not have to leave people mired in poverty. In fact, she said, high birthrates could generate more food to support more babies, and more babies added more brains to innovation, creating a growth machine like no other. Boserup believed that parents who produced a great number of children should be praised for adding more "natural resources" to the earth. Babies were not the problem, she argued; potentially, they were problem solvers who could figure out how to produce more food and other necessities. Indeed, it was precisely because of population growth, she declared, that a hungry world had reason to hope. Growth was needed to overcome poverty. More people would allow humans not only to survive but also to overcome the limits of the earth.[29]

Society's goal, Boserup maintained, should be always to cultivate the earth more and more intensively. Poor farmers should seek to shorten the fallow period in their fields to ten or five years or, ideally, do no fallowing at all. That might require a lot of intensive labor on the land, but she was sure that the earth would always respond positively to human effort. Every possible hectare might one day be needed for food production. Boserup was speaking the language of "cornucopian" economics, which after World War II became popular in many countries. The earth, the cornucopians believed, could become a never failing horn of plenty, spilling out an endless harvest of abundance—that is, if humans were willing to work hard and turn all the land into farms.[30]

Mark Cohen was not a Boserupian through and through. He did not share Boserup's radically anthropocentric faith that the earth can be made forever bountiful. He also did not argue that Boserupian intensification of land use would end in disaster. Current problems were not his main concern. As a scholar he was intent on explaining the origins of agriculture rather than examining what it had become. His conclusion about those origins was that "population growth is an inherent factor in the adaptive histories of many, if not most, human populations and . . . such growth can be used to explain aspects of the development of agriculture which are otherwise inexplicable."[31]

A plethora of books and articles have been written extolling the importance of agriculture, books by authors who like Boserup had been awestruck by the skill and virtue of farmers. For Boserupians, agriculture exemplifies the superior ingenuity, morality, and intelligence of *Homo sapiens*. "Here begins our progress out of nature" is their narrative, which has been a very influential mantra. Richard MacNeish, a leading anthropologist, for instance, has called agriculture the "great leap forward."[32] Similarly, the British archaeologist Graeme Barker praises agriculture for bringing "profound changes in the relationship between people and the natural world." Agriculture, he adds, was "the precondition for the development of the first great urban civilizations in Egypt, Mesopotamia, the Indus valley, China, the Americas, and Africa, and has been for all later states up to the present day."[33]

But is that all there is to be said? Might we add that, because agriculture has allowed the number of humans on the planet to skyrocket, we have been pushed into an ant-like division of labor and an engineered life? Might we add that agriculture has brought a loss of habitats on which so many of our fellow species evolved?

Lately, that Boserupian narrative of agriculture has become less common. In fact, the old celebration of agriculture is now being blamed for some of the world's biggest environmental and social problems, ranging from injustice and poverty to pollution, global warming, and species extinction. That reappraisal may come out from the heartland of agribusiness or from an obscure village left behind by progress. What went wrong in the history of farming? This poignant question is asked more often these days, and the answers have become darker. On the evolution of agriculture hangs our whole narrative of human history on the planet. Are we moving forward or not? Are we part of nature, or not? Is agriculture "natural," or does it warn that progress through conquest can go wrong? Is there a better way to provide humans with food than we have so far found?

A new narrative, which sees agriculture as more flawed than heroic, has appeared, telling how the evolution of a new way of life led, through population growth, straight to modern agribusiness. As human fertility pressed against the earth, agriculture scaled up and destroyed everything in its path. Small, simple transformations became huge and powerful forces that were destructive even to those who were responsible. In food as in sex, fulfilling unchecked desires proved not always better. Rather than leading us to some noble commitment to progress, truth, and justice, linking our urge to eat to that other primeval human urge, sexual reproduction, has left us with a far less flattering tale to tell.

Today, agriculture is still active, but it has been transformed by the industrial capitalist mode of production. It has spread far beyond Mesopotamia and the Yellow River: if we include the grazing of livestock, agriculture now covers about 40 percent of the planet's land surface. An area equal to South America is being used for agricultural production, with much of that territory turned into a plant and vegetable oil factory while another 3.2

billion to 3.6 billion hectares are devoted to raising a meat supply for human consumption. As food demands have grown, as the malnourished have scrambled to find something to eat and the already well fed have stuffed themselves with more and more meals, as human babies have proliferated, any fertile land that remains unappropriated is almost sure to be turned into plowland or pastureland. Cities have encroached on farms, which we bemoan, but farms have been encroaching on ecosystems for ten millennia, and who cares about that? Yet today, our dilemma remains the same: hunger and even starvation drive us, yet after nations have boosted farm production to avert famine and raised export earnings to pay for education, housing, and entertainment, people are still hungry somewhere. No one ever planned that agriculture would become such a treadmill, but it has come to that, and in the process agriculture has lost supporters, practitioners, and its old sense of virtue.

As agriculture has kept intensifying, it has turned much of the planet into a homogenized and yet ruthlessly simplified manufacturing plant. It has diminished the beauty, diversity, and fertility of the planet. A mere dozen domesticated plants have come to account for more than 80 percent of the plant life under cultivation. Those domesticates include the banana, barley, maize, manioc, potato, rice, sorghum, soybean, sugar beet, sugar cane, sweet potato, and wheat, all of them having been selected thousands of years ago. Only five kinds of large animals can be found on most farms: the cow, sheep, goat, pig, and horse—all of which have become forms of technology.

Out of the hundred million species that have ever lived on earth, agriculture has come to depend largely on a mere dozen or so. The rest have become expendable. Perhaps humans have not tried hard enough to domesticate more species, but more likely modern producers have overemphasized those favored few because with them they can produce more food.

Most of us are dependent, passive consumers of food. Out of a population of nearly 350 million, the United States depends on about two million

THE AGRARIAN WHIP

farmers to furnish its nutrition. Thus, agriculture, rather than the earth, has become our true mother. Or we should say that agriculture has become our "half mother," for according to *Our World in Data* about half of the world's habitable land is used for agriculture.[34] Even the seas have been replaced on their margins by fish farms that mass-produce salmon, trout, catfish, and shrimp. On what is left of the unplowed, unfarmed earth we are building "wind farms" and other energy-producing businesses, or we are mining the land for minerals and fuels.

Yet, surprisingly, a substantial amount of wilderness still survives on this heavily populated and intensely farmed small planet.[35] Where it survives on the margins of Russia, China, Canada, the United States, Australia, and Brazil, the earth may still seem to be a fertile mother, but even there human residents may find her bounty stingy and scarce. Our own fertility has diminished the fertility of the planet.

As we have come to depend more and more on our agricultural "half mother," we have acquired a taste for the same foods raised across the planet. From the Middle East we have learned to plant and harvest such foods as wheat and barley (both grains), peas (a legume), and olives (a fruit), along with raising sheep and goats. China has given us rice, millet, soybeans, and pork, while Native Americans have added corn, beans, squash, pumpkin, tomato, potato, and manioc (cassava), along with dogs, llamas, and guinea pigs as mammalian domesticates. Through migration and trade, all of those foods have become part of the modern consumer's hodgepodge international cuisine.

Thousands of years ago many hunters and gatherers resisted the agricultural transformation because they feared it would lead to a drastic alteration of their lives. They complained about the big changes required in their diet and habits. Grains were the easiest food to manage for higher productivity, but they may have led to enhanced state power. Although grains were rich in carbohydrates, calories, and sometimes proteins, they were low in other vital nutrients, so why were they so widely adopted? Was it because grain agriculture was helpful to those in power, enabling them to create centralized states? "Only the cereal grains," James C. Scott argues, "can serve as a basis for taxation: visible, divisible, assessable, storable, transportable, and 'rationable.'" Heavy taxation based on grain cropping may have gained elites more power over the people.[36]

Indisputably, evidence from skeletons exhumed from early farming settlements suggests that a wide nutritional degeneration came with agriculture. Eating cereal grains in particular meant increased tooth decay and gum disease, along with loss of tooth enamel, all indicative of malnutrition. Human skeletons, after grain consumption increased, showed a loss in average individual height of six inches among men, five inches among women. Life spans that had been very brief under foraging became even briefer. According to George Armelagos, a leading expert in paleopathology, "life expectancy at birth in the pre-agricultural community was about twenty-six years, but in the post-agricultural community it was nineteen years."[37] Fear that agriculture might be unhealthy and dangerous was widespread among foragers, who preferred clinging to their life even in the face of diminishing returns. Opposing them were all those who wanted more of their children to survive infancy and live longer than thirty years, a calculation that persuaded many to applaud the shift.

Foragers acquiesced in the transformation because their traditional hunting and gathering was bringing in less and less food. Men were forced to chase after smaller, scrawnier species of animals—birds, reptiles, fish, rodents, and even insects—to get enough meat. Women, who contributed mainly by collecting wild plants and practicing horticulture, had to walk farther from home and harvest plants that were less nutritional. Marshall Sahlins's "original affluent society" was in fact steadily becoming poorer and poorer. Yet even then, there were some who resisted making any changes to the foraging way of life. Eventually most of them lost out, but only gradually, and they did so only because they could not keep up with their own fertility.

Gaining more calories through agriculture, however, did not necessarily mean better health; vitamins, trace elements, and amino acids are also essential for strong bodies. Rice, wheat, corn, and other grains, the main plants selected for human management, were all loaded with calories but scarce in amino acids. Yet what alternative did a highly prolific people have? Shifting to a diet heavy in grains had almost no effect on their procreation, for they could still get enough energy from cereal crops to have sex and make babies.

The imperative that drives all kinds of reproduction was, in the end, the deciding factor in the agrarian transformation, for plant and animal domestication provided the only feasible way to feed growing families and bands. Despite the risks of skeletal and dental deterioration, despite vitamin and protein deficiencies and shortened lives, humans obeyed that inner imperative and accepted farming.

Foragers should have feared, and probably many did fear, an oversimplification of their environment; after all, they had long depended on natural diversity to survive. Did they also fear, or even understand, that the food species feeding a forager were mostly perennials, not annuals? Year in and year out the perennials had been the most reliable suppliers of food. A plant collector instinctively sought to spread her risks while supplying her progeny. Agriculture, however, led to an ever more draconian oversimplification of nature, reducing many complex ecosystems to highly simplified stands of annuals, even to monocultural landscapes populated by annuals. Annuals get their name because they spring up for a single growing season, after which they die, maybe reappearing next year or maybe not, depending on environmental conditions. On the plus side, annual plants can respond quickly to an increase in rainfall or temperature, so that when conditions are right they can yield more in a single year than perennials do in a decade. But it was the perennials that put people at a lower risk year in and year out. They still are a safer bet for sustainability. Perennials put down deeper roots, so they can withstand any shifts in the environment, and tap a deeper fertility. By focusing on a few annuals instead of many perennials, farmers may have gained more harvest per hectare, but the hidden cost was more and bigger risk.[38]

Another drawback in the transformation came from the heightened susceptibility that agriculture brought to infectious diseases and epidemics. Generally, the new farmers lived packed closely together in settlements, not unlike the nests of ants—but that meant more exposure to dangerous microbes. When people lived scattered about the landscape, they got sick less often. With agriculture and a more sedentary life it took many generations of genetic adaptation to overcome a big early increase in death rates. Eventually humans evolved new immunities or learned to stay clear of the most germy villages and deathtraps. They adapted but kept looking back at what seemed to have been a more stable, free, and healthy relationship with nature.[39]

In the end farming offered one big advantage that, for all its drawbacks, could not be resisted: it produced more food per person, which in turn supported more children and thus promoted the species. A hectare of agricultural land might yield fifty to a hundred times more food than a wild landscape. And then, as knowledge improved and harvests became more bountiful, the brutal practice of infanticide and geronticide could become less necessary and common. Parents could keep more of their infant girls alive and not be daunted by five or ten children per family. After all, with that bigger brood of offspring came a larger supply of house and farm labor.

Demographers calculate, as noted earlier, that there may have been between 5 million and 15 million people alive some ten thousand years ago, at the dawn of agriculture. By the year 1 CE, by which time agriculture had become the norm, the human population had swelled to 252 million, and it kept on swelling, despite occasional floods, plagues, and famines. By 1750 it had reached nearly 771 million and by 1950 around 2.5 billion.[40]

What an incredible miracle the first great transformation wrought! What other species could match it? Perhaps only the ants. As human numbers grew, people could feel assured that the great gamble of agriculture was paying off in more meals for more people, and who knew what other gains might follow that success?

For nearly two hundred thousand years the Twice Wise lived directly on nature as foragers. During that time, they expanded into many regions, reproducing themselves under sometimes severe constraints. When their populations changed, farming proved inferior to foraging in protecting the planet's natural resources. Foraging was nature's way of feeding all its species. But foraging was not a good way of life for managing human fertility.

Any of the good results that have flowed from agriculture become less positive when we scrutinize the word "domestication." It is a term used freely by many scholars and lay people, but few ask what it implies in our relations with nature and each other. "Domestication" is, quite simply, a euphemism for greater human control over the rest of nature. We think of domesticated land as a place that has been "tamed," from which wild creatures and plants have been driven off or killed. It is any place that we have made over in our own image. In logic and history, "domestication" is closely related to another word, "slavery." In our time slavery has come to be viewed as an unacceptable practice, and rightly so, calling up centuries of racial injustice and discrimination. Yet plant and animal domestication continued to enjoy an honorable status, even among the ethicists and moralizing poets. Now we have begun to ask what domestication and slavery have in common.

Agriculture from its early days featured the seizing of wild plants and animals and placing them inside controlled spaces—gardens located near a farmer's house, fields bordered by fences or walls, places where the farmer could control other forms of life and especially their reproduction.

THE AGRARIAN WHIP

Agriculture involved reducing animals to little more than quantities of meat, beasts of burden, pullers of plows, and even instruments of war. They became "domesticated," which involved being owned and incarcerated. The one who owned might brand his living property with hot irons, force rings and plugs into their noses, and strap harnesses over their shoulders. Domesticators grew accustomed to such practices, until one day they extended similar treatment to human beings as well. It is hard to say when human slavery began, but clearly it grew out of agriculture, and the production of more food or fiber was commonly the justification for both slavery and domestication.

All over the world we have tended to ignore the central role agriculture played in creating a legacy of slavery. Our myth makers tell us nostalgic stories about yeoman farmers, toiling peasants, and blooming gardens; they write songs and verses to celebrate rural life, whether it was lived in a small grass hut, a half-timbered cottage, or a mansion overlooking fields of plantation cotton, sugar, or tobacco.[41] As farming spread, so did its mythology, and so did the practice of slavery, both of humans and nonhumans. Plant and animal domestication, the myth makers have decided, is conducive to social order and family happiness and so-called symbiotic relations with the nonhuman. They have overlooked the darker reality that the farmer quite often used a whip, plow, harness, saddle, shackle, or tether. Plants were not subject to such instruments of control, but they too experienced the heavy hand of man, as he weeded, snipped, sawed, and fenced, deciding which trees or sprouts would survive and which would not.

Over time all the capturing, saddling, harnessing, and whipping of other species had this seldom-noted result: some people began to wield a new kind of power over others of their own species. As a form of power, slavery was not one single relationship, and it was not confined to humans. It varied materially (slavery organized along lines of genes, body shapes and sizes, skin color, economies, or technology) and culturally (according to social

THE AGRARIAN WHIP

constructs of race, class, or gender, or the wild and the tame). To be sure, the first social elites on the planet were not agriculturalists; they were the alpha males found among many species. But the agricultural transformation gave rise to new forms of hierarchy among humans.

One of the great poets of classical Greece, whose writings inspired readers for centuries, was the bard Hesiod. A contemporary of Homer, he is thought to have lived between 750 and 650 BCE, thousands of years later than agriculture's first emergence. We know Hesiod owned a farm worked by many slaves, and those slaves included a variety of species. Among Hesiod's most popular writings is "Works and Days," an epic in verse that features a fictitious brother who has become idle and is urged to follow the example of a farmer, casting aside a life of debauchery and making the earth yield its abundance. The poet does not want to make that life seem too onerous. The good farmer, he suggests, is one who manages to shift the hardest labor onto others, both humans and nonhumans.

Here is Hesiod telling how to manage a farm not very different from those that had first appeared among farmers of the Jordan River or Yangzi valley:

> [Get yourself] a house first of all, a woman, and an ox for plowing—the woman one you purchase, not marry, one who can follow well with the oxen. . . . Acquire two oxen, nine years old, male, that have reached the measure of puberty, for their strength has not been drained away yet. . . . When the plowing-time first shows itself to mortals, set out for it, both your slaves and yourself. . . . Pray to Zeus of the land and to hallowed Demeter to make Demeter's holy grain ripen heavy, as you begin plowing at the very start, when you have taken the end of the plow-tail in your hand and have come down with the goad upon the oxen's backs.[42]

This poet-farmer-slaveowner claims that he loves the earth as his mother. At the same time, he is very clear that good farming requires an exercise of power over the earth and its children. The ideal manager is one who employs whips and harnesses to make nature work for the collective good.

In the early days of the first great transformation some tried to escape the whip as they tried to escape agriculture itself. They refused to settle down in one place and stay there forever. They rebelled not because intellectuals told them that freedom should be cherished, but because their instincts told them to rebel. They were, nonetheless, caught in a trap of their own making, as their old way of life became impossible to sustain. Agriculture emerged as an evolutionary variant, but it took some whipping to get the variant working in place.[43]

The first ship carrying African slaves to the Americas to serve as a labor force for capitalist plantations sailed in 1526. Before the slave trade was stopped, some 12.5 million people were put on ships and delivered to the other side of the Atlantic, with almost two million lost to shipwreck, disease, and maltreatment. That trade declined toward the end of the eighteenth century, until by the 1820s no more than eighty thousand people a year were leaving Africa in slave ships, a large majority of whom were taken to Brazil. The British outlawed human slavery in 1833, setting free nearly one million slaves in their colonies, almost all of them transported there from Africa. The United States followed suit in the 1860s, setting free about four million slaves, most of them working in southern cotton fields. Thirty years later Brazil, which owned more slaves than any other nation, became the last place in the Americas to end chattel slavery. Before those acts of liberation, civilization had long been associated with slaves, social hierarchies, and caste systems, all of which were considered natural, reasonable, and quite necessary.[44]

Today, agriculture powered by fossil fuels has taken the place of slave labor on the land, yet the cries of animals being beaten with whips or confined in cages continue to be heard. If we are unmoved by such signs of exploitation in the countryside, it is because we still depend on farm animals for food and cannot imagine how to free ourselves from that dependency. Someday, all societies may turn away from every kind of slavery by figuring out how to produce food in a more bloodless way, perhaps by deriving meat from molecules of oil. Then at last it may be possible to liberate all humankind's animal kinfolk.[45]

Despite its coercive tendencies, or because of them, agriculture brought a substantial reward: it allowed people in many places to achieve a higher level of cultural development. As they gained in wealth and productive skills, they put some of their gains to the support of poets, artists, teachers, philosophers, doctors, soldiers, engineers, lawyers, and theologians. Agriculture made possible all those civilized occupations, along with cities, roadways, schools, theaters, sports, and entertainments.

Charles Darwin famously defined agriculture as "artificial selection," a type of evolution, like, but distinct from, "natural selection." Artificial selection, as he understood it, came from the differential survival of natural varieties (Darwin did not know what a gene or genome was, for these are twentieth-century terms referring to the basic physical and functional units of heredity, made up of DNA). Artificial selection, in contrast, was the purposeful effort by farmers and breeders to produce pigeons, dogs, vegetables, fruits, flowers, and livestock to suit their needs. Today, that nineteenth-century distinction between artificial and natural selection, however obvious it seemed in Victorian times, has become harder to draw.[46]

What is natural selection, and does it still go on? Have all humans become artificial selectors—have we remade the whole planet? Has artificial selection now taken the place of natural selection? If artificial selection is now dominant, then can we say that changes in organisms can resemble any innovation or social or technological change? Darwin did not consider such confusing matters. About ten thousand years ago, artificial selection, as Darwin understood it, seemed necessary for human advancement, and so it still does in our day. But if the farmer's tools and crops have all become "artifices," then what is not artificial? Should we care which kind of selection is going on?

Answers depend on whether we think hope comes from inside us, from our super large brains, or from the spontaneous, unmanaged fertility of a special planet and its species. Is it possible for hope to renew itself in a human nature that no longer sees itself as part of nature? Or do we need the planet to find hope?

CHAPTER 3

Humpty Dumpty and the Fate of Power

Out of the mouths of babes come wise and charming fables. Take the English nursery rhyme "Humpty Dumpty," which tells about a guy who sat on a wall and "had a great fall. All the king's horses and all the king's men couldn't put Humpty together again." The first printed versions of that rhyme date back to the eighteenth century; after that it was regularly applied to many failed political figures, including Britain's King Richard III and Cardinal Wolsey. But it could also be applied to any rotund, smiling fellow who represented power, including states and empires. They gain power, they crack apart, they collapse.

Children conceived of Humpty as an egg that could easily be broken, and that was how he was depicted when cartoonists drew him—a male figure with the shape of an ostrich egg, a gentleman dressed in a nice suit of clothes but doomed to fail. He was a cartoon version of all patriarchs, states, and empires, which eventually lose power and cannot be put together again. Any structure of power is vulnerable to internal and external threats, including microbe invasion, soil exhaustion, or a failure to secure food supplies and protect families—a vulnerability illustrated in this chapter by the rise and fall of the Roman Empire.

Few states in fact survive more than a few decades or centuries. At their height they may seem invincible, but even so they eventually vanish, and quite often they do so because they miscalculate the nature around them. Often it is their ecological ignorance that defeats them. Consider this

HUMPTY DUMPTY AND THE FATE OF POWER

famous warning from the poet Percy Bysshe Shelley: "My name is Ozymandias, King of Kings/Look on my Works, ye Mighty, and despair! Nothing beside remains." Ozymandias (the Egyptian pharaoh who called himself "king of kings") turned out to be ignorant of the fate of all statuary. His pompous effigy, meant to show his power, was safe from fire but not from entropy or erosion. Those holding power may think they are immortal as they sit on their high walls, looking down on their realm. But then their walls and statues weaken and collapse, as nature brings them to ruin. The more complex and concentrated their power, the more unstable they may be.[1] Concentrated power, like everything in nature, is subject to entropy, the force of gravity, the blast of winds, the danger of invasion.

If we had more sympathy for the environmental vulnerability of those in power, we might regard them with more patience, tolerance, and charity. We might even see them as would-be benefactors rather than dark, evil conspirators. Their power often depends on whether they can defend their subjects, provide safety and security, and relieve the fear and uncertainty that thwarts desire. A state may renege on its promise to defend the people from natural dangers, foreign armies, or thieves. It may fail to distribute wealth more fairly. It may not provide sufficient support to parents or progeny. States make promises that surround us like a wall, and without those promises we would never have advanced beyond simple farming. Ordinary people have willingly permitted state and imperial authorities to take command over their lives, thereby legitimating their authority.[2]

Like eggs, some states and empires grow up with tougher shells than others and are less easily broken. To survive over the *longue durée* they require a citizenry that is numerous, industrious, talented, and loyal, and a nature that is richly endowed, healthy, and resilient. Given both requirements, states can endure for centuries. Whenever a powerful state lacks those requirements, no amount of propaganda or firepower can save it.[3]

What do we mean by that power we call the "state?" Robert Carneiro, a distinguished anthropologist at the American Museum of Natural History, provided a terse definition: the state is "an autonomous political unit, encompassing many communities within its territory and having a centralized government with the power to collect taxes, draft men for work or war, and decree and enforce laws."[4] A state may rule over a single valley or many valleys, but always it must achieve unity out of diversity. States have been unnecessary among primitive foragers, for their needs were simple; a very limited kind of power was held loosely by a hunting and gathering band in which a few males exercised limited authority over others or over nature. When bands turned to agriculture, however, they began accumulating more food and wealth but ceding responsibility to others.

According to scholarly consensus, the very first state appeared six thousand years ago where the Tigris and Euphrates rivers merge and empty into the Persian Gulf. There, humans had become more populous over thousands of years, evolving from hunting to simple farming and then to life under more centralized management. The first state was Sumer—both a city *and* a state literally constructed out of river mud baked into bricks. Over time Sumer came to be surrounded by other states, and then all were merged into a single unified empire, the Akkadian. Subsequently, that empire grew large and ambitious and was absorbed into the Mesopotamian and Babylonian empires. The entire river valley came to be governed by one grandiose egg who promised to make safe all the farmers and all the small, fertilized eggs that had been produced in mothers' wombs. The people of Mesopotamia may have been peacefully induced and persuaded to become subjects, a persuasion that may have taken millennia to accomplish. Even though the power might be wielded with a soft touch, it could become harsh and violent, but always it was supposed to keep families and children safe.

An empire is simply a bigger version of the state, involving the merger of several smaller states into one, changing the scale but not the promise of security. Sumer grew by engorging villages, farm fields, and cities up and down the Tigris-Euphrates valley, until the whole watershed came to be ruled by a single man, Sargon the Great (2334–2279 BCE). That happened thousands of years after the first agriculture had appeared in the Fertile Crescent. Sargon managed to sit on his wall for fifty-five years before he tumbled down. Before that end, he diverted rivers for enhanced agricultural production and offered other protection for the first civilization. His empire extended from the upcountry headwaters all the way down to the Persian Gulf. We call that first empire Mesopotamia, a name that can be translated as "power arising on the land between the rivers."

Today the once grandiose imperial civilization of Mesopotamia lies broken into warring fragments. The alluvium left by the rivers no longer provides a strong agricultural basis for world greatness. The old rivers still flow in the valley, but they are much diminished and no longer renew the land's fertility or produce the food surpluses they once did. Now there are too many people crowded into too small a space, and the lands and waters have become less productive than they once were.

In the 1950s two scholars arrived at what had been the center of the Mesopotamian empire. They came at the request of the newly established government of Iraq to find out why there had been such a dismal fall from grandeur. One of the scholars was the Danish-born Thorkild Jacobsen, head of Chicago's Oriental Institute and professor of antiquity at Harvard; the other was Robert Adams, one of the leading archaeologists of his day, a professor at the University of Chicago and head of the Smithsonian Institution in Washington. The pair set out to uncover the deep environmental history of the region.[5] What they discovered was that under the early state the lowlands had become poisoned with salt washing down from the mountains and accumulating in the soil. People, including Sargon the Great, had allowed that to happen. The two scholars' report was careful and objective, but it did not lead to any political or economic revival, and perhaps none was possible without financial aid from newer centers of wealth and power. In this long-degraded place, there were too many people pressing on a shrinking environment, offering a tragic lesson for the planet: without some restraint of sexual desire, both the people and the land suffered.

HUMPTY DUMPTY AND THE FATE OF POWER

In the process of building the world's first centralized political and economic power, both settlers and heads of state in the Tigris-Euphrates valley degraded their natural assets. They had followed a pattern that earlier and later peoples, powers, regimes, and civilizations followed. Driven by the urge to multiply and replenish the earth, they became more and more densely packed in a narrow space. They might have sought to restrain themselves at some point and to live with fewer offspring sustainably among the marshes and along the banks, or they might have tried new ways of living. They did neither. Undoubtedly, there were too many of them to allow restraint, and innovation failed. They could see no new lands nearby to which they could migrate. The long, intricately connected canals and ditches that the state had helped them construct had become filled with toxic sediments, especially salt. Wheat could not tolerate the high levels of the mineral that permeated the valley. When the rivers had flowed naturally, the excessive salt and silt had been flushed into the sea, but as the farmers' demand for water expanded, salt built up in the fields, poisoning the root zones. There was no easy way to get rid of it. Many fields had to be abandoned, until the foundations of prosperity and power collapsed. This first Humpty Dumpty fell because farmers looked to an incompetent state to manage their environment.

The fall of Mesopotamia and its power elite was blamed by the visiting experts on too intense a use of land in a bright, hot climate with high evaporation rates, which left salt crystals behind glistening like snow. Natural erosion had created a broad, rich delta at the head of the Persian Gulf, but now the cultivated valley produced violent torrents of mud that covered dwellings, plugged irrigation canals, and left a residue of salt. The scholars calculated that toxic silt now covered some of the ancient farming fields to a depth of ten meters—a degradation that has plagued much of the world's irrigated acreage, with consequences that may endure for thousands of years. As damage continues, fields get so spoiled that the remedies become too costly and impractical. The process is called desertification. According to the United Nations, "Desertification is not the natural expansion of existing deserts but the degradation of land in arid, semi-arid, and dry sub-humid areas. . . . Among human causal factors are overcultivation, overgrazing, deforestation, and poor irrigation practices. Such overexploitation is generally caused by economic and social pressure, ignorance, war, and drought."[6]

By "social pressure," the United Nations means too dense a population that state and local managers of the environment cannot control. Today some two billion people worldwide suffer from desertification. They usually live in severe poverty, and there is no other place to go.

Many thousand kilometers east of the Tigris-Euphrates valley, a similar story of excessive population pressure and inept government oversight can be found along China's Yellow River. Here is another semi-arid environment where people have long been attempting to grow crops. Like farmers in the Tigris-Euphrates valley, they initially crowded into well-watered bottomlands where there was plenty of wild food to hunt and gather and where there were good rich soils to grow crops. Near the Yellow River was an immense plateau made of loess, a light soil that had been deposited by high winds back in the Pleistocene epoch. The loess country was naturally dry; its low annual rainfall was highly destructive to land wherever the vegetative cover was sparse, and then it became worse after the land was deforested, burned, and plowed. Rain then washed soil down from the plateau to the river, bringing a potential bounty of fresh nutrients but also spoiling the planted crops. At first, an increase in erosion did not seem to matter; after all, erosion was what had made the valley attractive to foragers and farmers in the first place. But over time the region became a world-class disaster.

Along the Yellow River a succession of powerful states grew up, bearing such names as Xia, Shang, Zhou, Qin, and Han. As in Mesopotamia, independent villages came to be united under concentrated power. The first Chinese state was founded by Yu the Great four thousand years ago. The most successful state was the Han Empire, which lasted four hundred years.

At its peak it exercised dominion over sixty million people, one fourth of the world's population. Almost all of them were small farmers, the largest concentration anywhere on the planet. That amazing gain in human numbers allowed wealth and power to flourish here until, once again, erosion covered the fields with sand and silt.

Political and economic development could occur along the Yellow River because it offered an abundant supply of water rich in suspended nutrients, good for renewing the soil. In addition, the people worked hard to make a more and more intense use of the land, just as economists like Ester Boserup would later recommend. As with the Tigris and Euphrates empires, China's powerful state took control of the river, promising to protect farmers from its dangers, helping them produce food more efficiently, and now and then redistributing the wealth in the form of disaster aid.[7] But here, too, a great river became so disturbed that it threatened the farmers with raging torrents of floodwater and smothered their crops in silt.[8]

None of the world's early states or empires succeeded to the extent they promised in making nature obey them. They lacked sufficient knowledge and skill. No one in their time understood well such matters as dryland ecosystems, stream hydraulics, soil formation, and fluid dynamics. China's officials may have fared better than those elsewhere; certainly, they had experience governing a large territory filled with rivers and valleys. Abundant water flowed down from the Tibetan "water tower," a high plateau lying to the southwest, arguably the key source of China's early greatness. The first Chinese state was established in the Yellow River watershed, but thanks to those other rivers, that model was replicated in many other valleys that offered food, homes, and wealth to a growing population. As farmers kept migrating southward away from battle zones, the Yangzi became a second center of power, symbolized by the move of the Song capital away from the Yellow River to the Yangzi delta in the twelfth century CE.

The early Chinese state did not draw up any grand plan of river conquest. It did try to move surplus farmers to the northern frontier as a shield against the pastoral barbarians coming down from the drought-plagued steppes of Mongolia, who in their crisis created one of the largest empires in history. China's farmers resisted being moved north because they understood, if the state did not, that the land on the northern frontier was too dry, the soils too erodible, the floods too devastating, the diseases too common, and the barbarians too hard to stop. Sensibly, many chose to ignore the state and move in the other direction—to the Yangzi, the Sichuan Basin, and the Pearl River.

Farmers learned to innovate as they moved—constructing irrigation paddies where they grew the many-colored rice plant, *Oryza sativa,* and earthen terraces to stop hillside erosion. The state promised protection from enemies, and the people continued to demand that protection, in effect expanding the empire in all directions. Many dynasties rose and fell over succeeding centuries, as China, in the words of the historian Mark Elvin, wrote a story of "three thousand years of unsustainable development."[9]

About the same time that state power was growing along the Yellow River and elsewhere, another civilization was emerging in what we now call Egypt, along the brown ribbon of the Nile, which flows northward from African highlands to the Mediterranean Sea. The Egyptian state and civilization were directly influenced by the Tigris-Euphrates model, but they acquired some unique features from their relations with the great river. The Nile is quite unlike the Yellow, the Yangzi, or the Euphrates in that its floods come with almost clocklike precision, reflecting the natural regularity of monsoon rains that fall from Southeast Asia to East Africa. The Nile slopped over its banks every year, but it did so reliably in the late summer and early fall. Farmers learned to trap its floodwaters behind low retaining walls and to domesticate the gentle giant. Any excessive flows were carried away and deposited in the Mediterranean.[10] But here again, a state regime arose to rule over a very large and fertile valley threading through a severe desert.

Again and again riverbanks furnished the material setting for what Robert Carneiro calls "the most far-reaching political development in human history, the most important single step ever taken in the political evolution of mankind—constructing the first states."[11] For a while, those river-controlling states grew bigger and bigger, but none of them, including classical Egypt, proved able to last forever. By the twentieth century only China held much power, though world politicians were still eager to bring order and prosperity out of flowing water.

Today there are nearly two hundred sovereign states competing to exploit the planet's natural wealth, from soils and rivers to the fossil fuels. None of them wants to be called an empire now, for such power has come to be seen as exploitative and backward. But whatever label they wear, every one of those two hundred rotund eggs has tried to gather power from the earth, yet all have ended up increasing their vulnerability.

Carneiro concluded that all states and empires, whether ancient or modern, have had their origins primarily in human nature and only secondarily in moral values or social ideals. States were not created by wicked people seeking to rule over the common folk. Rather, the folk, feeling endangered and fearful, demanded more security for their families and children. Trying to evade those threats, they turned to states and yielded power to them. Thus, a paradox bloomed across the ancient world as states sought to protect farming communities from the power of nature but then used state power to impose burdensome taxes and hard labor on their subjects. To some extent, states did protect people from their environment, but they did so at the cost of a loss of local autonomy. Again and again, people felt driven to make a true Faustian bargain by yielding to the blandishments of states.

As populations grew, power elites increased in size, reach, and ambition. At the top were generals, governors, and emperors, all of whom recruited armies, technical experts, and tax collectors; further down were engineers, water controllers, and priests. Too many people competed for the same water and soil, a problem that the state tried to rectify by waging war against other states as well as against rivers, always hoping to add to its territory. The leaders may have thought in terms of loot and glory, but their success came from securing the crops and populations of ordinary people. Thanks to the protective shield of the state, people dared to believe they could settle down and tend their gardens, so long as there were governments to keep them safe. Peace reigned at the village level, but violence increased elsewhere, up and down the river valleys, as rival armies clashed over water, land, and other resources. One could say that both the weak and the powerful needed each other, and in that shared neediness each party hoped to benefit from state development.[12]

Evolutionary science tells us that there is no escaping competition and violence, though both can be checked by cooperation and peace seeking. Humans, like other species, have an ambivalent nature and desires. The latter can be so blinding that even when we think we are free, we may in fact be building a wall that will become our prison.

Scholars have shown that violence among humans goes back as far as we can see, although foragers lived comparatively peaceful lives within local kinship groups and practiced, at least internally, a great deal of mutual aid. Life got more dangerous and conflicted when a foraging band or group of farmers encountered others who sought more land to feed their numbers. Then rivals rushed to fight with whatever weapons they could find. Evidence of violence shows up in early skeletons exhumed from the earth—skeletons missing a few limbs or with fractured skulls or broken femurs. In a paper published in 2016, a team of social scientists concluded that historically "violence is explained by resource scarcity and not political organization."[13]

Such violence, like the counter-propensity for cooperation, preceded the state. To credit states or empires for making life more violent would be a mistake, for it was the violence of human desire that produced states. Hiding behind a government's iron shield, farmers could leave much of the fighting to military professionals. Consequently, fewer and fewer people experienced in their daily lives much physical danger. But to secure that peace, they had to raise enough food to support the state as well as their own children. This they tried to do by growing as much grain and other food as they could and paying for protection with their crops.[14]

Additionally, some physical dangers came from the nature of the planet, such as volcanoes or earthquakes or pest invasions, any of them liable to overwhelm societies. Those dangers got worse whenever people ignored or exceeded their local limits, through soil salinization, siltation, or depletion. Here were the root causes of insecurity, rivalry, and unhappiness, and here were major reasons for the rise of states and empires. A realistic view of planetary history must acknowledge that human life, before and after the state, has been a rough journey.

Carneiro saw the natural environment as a "circumscribing" material reality that led to state formation.[15] States, according to his theory, arose wherever and whenever soils, forests, fisheries, minerals, or energy came to be in short supply, placing a material restraint on human fertility. But not all circumscription was imposed by outer nature; often it came from inner drives that turned abundance into scarcity. Circumscription could develop almost anywhere humans went. It could be found in places where once there had been lush possibilities that over time people overran.[16]

Carneiro's theory of the state emerged from his comparative studies of the Brazilian rainforest and the drier coastal mountains of neighboring Peru. In the rainforest, no empires ever emerged, he pointed out, whereas in the Andean mountains and foothills one of the world's most famous empires, the Incan, emerged. The rainforest offered a large, well-endowed environment where nature was rich and abundant, and the humans who ventured into that place remained relatively few and widely dispersed. In contrast, across the Andes in what is now Peru, Carneiro found a different outcome. People who settled in mountain valleys running down to the Pacific Ocean found themselves living insecurely. They worked hard building houses, fields, terraces, roads, and bridges in stony canyons. As their populations increased, they turned to domesticating potatoes, quinoa, tomatoes, and avocados. They diverted water from the rivers flowing through the canyons and used them to irrigate their crops. But soon they felt the heavy hand of armies and states, which seemed necessary as their food system began attracting enemies. Carneiro wrote, "From this point on, through the conquest of chiefdom by chiefdom, the size of political units increased at a progressively faster rate. . . . The culmination of this process was the conquest of all of Peru by its most powerful state, and the formation of a single great empire."[17]

All that social evolution started with high fertility rates outgrowing a narrow terrain. Nature was a determinant, not only of human reproduction but also strategies adopted to sustain it. Did the Incans feel differently about their reproductive nature than people in the rainforest did? We have insufficient data to answer. What the anthropologist knew was that the Incan rulers acquired extraordinary power over much of the highly incised western coast of South America. Then at the climax of their power they were invaded by gun-toting armies from the faraway state of Spain, when people of another empire in the making were facing their own constraints. Soon after they arrived, the Incan empire collapsed, and a Spanish empire succeeded.

Meanwhile, east of the Andes, in the immense Amazonian Basin where there was a much less circumscribed environment, a radically different political system developed. Here there were no steep, eroding valleys filling up with people, no tiny plots of dirt carried in baskets on one's back and dumped to make terraces on hillsides. Amazonia, in contrast to the Andean highlands, was a wide open country through which flowed many tributaries, a densely braided water network offering multiple pathways into what must have seemed a wonderful refuge from competing bands.

Whenever the denizens of this terrain felt pressured by their own babies or by foreigners, they traveled upstream and made a new clearing in the forest, until that clearing became threatened and they moved to fresh ground, allowing the forest to regenerate behind them. Such easy transportation by waterways looping in and out of the forests allowed people to avoid conflict with one another. As foragers, they had a naturally lower birthrate than the sedentary Incans. Also, the environment enabled them to avoid turf warfare. They needed no state apparatus to maintain peace. Big battles were infrequent and usually not severe. Inhabitants of the rainforest might have followed the pattern of all foragers, becoming more numerous until they exceeded the forest's limits—but they did not, probably because their numbers remained dispersed over a much larger terrain.[18]

Carneiro's theory of circumscription offers a possible explanation for why the Chinese state, in contrast to the states of Mesopotamia or Peru, lasted so long, for China too enjoyed a bounty of arable land on all sides, enough abundance to prevent conflict but not enough to make the state unnecessary. Some places on the planet offered better support for human settlers than other places. China's state arose and prevailed longer than Mesopotamia's or Peru's perhaps because its habitat allowed a larger and more stable kind of power.

By the time of the Xinhai Revolution in 1911 CE, China's population exceeded four hundred million, and all its river valleys felt the pinch of too many people. Its soils and waters were overworked. Its farms had shrunk, on average, to only a few *mu* (fifteen *mu* equal an acre in China's traditional system). On those miniscule farms lived on average seven individuals (five children, two parents, plus in some cases a grandparent or two), along with assorted farm animals and plants. By that point a consortium of Europeans could easily invade China's agrarian society and establish foreign enclaves. There followed a series of revolutions that ended the agrarian way of life and pushed the country toward something new: an amalgam of industrial capitalism and industrial communism. Pure ideas, domestic or international, do not explain those revolutions; material conditions must also be acknowledged. Breaking free from its longtime agrarian and imperial past, China undertook to reinvent itself, creating a new kind of nation-state dominated by factories and cities.

A comparative view of the origins of states and empires makes both their differences and similarities compelling. Of course, we must allow for cultural differences in the form of ideas, religions, and philosophies, but we must also recognize the role played by the environment, human nature, reproduction, and food supplies. Like all forms of evolution, the course of power was determined by the planet and its people whose desires were at once universal and yet subject to change and diversification. States do not begin simply as abstract blueprints in the minds of a single person or a political party; they are not imposed on a blank slate. States, of course, may not like to acknowledge that their people are like people everywhere—the result of a common human nature and subject to the same natural laws. Even as states differ from one another, however, their differences cannot be reduced to differences in abstract thought. They develop from inner and outer nature interacting, and they do so in similar ways even when they claim to be unique and distinctive.

What early states and empires usually wanted was to multiply their populations. Where is there a state in ancient history that promoted birth control? From their earliest days states encouraged their subjects to bear lots of children, that is, until the second half of the twentieth century, when populations began skyrocketing. "Bigger families, more babies" was regarded as the best formula for expanding state power, even when it ran against environmental limits and shook that power severely. That does not mean that women and men had more children because some state told them to do so. In the end they followed their natural desires more than government mandates.

This view of history—realistic, materialist, and scientific—runs counter to a long-established tradition in the West that views the growth of states as deriving primarily from political philosophies. Consider, for example, Henri J. M. Claessen, a cultural anthropologist at Leiden University, who has offered an emphatic defense of that view. Different people, he says, have invented different values or ideals that became states. Ideas about nature, religion, the supernatural, and the individual's role within the group arose in many brains and then became "ideological," serving the purposes of elites.

States, in turn, give the people what rulers imagined the people wanted. "The commoners," Claessen writes, "paid in goods and services, and the ruler paid back in protection, law, order, fertility and sometimes some gifts; an exchange of goods for Good."[19]

What does Claessen mean by the "Good"? For him, it comes from abstract reasoning. The group first creates an idea of the Good, and then leaders take over and promise to deliver it. But an evolutionist would answer that the Good has one supreme, universal, inborn definition that transcends all cultural ideas: replenish the species, the tribe, the band, the family. With the shift to agriculture, the Good came to mean the raising of bountiful crops, the breeding of numerous livestock, and the plowing of the land. Behavior did change, but only as ideals changed.

No doubt, as foragers and farmers added to their families, they imagined the heavens and earth populated with gods and spirits, all of them supposed to make human life more secure. The idea of Heaven was, no doubt, the work of some individual brain, but was it a brain that ignored or refused to serve the body? The most important of early man's imagined gods were those that protected human fertility. Through rituals, people beseeched their gods to help them conceive as many children as possible and to bless the harvests they needed to feed their progeny. The deities, whether they dwelled in the grass, forest, or sky, were identified everywhere. They were supposed to help people gain control over nature—to make both people and land more fertile and productive. The imagination thus answered a material need among humans. From there, it was a short step to believing that some mortal on earth who could help farmers secure food and sex might be godlike. Emperors could become one with the gods, wielding mysterious powers to aid a family's survival.

The state promised implicitly to protect women and men, improve the harvests, and furnish vital resources like water. Leaders knew they would be judged by whether they delivered on that promise. Therefore, those in power sought to encourage human fertility. By adding more workers to the

HUMPTY DUMPTY AND THE FATE OF POWER

labor pool, the state sought its own security. Yet even the most well-intentioned and benevolent leaders could miscalculate or lack important facts. If the people had too many children, the environment became degraded. Even habitats that once seemed overflowing with abundance could become crowded and impoverished wastelands of depleted or poisoned soil, polluted water, failing crops. Then might come the downfall of a state. If they made war on neighbors and added more territory to their domain, states might avoid that fate. But if the potentate ever slipped in his duties, his regime could experience a great fall.

Powerful states established cities as centers of administration and command, enclosing them with high walls for protection and control. Often they put those walled cities on or near a river, where there was a dependable source of a key natural resource. Did the people living inside those walled, riverine cities understand that they depended on a nature that was volatile, unpredictable, and as much inside as outside them? Did those who lived within the walls understand the challenges they had to face?

Here and in the preceding chapters, three questions have been raised. Why did humans leave their first homes in Africa and spread across other continents? Why did some of the new frontiers become centers of agriculture, while others did not? Why did institutions of power evolve when and where they did? The common answer to all those questions is that humans' inner nature pushed them to seek for themselves and their families a more secure place on a volatile but fertile earth.

The most fabulous, admired, hated, and debated state in history was surely the Roman Empire. Although many intellectuals and political leaders have taken Rome as a shining model of success, admiring its many accomplishments, others have decried Rome for its moral decadence, for going too far, in the words of a political philosopher, in the pursuit of "immoderate greatness." Another has summarized the Romans as notable not so much for their architecture or laws as for "murder, incest, and the wearing of expensive jewelry."[20] A broader list of Roman civilization's characteristics must include brutality, slaveholding, and military conquest. Long after its demise, Rome would serve not only as a warning to anyone aspiring to empire but also as a model to be emulated. We have never been able to decide whether that state was good or bad.

Why this great Roman egg appeared in the first place, dwarfing everything before it, and why it broke apart so decisively, ushering in the Dark Ages, have been popular topics for a thousand years or more, even before Edward Gibbon produced in the eighteenth century a best seller on the subject.[21] According to Gibbon, Rome came into the world espousing noble ideals but then fell into corruption and decadence. Few of his critics or admirers, however, have entertained the notion that Rome was destroyed through overpopulation, hunger, and inadequate knowledge of the Mediterranean Sea and its climate, soils, microbes, and ecology. Empires fall not simply because they are filled with good or bad people or because they are harsh toward their citizens, but because they are ignorant of the earth that supports them.

Gazing at a wall map of the Roman Empire, one cannot help being impressed by its intercontinental span and geophysical coherence. Few states have matched it for size, grandeur, or power. If we take as its high point the year 138 CE, when the emperor Hadrian ended his reign, we see the empire at its maximum, stretching from the Strait of Gibraltar northward across the Iberian peninsula and over the whole of France, Belgium, and England, all the way to Hadrian's Wall in the British Isles, plus all the lands south of the Danube River, including the Balkans, Italy, and Greece, and then also Turkey, the Levant, Egypt, and North Africa, right around to the forbidding barrier of the Sahara Desert. Other military victories would extend the control of Rome over the ancient Tigris-Euphrates watershed. That was the empire at its peak; within a few more centuries it had begun to spiral downward into disease, hunger, and chaos.

Altogether, the Roman Empire endured for about five hundred years, with an additional five hundred years added for the time needed for its gradual building-up and breaking-down. Many ruins were left behind from its glory days, including high stone aqueducts conveying fresh water, long paved highways, the ghostly quiet of ruined sports arenas, the tottering walls of old public baths, a few silted-in seaports, a derelict olive mill standing in what had once been a grove of olive trees, a sorry mix of tree stumps, depleted soils, and eroded farmland. They are all mementoes of Rome's past, remainders from the time before this greatest of all Humpty Dumpties eventually fell and broke apart. They remind us too that no one has ever managed to restore the Roman egg.

Dozens of reasons have been given for the fall of Rome; this is one of those overdetermined events where just too many possible causes exist to allow one simple answer. Dominant explanations can be fitted into two categories: either the Romans were victims of outside forces (particularly, the violent barbarians who invaded from the north) or they brought about their demise through inner moral failure (death by decadence). The incursions of the Huns and Vandals are familiar stories, but they came later than the other failings, so we can put them aside. Speak the names Nero or Caligula, two of the worst emperors ever, and the second kind of explanation gains a certain plausibility. However, if we want to avoid excessive moralizing and not impose the standards of our time on the past, we must focus on the material Rome that fell apart through state and popular ignorance. Who are we to decide what is evil and what is good?

There never would have been a Roman Empire without the defining presence of the Mediterranean Sea. Where the earliest states had evolved out of rivers and mud, Rome grew up on a mountainous peninsula almost surrounded by a briny sea. It developed as a sailor's empire, an expansion of a maritime economy that scaled itself up to match the huge size of that body of water.

The Mediterranean is almost completely landlocked; it has only one tiny outlet into the Atlantic Ocean. Today, the sea covers an area of 2.5 million square kilometers, with an average depth of 2,500 meters, though much of it is now heavily polluted by urban and industrial wastes and ranks high on the list of planetary environments in crisis. Two thousand or three thousand years ago, the sea was much cleaner, its air was bracing, and it must have seemed larger to people than it does today. It inspired the Romans to seek grandeur—but then the sea and its region became their nemesis.

At first the Romans called the surrounding waters Mare Magnum, or Great Sea, but after they made it the core of their empire, they started calling it Mare Nostrum, or Our Sea. They claimed every drop of its waters, and even those of the adjoining Black Sea. Yet the Mediterranean did more than present physical parameters for Rome's ambitions; it profoundly influenced the practice of empire as well. The sea was not an inert, passive background of mere H_2O but a powerful shaping force. We may, therefore, speak of Romae in Mare, or the Rome the sea made.

The Greek poet Homer, a quasi-mythical figure who was always popular on the Italian peninsula, emphatically proclaimed his love of the sea and made it a powerful character in his sagas. If he was in fact a real individual, he was also a blind man. He described the Mediterranean as the "wine-dark sea," yet on a typical summer day, it is gorgeously blue or blue green, not the red or white of wine. Perhaps Homer was thinking of a sea whose waves reflected a sky full of dust blowing from barren, abandoned lands on shore, giving the water a darker hue. Whether sightless or not, he like many others of his day lived unaware of some important facts.

Modern science has revealed that, a hundred million years ago, there was no Mediterranean Sea of any color or shape. Remember that well before humans existed, the planet's single landmass, Pangea, broke apart due to continental plate movements. Several smaller continents emerged from that breakup, and as they drifted apart a body of water opened through which one could have sailed an armada from Europe to Australia. Geologists call it the Tethys Ocean. That ocean no longer exists, just as its successor the Mediterranean will someday disappear, as continents continue to drift, determining geography and how we live. One day the Mediterranean may become a river connecting the world's oceans, and if it does, it may cease to be a major force of empire for perhaps another hundred million years.[22]

For a brief period, at the western end of the Tethys Ocean there lay a profusion of islands, which, as many ages went by, became the fragmented subcontinent that we call Europe. Bits and pieces were pushed together to form a patchwork of land, forming the western end of Eurasia. Meanwhile, further plate movements pushed Africa and Europe closer and closer together, almost closing the Tethys seaway and creating what we know as the nearly enclosed Mediterranean. All around that sea were low-rainfall lands cut up by mountains and valleys, subject to droughts, damned by many poor soils, now and then rattled by earthquakes, and for much of the year warmed by a fierce sun. Water became a bridge linking a patched-together Europe to the Middle East and Africa.

About 6.5 million years ago, the Mediterranean almost completely dried up because of global climate change. A long cold spell fell over the earth, creating polar ice and diminishing sea levels, resulting in an increase in deserts or near deserts.[23] For a while the Mediterranean was reduced to a series of rock basins almost devoid of water, and Northern Africa became a vast wetland, until another shift in climate brought back abundant rainfall and refilled those basins, giving the sea its present diversity and grandeur. The wetland, in contrast, dried up and became a new desert. African foragers discovered that sea as they trekked northward through sand dunes; by then it offered warm climates, a complex mosaic of soils with unique sets of flora and fauna, and underneath it all, a basement of dense strata, unstable volcanoes, and shoved-together rocks.

Donald Hughes, the Mediterranean's leading environmental historian, summarizes the region thus: "The Mediterranean Basin has varied patterns of land, but in most places, it is mountainous, with rugged and complex ranges. Between them are sheltered valleys and occasional alluvial plains. The typical aspect of the landscape in this region is that of a sea backed by mountains."[24] In other words, it was a natural mosaic beautiful to behold, although hidden in its beauty were some serious deficiencies that only a farmer would appreciate and regret. Less than one fifth of Greece, like the lands of Spain and North Africa, is arable, while the Apennine chain that dominates much of Italy has never been ideal for agriculture. According to the Roman naturalist Pliny the Elder, the predominant soil type is *terra rossa,* a reddish soil derived from limestone—silty-clayey in texture, well-drained, and good for growing grapes but low in the organic carbon that wheat requires.[25] For thousands of years, the region defied the grain farmer. Those who first came and settled here were foragers, not farmers. Their descendants stumbled into agriculture, as farmers did elsewhere, but even then they could turn only a few areas into high-yielding fields and crops. From the beginning it was a shaky conquest.[26]

Compared with China or Mesopotamia, there was no single dominant river system in the Mediterranean area, except the Nile. Instead, there was a sea, with its long horizons and high salt content. Then as now, the winters were wet and chilly, the summers dry and warm—a good place for holiday travelers but not for people seeking to produce protein.[27]

The sea itself is almost bisected by the Italian peninsula, the most Mediterranean place of all. Around it a few islands still can be seen, providing stepping-stones between continents. One of them, Sicily, sits like a small rock that the Italian "boot" is kicking aside. Sicily was not so dispensable, however; it turned out to be highly promising for agriculture, and therefore it became the first foreign land to be conquered and incorporated into the Roman state. Rome itself was founded in 753 BCE, with its capital only thirty kilometers inland from the sea. There on the banks of the Tiber River, men and women settled and planted grain, especially wheat, their staple food.

In the third and second centuries BCE, Rome's armies moved on from Sicily to attack the city-state of Carthage, founded by the Phoenicians in what is now Tunisia and tightly hemmed in by sea and desert, a state occupying a semi-arid plain and growing hungrier year by year. The Romans took control of the place and moved on to take control of Iberia's wheat fields, which could be made to feed Rome too. Then, with ruthless determination, the Romans proceeded to expand all the way around the Mediterranean, seeking on all its shores more soil, more wheat, and more granaries and using the broad sea to transport that foreign food back home.

By the time Gaius Octavius proclaimed himself first citizen of Rome and then took the title Caesar Augustus, a title he bore until his death in 14 CE, the Roman Empire had succeeded in gaining power over the entire Mediterranean region. It concentrated on lands bordering the sea, desiring to own the entire littoral, and thus the sea's waters became quite familiar as a mode of transportation, as familiar as the roads on the peninsula that linked Rome to its countryside.

Those imperial beginnings can be easily dated, but the end point of the Roman Empire is harder to pin down, for it declined by fits and starts, falling apart and then reviving again and again. We can say that it was finally dead, at least in the west, by the fifth century CE. That death came as inexorably as it had in Mesopotamia, but it might have come later had the Romans not made some blunders along the way. Among them was Rome's invasion of humid, forested lands lying beyond the Alps and along the Danube—another conquest dictated by domestic hunger but met with more fierce resistance by the "barbaric" tribes living there, who were struggling to maintain their own food supplies.

Rome's imperial expansion cannot be blamed on a mere fondness for luxury goods. There was such demand, to be sure, as there had been for a very long time across Eurasia, but it is hard to see how a few sybarites could have created such a vast empire and kept it going for so long. Food, not baubles, was the chief incentive and reward. To get food required finding fresh, fertile soils that could support a highly fecund people. There was also an intense hunger for timber products, minerals, silver, and slaves, the last needed to help subdue the earth and make it more productive. If the Romans were immoderate in their desires, we should not point a finger only at the pampered few who coveted such luxuries as pearls, spices, and silks, bought from traders along the fabled Silk Road that linked Rome to China. We should also put some blame on the ordinary people, who were naturally eager for more children and who demanded grain and flour to feed them. Domestic hunger was an important reason why the Roman leaders could get so worked up about owning every piece of real estate they came across. They sought to acquire colonies especially where wheat could grow—sunny, well-watered lands with better soils—and they were willing to fight hard to get and hold them.

Roman leaders did not know much about the specific places they acquired, but in general they understood those lands from a broader perspective than did the peasants. The empire relied on agricultural experts and naturalists, who gathered heaps of knowledge about distant soils, waters, forests, mountains, and sea. Yet in the end that knowledge did not help Rome find a true sustainability; it was primitive knowledge. It became a bottleneck affecting the entire Mediterranean region.

The wheat that was central to the agricultural economy of Rome had been first domesticated in the Tigris-Euphrates basin, deriving from a wild grass, einkorn. Rome's founders took a while to discover that their *terra rossa* soils were not well suited for growing wheat. Better places would one day appear in the Ukraine (with its Chernozem soils), on North America's Great Plains (brown soils), and even in the French and German deciduous forests (grey brown podzolic soils). Only the last of those soil types, however, was within reach of the Roman armies, and many barbarians were living on top of them, ready to fight hard to stay there.

Although it may have seemed much larger and more fertile than the Tigris and Euphrates valleys, the Mediterranean region shared some of the old vulnerabilities. It too suffered from siltation and salinization, although its biggest problem was nutrient depletion, especially of nitrogen, potassium, and phosphorus (NKP) in the red soils, resulting from too many years of plowing and planting in the same place.[28] Adding to that problem was a worsening climate and a succession of severe pandemics. With that perfect storm of problems, the situation of the Romans became more and more dire until it became terminal. Neither the conquering barbarians nor the dissident Christians and Muslims of the Mediterranean region would ever be able to put a sea-based empire together again.

In 1916, a brilliant economist at Columbia University, Vladimir Simkhovitch, argued that, because of widespread soil depletion, the Roman system of agriculture proved unsustainable.[29] Simkhovitch stressed particularly the failure of small farmers to produce enough wheat as the leading reason for the fall of Rome. He was largely right—but the chain of explanation only starts there and becomes a rather complicated story of ecological vulnerability. The failure to produce sufficient wheat on the Italian peninsula led to a string of foreign military campaigns, and then to an overdependency on an imported food supply. Importing a big portion of their wheat left the Romans at grave risk, because importation opened the sea lanes to deadly but invisible microbes, which were brought home along with the wheat and killed many people and the Roman state.

Early on small farmers near Rome supplied wheat to the masses. But as they intensified local production, their yields began dropping, until they fell so low that many farmers stopped planting. By that point, Simkovitch writes, farmers were harvesting on average a mere four or five bushels per acre, or about ten to twelve bushels per hectare. How discouraging that must have been; farming did not seem worth a family's efforts or perseverance. Rome responded by giving people money to purchase food, but by then the farmers had little to sell. Often they could not produce enough even to feed themselves and their children, let alone any surplus for others. To survive on their depleting fields, they needed to rebuild the soil with fertilizer, but there was not enough fertilizer to cover the problem. They were forced to borrow money even to pay for their daily food. With such dim prospects, farmers began deserting the homes for the city, adding to the growing numbers of the urban poor.

"Nearly all agricultural writers of antiquity," writes Simkhovitch, "viewed their contemporary agricultural situation as due to the exhaustion of the soil; or, as they put it, as the result of the soil's old age."[30] Those old writers got it right: soil was the chief problem. But to come up with a remedy required more and better knowledge. They could not figure out how to prevent that natural aging, which was in truth man-made soil exhaustion.

Pessimistically, Roman writers of the imperial period concluded that nature is like a woman who in her early years is highly fertile but then, as she gets older, becomes barren. Aging, they said, was nature's law—and nothing could be done about it. They concentrated, therefore, on looking for younger, more fertile soils somewhere other than Italy, somewhere near the Mediterranean shipping lanes. The state agreed and launched into an imperial phase, seizing foreign fields, growing food on them, and exporting it across the sea. They could imagine no other course of action.

The philosopher Lucretius Carus (born 99 BCE, died 55 BCE) echoed this fatalistic thinking in his long poem *De Rerum Natura,* published after the problems had already become visible. Mother Earth, Lucretius wrote, had once provided plenty of wheat, wine, and olive oil, even "without the tiller's care." But what he saw and heard about in his day was that yields were falling. "The farmers with a sigh complain, That they have labor'd all the year in vain." Lucretius, like others, blamed the farmers' plight on the natural aging of the earth. He knew that the average Roman farm covered a mere two hectares (or seven *jugera*), from which a good farmer might harvest twenty bushels of wheat per year. Even after grazing the stubble left in the fields, he and his family could not feed themselves and their animal workers, much less send a surplus to the city. Households at the time averaged five or six babies (half of them growing up to adulthood, the rest dying young) plus various kinds of livestock and, occasionally, a human slave or two. That was a lot of mouths to feed on two hectares. Frequent plowing to bring up the subsoil and frequent replanting of the same crop year after year left the soil exhausted all the way down and left the farmers discouraged and destitute.

The land, of course, was not really getting old—geologically, Italy was still a relatively young place. The problem was that the land was overworked, and its soils could not sustain the food that a growing population needed. What had once been a rich if circumscribed ecosystem, stocked with nutrients, bacteria, worms, and other invertebrates that help turn over soils, had been turned sterile and unproductive.

This happened, we can see with hindsight, because of ignorance and inexperience but mostly because too many people were demanding that the land produce more wheat for making bread. The state was convinced that a dense population was good, when in fact the opposite was true in the absence of practical innovation. The farmers may have learned a lot about their soils, but they were caught in a demand spiral that no one could stop. In the end, Roman farmers began selling out to those who were flush with money. This was especially the fate of hillside farms, where soils had not only been depleted but also washed away by winter rains. Erosion might have been countered by hillside terracing, but that required heavy labor, and many farmers chose instead to leave the land.[31]

Rome's leaders tried arresting farmers, forcing them to continue planting and cultivating. Such harsh methods met with little success yet stirred much resentment. Making slaves of one's own people was not likely to win their support, and doing so would not reverse the falling yields. Once begun, this hopeless strategy would elsewhere take on more elaborate, formal shape after the Roman Empire had completely collapsed. Social coercion would become institutionalized as the medieval feudal system, which once again bound people to the land without controlling their reproduction. Many generations had to pass until Europeans realized that turning people into serfs did not make them better farmers. In 1861, Russia became the last state to abolish serfdom, but by then imperial Rome had long vanished.[32]

The concentration of land in the hands of a wealthy elite class has been blamed for Rome's failure to feed itself and for turning Italy's diminishing number of farmers into near slaves. Those new owners bought and merged small, degraded farms into *latifundia,* or large estates. Increasing the size of farms would not, however, provide an answer, although no one had a better solution. Simkhovitch argues that the wealthy ended up saddled with the task of making money out of lands that had been badly damaged by overcropping. Buying such land was a poor investment, for the buyers, like the small farmers, did not know how to restore exhausted soils. All they could do was to try altering the crops raised on that land, switching from wheat and barley to grapes and olives, or making degraded fields into sheep pastures. None of that, however, solved the food crisis.[33]

Contrary to Ester Boserup's rosy belief, a denser population does not always lead to more efficient or knowledgeable land management. What every landowner, small or large, should have done was to let the land rest for a few years while larding it with a copious supply of fertilizer. There were just too many people pressing on the food supply, however, to allow such a strategy.

Nutrients like nitrogen and phosphorus can come from organic wastes like stable straw or animal excrement.[34] Farmers did keep a few domestic animals on their plots, but the supply of manure they collected from those animals was never enough to restore so many depleted wheat fields. All of Rome's privies together could have furnished only a small part of the restorative elements needed in the fields, and little of that human or other animal waste was ever collected and recycled.

The best solution, therefore, appeared to be a shift of food production to new lands. There was little virgin land in the Mediterranean region, but there were a few better places found that could grow wheat. In taking over much of North Africa, the Romans acquired Egypt and began to plant and harvest wheat there. The Nile seemed to be a dependable ally, bringing down copious amounts of good water and good soil from the Ethiopian highlands and spreading them over the narrow strips of fields on both banks before running into the sea. There were uncertainties in that flooding, to be sure, for the river was dependent on monsoons from the Indian Ocean. Yet for a while Rome reaped the benefits of the Nile, exporting Egyptian wheat to the capital. Egypt became the empire's new breadbasket. The state hoped to add more such producers in Romania, Germany, and France, though it was far less easy to import grain from those producers because mountains stood between them and the sea. With Egypt and North Africa, however, there was safe, cheap water transport. The Nile together with the Mediterranean offered what seemed a brilliant solution to Rome's food problems.

Before Emperor Septimius Severus died in 211 CE, he made sure there was enough grain in Roman granaries to feed the city for seven years, which meant storing much of the production. By then seventy-five million people were living under Rome's rule, a large percentage of whom depended on the distant Nile Valley breadbasket. How many additional granaries like the one in Egypt, the leaders asked themselves, were needed? As many as they could get! How many Niles were there in the known world? There was only one. As one observer gratefully put it, "the Nile provides us with a flood of the customary level, and a bountiful harvest is produced among the Egyptians."[35]

To keep both its central and peripheral peoples satisfied, Rome constructed a fleet of cargo ships to convey grain across the Mediterranean on regular schedules. Transportation by water was the least expensive option, far cheaper than using oxen to pull heavy wagons loaded with wheat over rough dirt or stone-lined roads and across the Alps. But the basic problem would not go away: soils at the empire's core had become thin, weak, and deficient in nutrients. The empire could be saved by importing food, but for how long?

The Roman Empire, unlike its Fertile Crescent predecessors, was launched in what might have seemed an *un*circumscribed environment—a peninsula surrounded by a huge watery basin that seemed to offer opportunity as wide as the world. But the land base was thin. Although initially there seemed to be enough good land, there were hidden constraints. As the empire became even more densely peopled, those limits began closing in.

Soils, it must be emphasized, can be a serious limitation to any empire, ancient or modern, along with water supplies in a narrow river valley or along a coast. Adding to the need for good soils was the Roman reliance on wood—lumber to build all those ships, firewood for heating homes and public baths, fuel to smelt metals and fire pottery. By the third and fourth centuries CE, wood had become so scarce in the Roman empire that citizens were, in the words of John Perlin, "burning anything that would bring forth heat: twigs, shoots, stumps, roots of vines, pinecones, and wood left over from construction sites." Here again, as with grain, the empire was compelled to turn to ever more distant sources, but those sometimes far-off, inaccessible forests were already claimed and defended by local populations, and relying on them would only add to Roman vulnerability.[36]

Modern science has recently suggested still another source of environmental danger for an agrarian way of life. A good agriculture needs a good climate—for growing either wheat or forests. Climates are, of course, always highly volatile patterns of temperature, moisture, and energy. Around 200 BCE the climate in the Mediterranean region entered a prolonged period of warming. Nothing was unusual about that—warm and cold spells had occurred through all of history. But perhaps the Romans were unaware of any danger in the warming. Increasing evaporation from the sea as a result of global warming meant more clouds and more rainfall, all of which may have seemed good for farming. Scientists call this change the Roman Climate Optimum (RCO). In a sense, it made imaginable the grand project of building an empire around the Mediterranean Sea, but it did not ensure its long-term success.[37]

We cannot attribute Rome's fortunes and misfortunes wholly, or even mainly, to climate change. The empire was established in 27 BCE, when it acquired its first emperor, two centuries after the warming had started. Then the empire ended, at least in its western parts, in 476 CE, when Romulus Augustus was defeated by the German Goth Odoacer—three centuries *after* the RCO ended. The dates do not coincide, and climate change cannot explain the falling yields on the Italian peninsula or the shift to importing grain from the Nile. Once again, it was an expanding population and dwindling food supply that presented a complex, dangerous challenge.[38]

Besides threats to the network of overseas food suppliers, a plethora of other environmental problems plagued the Romans, including industrial air pollution and lead poisoning concentrated in urban areas and mining towns. Air pollution had existed as far back as caveman days, but the Roman Empire created more pollution than humans had ever seen before, as the Romans added industry to their basic agrarian economy. Around the Mediterranean Basin sprang up many new industries, an anticipation of nineteenth-century industrial mining, smelting, and manufacturing.

Pollution by lead was especially dangerous to the land and human health. Lead was used in making glass mirrors, pipelines for carrying water in and out of houses, and drinking vessels from which wine was consumed—all wonderful inventions at the time. But lead in the domestic environment meant poison in Roman bodies, especially wealthy bodies. It was their homes that became particularly contaminated with the metal. The Roman *domus,* a single-family home designed for the superrich, was the glory of the empire, but the heavy use of lead under its roof caused brain damage. On the positive side of the ledger, the empire produced a lot of clean water, but some of it flowed to houses through lead pipes. Fresh water came from state aqueducts, and state sewers carried away wastewater and human excrement; overall, sanitation improved for some while pollution worsened.

The urban population experienced both serious pollution and overcrowding. The empire had a penchant for packing people into small spaces. Besides the capital city of Rome (numbering at its peak one million residents), the empire included such large cities as Pergamum, Antioch, Alexandria, and Carthage (respectively located in Turkey, Egypt, and North Africa).[39] All those places were populated by poor people, many of whom were afflicted with contagious diseases.

After soil depletion, surely the most serious environmental problem among the Romans was the arrival of foreign microorganisms causing disease and epidemics. Those organisms became threatening only after they became an unseen part of exchange and trade around the Mediterranean Sea. Animals in the wild had long been victims of overcrowding, but now those getting sick were people who lived among their livestock. Horses, sheep, pigs, cows, and chickens were all carriers of pox. Then the Romans unwittingly increased the spread of microorganisms by sending ships across the Mediterranean Sea, even into the Indian Ocean and connecting with the interiors of Asia, Africa, and Europe. In doing so, they created new, easy pathways for once isolated microorganisms to travel straight to Roman cities. Microbes came along with the shipments of wheat, spices, silks, and other trade goods into urban markets, arriving in the holds of ships that brought merchants and military leaders to Rome. Like tiny, invisible Goths, the microbes proliferated all around the Mediterranean, some coming from the tropics, others from the interior of Eurasia. Here, in short, was a new human-made ecological threat that unsettled the empire and helped bring it down.

"If there were a material force at work in the fading fortunes of the Roman Empire during the late second century," writes the historian John Brooke, "it was disease—the Antonine Plague of A.D. 165–180, Cyprian's Plague of 251–266, and the Justinianic Plagues starting in 542."[40] Brooke is right about the insidious power of disease, but we must add that it was a very large human population clamoring to be fed that made epidemics more likely than before, weaving a web between organisms of many kinds and allowing sickness to spread more easily.

The best guide to this tragic tale of microorganisms is Kyle Harper's *The Fate of Rome*, a work that should change the way we view all states and empires. Harper describes the first century of the Roman Empire as "the happiest age." Relatively, at least, it was benign, stable, and prosperous. Everywhere food and other commodities seemed to be increasing, due in large part to a favorable climate. Farm fields, barnyards, vineyards, child births, and the general economy were all doing well. Thanks to growing prosperity, Rome could fund thirty legions of soldiers, totaling some five hundred thousand men, which it sent to pacify the frontiers. Some were sent to secure new territory, others to protect faraway fields and granaries. Only two legions were deemed necessary to secure North Africa and Egypt, while the rest were spread across the more fiercely contested northern and eastern borders. So many troops were possible because Rome's population had increased at the rate of 1.5 percent a year, a rate that could double a population in five decades. "Like a swell rising from the deep," writes Harper, "the populations of three continents under Roman rule rose in a great, synchronized wave of growth that crested in the age of the Antonine emperors [in the second century]."[41] By the reign of Caesar Augustus, from 27 BCE to 14 CE, there were sixty million Romans. The largest portion of them were concentrated on the Italian peninsula and nearby islands, but citizens had been added in Gaul, Germany, and Asia Minor, while Egypt alone counted five million. The increase in Egyptians was an especially important jump, for almost all of them were farmers packed along the Nile, making it among the most densely settled regions of the empire.

More people did not signal better health. Roman life expectancy at birth stood at twenty to thirty years, no better than it had been in the time of foragers and perhaps worse. Nutrition was not improving either; consequently, Rome's men and women were declining in stature, until their average height was about 160 centimeters. We must conclude that, despite the foreign wheat supply, a lot of people were not eating all that well. Shorter, thinner, and less nourished, they were losing their vigor, though they could still produce plenty of children and continued doing so.

The state promoted human reproduction by offering, in Harper's words, "powerful inducements to high fertility in its natalist policies, penalizing childlessness and rewarding fecundity." Women who had given birth to many children were rewarded with legal privileges. Contraception methods were quite unreliable and sometimes dangerous; they were not in general use or public favor. In fact, birth control was officially restricted and discouraged. "Natural fertility," says Harper, "was the reality in the Roman world." Women, despite living a very short span, bore an average of six children, although as many as half of those babies would never see adulthood.[42]

Perhaps the greatest achievement of the Roman state was providing more homes and jobs, "without sputtering from the glut of labor." In fact, wages rose dramatically for a full century, outstripping the costs of wheat and land, although they too were rising.[43] Because of state control, people could afford to buy imported food, even though they ate it in often insalubrious dwellings. Despite some success in increasing the food supply, malaria, typhoid, dysentery, tuberculosis, and diarrhea became more common than ever, casting a pall over urban neighborhoods. While the richest citizens always could find a way to leave town during disease outbreaks and retreat to their landed estates, the not so rich were trapped; they had no other place to go. Either they acquired immunities to the diseases around them or they died, but even those with immunities could feel a loss of vital energy. They missed many workdays and there was only the most primitive medical help. "The Romans were helplessly caught in the vice grip of their own progress with its confounding ecological repercussions," writes Harper. "All signs point to an empire whose people were groaning under the weight of an exceptionally burdensome pathogen load, despite and in some ways because of the success of the Roman empire."[44]

That was how things looked in the first glorious century or two of Rome's empire building. Worse conditions followed. In 165 CE, during the reign of Marcus Aurelius, the great Stoic philosopher, a hideous plague erupted on the Egyptian coast and spread to Rome. Its symptoms have been diagnosed by Harper as smallpox, caused by the *variola major* virus that had long been present in the land of the pharaohs; three-thousand-year-old mummies show its scars, though how the Egyptians became infected remains poorly understood. The origins of the smallpox virus go back possibly to 10,000 BCE. A highly contagious disease, smallpox may have been endemic among wild rodents living in Africa, particularly in the Sahel, a dry savannah south of the Sahara Desert, which was populated by a few pastoralists who may have first contracted it before passing it to the Egyptians and Romans.[45]

With the enlargement of the empire and more activity along its shipping lanes, the smallpox virus now had quick and easy access to the center of empire. It was spread most likely by the naked-soled *Gerbilliscus kempi*, a rodent that previously had lived far away from Rome but was spilling out of its usual habitat and may have infected imperial armies passing through the Red Sea. Those armies would have carried the pox back to Italy, from whence it spread to the rest of Europe. The empire, through its maritime fleets, brought on itself an epidemic, which lasted from 165 to 180 CE and killed some seven million people, or 10 to 20 percent of its subjects.

After the smallpox epidemic subsided, life in imperial Rome seemed briefly to recover some of its former élan. Wars of conquest resumed, legions returned to full strength, gladiators once again entered the sports arenas to slaughter dangerous beasts before cheering mobs, and wheat was shipped from Egyptian fields to Roman consumers. The empire's population recovered from its demographic losses—a mere decade was enough to replace the dead. Neither the people nor their imperial leaders, however, quite grasped how their lives and their regime had become endangered. They had crossed into an era of recurring pandemics, yet they remained uninformed about the causes.

Many leaders blamed the new vulnerability on capricious gods or vengeful nature. But the enemy was a little rodent living in a barren, semi-arid, rock-strewn land, struggling to survive in a very tough environment and in no way intent on destroying Romans, many of whom did not know the creature existed.

Seventy years after the Antonine plague came a second devastating pandemic, the Cyprian, which lasted another fifteen years. What caused it is still not clear. Perhaps it came from an Ebola-like virus originating in sub-Saharan Africa and then infecting Ethiopians and Egyptians before entering the Roman bloodstream. Vomit, bloody discharge, and fever were among its symptoms. This second great epidemic in imperial Roman history was, argues Harper, caused by an unfamiliar virus spreading throughout the empire. Along the distant northern frontier, armies caught the sickness and Roman lines of military defense collapsed. Among the victims may have been Emperor Claudius II, who died in 270 as the plague was raging.

One unexpected consequence of this second big epidemic was that a new religion called Christianity gained popularity all over Asia Minor and Europe. That happened as the followers of Jesus Christ, who had been crucified more than two centuries earlier, blamed the pandemic on Rome's pagan gods. Those gods seemed to offer no protection, they argued, while Jesus would protect his followers. Christians warned that a day was approaching when the One True God would push aside all the minor, competing deities and declare a final judgment day for humanity, when it would be better to be on Christ's side and enjoy disease immunity. During the third century CE that apocalyptic message gained a big audience, as its prophets lambasted Roman leadership, the Mediterranean empire, and the reigning state religion. Almost miraculously, the empire recovered from the Cyprian epidemic, though once again it had been badly wounded. The empire not only survived but even went through another spurt of economic and demographic growth.

Recovery from the "Ebola invasion," however, proved short-lived. There were still those depleted domestic soils, there was still a gnawing hunger in Roman bellies, and those wheat-laden ships were still sailing back and forth between Italy, Africa, and Asia, bringing deadly microorganisms into the heart of western civilization. For another century and a half, the Roman Empire managed to totter along, but then it collapsed once again, as the Romanian-born Alaric, king of the Visigoths, invaded, sacked, and slaughtered. What role did the epidemics play in his victory? The answer may never be known, but battered by so many enemies, the Roman Empire—enervated, demoralized, anxious, and overpopulated—began to slide downward into terminal decline.

Before it reached the final stage, the Roman state abandoned Rome and migrated to Constantinople, where it hoped to revive its fortunes and health. And for a while it seemed to get a new lease on life. A new emperor, Constantine (ruling from 306 to 337 CE), breathed life into the badly cracked egg. He did, however, surrender to the Christians, accepting their religion as the state's official faith, a shift in deities that did not protect anyone. In 542 CE, a third epidemic swept through Constantinople. This time the killer was the bacterium *Yersinia pestis* (the bubonic plague), which was spread by fleas and rats through trade networks that now reached as far eastward as the Tibetan Plateau and Kazakhstan as well as the Indian Ocean and Africa. This third wave has been called the Justinianic epidemic. It killed more people than any other in human history. It was caused by the bubonic plague, which finished off the Roman Humpty Dumpty and then for many centuries afterward kept coming back for fresh bodies.

For nearly a thousand years the Mediterranean region had been ruled by the most affluent, technically advanced, and well organized state in the early history of humans, yet the empire ended in shambles. High fertility rates among the Romans were the ultimate cause of that ending—the packing of more and more people on lands connected by a virus-corrupted sea. Overpopulation led to soil depletion in the countryside, farmer displacement, and social disorganization. New food resources had to be found, and Romans found them along the Nile. As yields at home continued low while populations kept recovering and growing, the state had to import more and more food from its sea-linked colonies, but the practice of importing food allowed pathogens an easy way into the heart of the empire. There were other cracks and weaknesses, but it was those agricultural and epidemiological materialities that mattered most. Fundamentally, they weakened the state, and it never recovered.

This was not, to be sure, how Rome's leaders wanted the people to judge their regime. They wanted to be seen as masterful architects of abundance and security. Such was the picture that Rome's most eloquent figure in politics, Marcus Tullius Cicero (106–43 BCE), tried to promote as a senator. Ignoring all the environmental problems discussed here, Cicero thought Rome deserved credit not only for promoting art, music, and literature but also for supporting the "arts of necessity," including the production of "a variety and abundance of food" and better health care. In a moment of high exuberance, Cicero trumpeted the greatness of Roman agriculture: "We enjoy the fruits of the plains and of the mountains, the rivers and the lakes are ours, we sow corn, we plant trees, we fertilize the soil by irrigation, we confine the rivers and straighten or divert their courses. In fine, by means of our hands we essay to create as it were a second world within the world of nature."[46] Cicero was right about Rome's many achievements, which added up to a higher level of civilization. But there was a lot of boasting in that passage, a blindness to the darker side of success.

Take note, however, that this Roman humanist, so full of self-congratulation, ends with a more somber conclusion: we should celebrate our human achievement, he cautions, but we should keep that achievement securely within and subordinate to nature. The empire may have aimed at a second world within nature, but it did not replace the first world, for the latter continued to evolve on its own. Had the Romans understood that first nature better, Cicero hinted, they might have achieved an even greater triumph. Later readers have not noted his final cautionary tone; they have dreamed naively of *replacing* first nature with a wholly man-made earth. That ambition, far from satisfied, would go on expanding until it became the modern project, which is nothing less than to elevate God (in the form of Man-God) permanently and categorically over the natural world.

Absolute moral and technological control over nature has become a common aspiration among modern societies, but what humans can show for their efforts so far remain superficial, temporary changes in the visible landscape, such as diverting rivers or capturing and breeding a few plant and animal species. A radical change in the planet's climate has so far not yet occurred; it may be lurking around the corner, but we don't really know its scale or certainty. Even that change may turn out to be minor in comparison to what plate tectonics and other biogeochemical forces accomplish daily. Moderns assume too easily that they now control all of nature, until new pandemics and food shortages demonstrate a humbler, more complex truth.

Sapiens did succeed, despite the fall of Rome, in expanding their food production and birthing more people. The human population, according to some demographers, nearly doubled between 500 and 1300 CE—but then the bubonic plague roared back into Europe and across Eurasia, making a huge dent in human numbers. The first repeat of plague hit Europe from 1347 to 1351, killing at least a third of the population, or some twenty-five million Europeans. But that was not the end. One of the worst plague events began in China's Yunnan province in 1855 among miners seeking copper in the mountains; from there it spread to Canton, Hong Kong, Taiwan, Mongolia, and the west coast of the United States, becoming endemic for many decades. It rocked the British Empire, inflamed racial prejudices worldwide, and killed an estimated fifteen million people in India alone.[47]

Such is the resilience of human reproduction that all those horrible losses could seem to be mere blips in planetary history. Demographically, the millennium that followed the Roman Empire follows the familiar story of rapid rebound and recovery. Centuries later, following the Black Death, the world's numbers were initially suppressed but only for a century, and then they climbed back and even surpassed earlier peaks. By 1500 CE the human population was pressing hard once again on the limits of nature. And then, after the reopening of the western hemisphere, the population exploded once more, reaching one billion by the early nineteenth century.

Nature, Cicero subtly reminded his listeners, is a check on the self-confidence of human politics, technology, and reason—a material reality eluding our understanding and control. Although the Roman Empire made it possible for some humans to feel more secure, even the most powerful state before the present proved defenseless and witless in the end.

If we followed Cicero's distinction between two worlds, one encompassing and the other encompassed, we would have to concede that the Roman Empire, great as it was, could not sustain itself. It raced to embrace its fate. We might go on to conclude that, though the outcome was tragic for many, Humpty Dumpty's fall made it possible for other states and empires to rise and thrive for a while.

If we believed that humans and their institutions must follow the basic laws of natural evolution, we might begin to understand history differently. We might agree that all social or cultural innovation is by nature imperfect and impermanent. We might end up writing narratives free of excessive moral judgments. A planetary history might instead become the integrated, broad-minded study of states, gods, ideologies, values, and ecologies, all rising and falling polyrhythmically, world without end.

CHAPTER 4

The Discovery of Second Earth

After the fall of the Roman Empire, according to standard narratives, came the Dark Ages, a time marked by social stagnation, decentralized economies, and scattered, feeble efforts to recover lost pomp and prosperity. Overall, it was a time of high religiosity. Human numbers went on increasing, despite the spread of authoritarianism and unreason, adding more and more bellies and gonads, until one bleak day there arrived a full-blown sustainability crisis. That tipping point appeared first in Great Britain and the Iberian peninsula, prominent points of an Atlantic-facing region we can call the Maritimes—Eurasia's westernmost shores and islands. We can use 1500 CE as the approximate date of the tipping point, which eventually unsettled every continent, throwing them all into upheaval.

By 1500 the most telltale indicator was that the agrarian way of life was beginning to crumble, even though it would never disappear altogether, just as foraging has never completely vanished. A new way of life began to evolve that we can call the industrial capitalist way. We cannot find the hand of providence in that development, but we can see how, why, and where it happened. We can learn how, by leading the change, the West recovered its power and confidence, lost since the fall of Rome. New western empires, far exceeding those of Rome, were established by the British, Spanish, French, and Americans, all influenced by capitalist logic, international trade relations, and profit seeking. Any such big transformation is multifactorial, and so was the industrial capitalist one. But its most powerful drivers were material changes in population accompanied by growing hunger and growing knowledge of the planet.[1]

To be sure, by 1500 humans had become, more than ever before, culture-bearing and culture-centered animals, expanding their capacity for imagining and shortening the time they needed to generate and spread new ideas. They gained, through cultural evolution, new ways to communicate, including what the biologist Richard Dawkins has called memes—that is, cultural elements that like genes can be imitated and replicated through books, magazines, newspapers, schools, movies, radio, or the internet.

Around 1440 CE a German goldsmith, Johannes Gutenberg, invented a new printing press, which, although it came slightly before the second great transformation began, accelerated the shaping role of culture in human evolution by magnitudes.[2] Previous cultural adaptation had proceeded slowly, as memes took thousands of years to spread, compete, and win acceptance. If we want to understand evolution in all its dimensions, we must see how the interaction of human numbers, food supplies, knowledge, culture, technology, and environment began to make changes more and more quickly.

In geographical terms, the new burst of change began first in the Maritimes of western Eurasia. Although spanning ten thousand kilometers from east to west, covering some 36 percent of the earth's total land area, the Eurasian supercontinent had long played a key role in stimulating the spread and development of humans and their genes and memes. As their numbers increased and Pleistocene ice and cold diminished, the Twice Wise spread across that entire supercontinent. But their numbers became a problem again, at different times in different places, leading to an intensification of agriculture, which in turn led to the spread of cities, states, empires, written languages, recordkeeping, even formal philosophy and religion.[3]

The eastern part of Eurasia had been in the forefront of the first great transformation that humans went through, the turn to agriculture, but after 1500 the dynamic center shifted to the western end of the supercontinent, to its maritime edges. There, humans had reproduced far beyond the biblical mandate to be fruitful and multiply, until they overwhelmed the capacity of their environment. Expanding knowledge, especially the knowledge of how to produce more food, enabled communities to enlarge their numbers further, but that capacity would be severely limited. It was then that a few individuals discovered a brand-new world beyond their shores, one that seemed without limits—the western hemisphere. This discovery led to another profound material change that affected almost all the world's people.

World demographic patterns suggest why around 1500 a tipping point became inevitable. Back at the dawn of agriculture, around 10,000 BCE, the population of the world stood at an estimated 5 million to 15 million. By 1000 CE, despite many oscillations, the world counted 250 million, and it continued growing until around 1800, when dropping fertility rates began to appear under industrial capitalism. Only a few of those millions alive in 1000 CE knew how to read and write, or anything about people living elsewhere. By that date Eurasia was home to nearly 200 million people—Europe counting 30 million and Asia 150 million. Five hundred years later, the planetary total reached 461 million, and *sapiens* were beginning to make and read books and learn about the whole planet and its possibilities. According to the French demographer Jean-Noël Biraben, Europe led the world in the percentage of population increase, adding 37 million from 1000 to 1500. Asia added 95 million. Africa reached a total of 87 million, becoming so crowded that its leaders intensified the tilling of the soil and the selling of their own people to slave-trading Arabs and Portuguese.[4]

No other large animal species has ever multiplied as fast as humans were doing. Epidemics, poor harvests, climate changes, and the collapse of states and empires might temporarily affect those totals, but almost always populations grew. The rate of increase may seem unimpressive compared with more recent experience, but century after century the numbers grew exponentially like interest on a bank account. By 1500, there were more than two Europeans living where only one had lived in the days of Caesar Augustus. The addition of millions of new brains stimulated a burst of innovation and social change. What were the consequences of that innovation? They ranged from printing presses to long-range sailing ships, compasses, maps, and new sources and varieties of food.

In nature as in society, minor-seeming increments can aggregate until they reach a point of sudden release. A glacier, for example, can melt at an almost imperceptible rate until suddenly it cracks in two, and the resulting pieces break free and drift away. Or take the thresholds of permafrost: climatologists tell us it may melt gradually until it reaches the point where long-buried methane can escape into the atmosphere, causing a huge and sudden spike in greenhouse gases. Scientists cannot anticipate exactly when such moments will occur; historians cannot say with high confidence when the slow accumulation of millions or even a billion humans may bring societies to a momentous time of change.

A temporary reversal in population gain, as we have seen, was caused by the bubonic plague, which swept through European countries from 1347 to 1353 CE. Losses from the disease were severe, but recovery was rapid. By 1600, another 20 million people had been added to Europe's pre-plague totals. In the next century another 20 million were added, until around 1800 the European population stood at 120 million—while the world population passed for the first time one billion. By then large numbers of Europeans were leaving home or already living in colonies and settler societies as far away as the Antipodes or the Americas. Why did they uproot themselves, and what were the consequences of their exodus from the old world?[5]

The most dynamic center of the world's second transformation was Great Britain, which after the Pleistocene had become a land densely packed with farmers. But that condition reached a breaking point when the agrarian way of life began to totter. After the Pleistocene, as a warmer, wetter climate ensued, tundra gave way to thick forests and grasslands. For a brief time, any species could still get to Britain easily by foot or wing, until the seas began to rise from glacial melting, making Britain an island separated from the rest of Eurasia by a wide saltwater channel. Not every part of that emerging island offered good habitat to migrants, for the landscape was dotted by many infertile mountains and moors, some of them returning to vegetative wildness—desolate sites like Dartmoor that no one has ever managed wholly to domesticate.

According to evolutionary theory, geographical isolation promotes biological diversification. The now familiar variations called foraging and farming had appeared on the earth's surface in isolated places and then diffused. Poets later found in that isolation something to celebrate. William Shakespeare, for example, proudly embraced Britain as an Eden separate from the Eurasian norm:

> . . . this sceptered isle,
> This earth of majesty, this seat of Mars,
> This other Eden, demi-paradise,
> This fortress built by Nature for herself
> Against infection and the hand of war,
> This happy breed of men, this little world,
> This precious stone set in the silver sea,
> Which serves it in the office of a wall,
> Or as a moat defensive to a house,
> Against the envy of less happier lands,
> This blessed plot, this earth, this realm, this England.

The lines are spoken by the character John Gaunt in Shakespeare's play *Richard II* (Act 2, scene 1), to which Gaunt adds a stinging rebuke: "That England, that was wont to conquer others / Hath made a shameful conquest of itself."

What Shakespeare did not seem to realize was that England's "happy breed of men" were becoming less and less happy as they were being squeezed more and more by their own fertility, forcing them into fierce competition. In that regard they were no different from nonhuman creatures. Experiencing too much growth, the English began to feel the limits of their environment closing in, threatening a future of intense rivalry, unrest, and violence.

The saltwater channel that separated England from the Eurasian landmass inspired splendid poetry, but it could not keep out all the land-hungry migrants who kept arriving, century after century. They came in several waves, first as foragers, then as farmers seeking fresh lands. Foragers, waving their spears about, were pushed aside by whip-brandishing agrarians. All the better soils soon passed to a set of self-aggrandizing owners, who came to occupy most of postglacial Britain. Then, as in the case of classical Rome, some of the newcomers began seeing themselves as an elite class of people, sure that they deserved above all others to be the land's possessors. What was nature and what was culture in that fierce possessiveness cannot easily be separated.

As the human invasion continued, a long-term shrinkage in Britain's biological diversity set in. We have excellent evidence of that shrinkage in the *Domesday Book,* a manuscript record of England and Wales completed in 1086 CE, which estimated that one million people then lived on the favored isle. The *Domesday Book* reported that forests had been removed from 85 percent of the country, and an even higher percentage from land lying below one thousand meters where soils were well suited to agriculture. Similar forest destruction to make room for agriculture had gone on across all of Eurasia, but Britain offered an especially severe case of internal change. By 1400 its tree cover had managed to recover somewhat, thanks to the bubonic plague, but then as humans resumed reproducing and added more mouths, the forests began to shrink again, until by 1850 they covered less than 2 percent of the island nation, a massive environmental change that explains why new innovations in culture and technology became necessary.[6]

A similar shrinkage of habitat occurred in another part of the European Maritimes, Iberia, a peninsula jutting out from the European subcontinent, split between the nations of Spain and Portugal. Surprisingly, that rather dry piece of land was for a long time more forested than Britain, but Iberia's woodlands were by no means thick or permanent. Here was a semi-arid environment, where deforestation had gone on even before the Romans began cutting down trees for supporting timbers in their mines, for making charcoal, for building houses, and for opening the land for farming and herding. Across the uplands, where grain was not a feasible crop, large flocks of sheep were set grazing, preventing forest recovery. Iberia, like Britain, had a history of humans pushing ecosystems to their limits and beyond. One especially vicious result was that the Christian Iberians, feeling the shrinkage in their environment, began to chase out competing Muslims and Jews. Any parcel of land that could grow food had to be devoted to feeding God's chosen people.[7]

The rest of Europe may have enjoyed better natural conditions than Britain or Iberia. Europe's old agrarian economies based on feudalism remained productive, but social inequality was increasing as population growth pressed on resources. Some parts of Eurasia and the Middle East, however, presented more drastically diminished opportunities for human development. Nowhere on the supercontinent were crop yields high, for soils had been widely depleted. Some areas still offered a new frontier of abundance, but most of what remained intact were deserts, grasslands, or boreal zones. Across all of Eurasia a growing number of farmers were finding less and less opportunity for expansion.

The power of environmental limits has long been ignored by most historians, perhaps because they assume too confidently that miracles of technology will always appear and rescue people from fate. A crisis, nonetheless, was approaching on many fronts, and it would have many unanticipated consequences. As their numbers kept growing, peasants intensified their plowing and cropping, and they adopted more and more innovations in cultural attitudes and methods of production. Although such efforts may have bought more time, they seldom helped for long.

Anthony Wrigley has labeled pre-modern Europe an "organic economy . . . a traditional economy bounded by the productivity of the land."[8]

That economy was also bounded by deficiencies of knowledge and skill. The organic label, however, glows with nostalgia, suggesting a stable, happy relation of people with nature, but in truth it was anything but that.

All farming, ancient or modern, is organic, for all farming depends on living organisms. Wrigley meant that no fossil fuels were in use, but even those fuels once were organic—we might call them "ex-organic." Even today's high-tech agriculture is organic in the sense that it depends on living seeds planted in soil and energy that comes from the sun and is mediated by photosynthesis. Or it depends on long-buried plant and animal remains. In fact, there is no alternative to organic farming or organic life. Necessarily, all agriculture and all foraging require either a living or deceased nature, creating a dependency that became more intense as more mouths cried out to be fed.

A more accurate term than "organic" for Europe before 1500 would be "agrarian," suggesting a mode of production based on plant and animal domestication but not yet based on industrial technology or urban resettlement. By that year the agrarian life was in serious trouble across much of Eurasia, and nowhere more so than in those low-lying, sea-girt lands bordering the Atlantic Ocean, including Britain, Iberia, France, and the Low Countries. There, human pressure on soils, water, and biota was reaching a peak. Famines repeatedly happened, and always there was the threat of microbial epidemics. Famines increased in part because of soil depletion, but they got worse whenever that degradation coincided with anomalous wet or dry spells. Add the danger of diseases spreading from one continent to another, and a growing state of crisis seems an apt description. Some of the more unhinged, harking back to ancient prophets wearing hair shirts, responded that an end time was coming when the gods would punish a sinful species. Armed with the Bible, mass printed in the vernacular, the worrying types could spread the meme of apocalypse and raise the alarm among their fellows.[9]

At the end of the Middle Ages, Britain was facing not a lapse in moral bearings so much as a fertility that was out of control. The population reached five million people around 1500, more than twice what it had been only five hundred years earlier. By 1800 the island added eleven million more. As for Iberia, its numbers also swelled over the same period, from eight million to fourteen million. And then there were the Scandinavian countries, which responded to their own hyperactive fertility by expanding over the North Atlantic, getting a permanent foothold in Iceland but only a temporary one in Greenland and Newfoundland. How, all those beleaguered peoples asked themselves, could they support their progeny? At the time, they were not ready to question their own urges or seek to control them. Instead, they responded by seeking new lands and additional resources.

Migration became a common response, especially among the poor who had no choice but to seek new lands to conquer and occupy, as *sapiens* had done since the era of Africa's Great Rift Valley and as the Romans had done in classical times. Predictably, the superabundant folk of the "scepter'd isle" set out to conquer nearby Ireland, which involved not the resettling of themselves so much as the acquiring of food to export back home.

Then up and down the Maritimes people began eyeing more seriously the ocean lying just offshore. The Atlantic had long been a kind of wall separating them from the rest of humanity, leaving them comparatively poor, marginalized, and ignorant. Rather suddenly, it became a doorway to new riches to the west. As that door began to open, those living in the Maritimes found themselves no longer among the poorest on earth but instead on the verge of becoming a people of plenty. They even dared to imagine that the new wealth they found might be infinite.

First, they sailed into the Atlantic seeking fish, especially the unexploited cod stocks of the Grand Banks.[10] Afterward they were drawn to the immense soils and forests of unfamiliar continents. After the Scandinavians, the people most inclined to dream of the possibilities beyond the ocean came from Iberia and Britain, notably not from Germany, Poland, Greece, or China. They began to realize that the western hemisphere offered nothing

THE DISCOVERY OF SECOND EARTH

less than a Second Earth. It was discovered out there across the sea, looming like an entirely new planet waiting to be exploited.

The Second Earth to the west offered a much more fertile Eden than Shakespeare's green isle. Although the new hemisphere contained only 30 percent of the planet's landmass, there were two huge, beautifully endowed continents that no one except their own inhabitants had ever realized were there. Seventy percent of Second Earth was covered by oceans—by waters deep and shallow, useless for farming but full of animal protein. Knowledge of those assets was sketchy at first, but in the centuries after 1500, Second Earth promised an extraordinary addition to the human masses.

We have understood *the facts* of the Great Discoveries for a long time, so long that they are now taken for granted, but not the implications. The western hemisphere was no cultural invention; it was first and foremost a huge material reality that had fallen into the laps of some very lucky people. It was western Europeans who took command over much of that hemisphere, which was so large and abundant that all description became hyperbolic.

Coming upon that bounty just as scarcity was tightening at home, the European Maritimers became fiercely determined to conquer and possess it. Wrongly, they took Second Earth to be nearly uninhabited or weakly defended by other humans—a most available frontier, they concluded, offering unfathomable riches of cheap natural resources, ranging from fish, timber, soils, and minerals to freshwater rivers and lakes. They soon discovered that Indigenous people were living in that "new world," but those people did not seem well armed. Long experienced in fighting among themselves for territorial possession, the indigenes would in fact fight long and hard to hold on to the hemisphere as their possession. Yet eventually they would be dispossessed just as other hominins and species had been dispossessed in the long wars that ended with human ownership of the Old World. Thus, history would repeat itself, and Second Earth would come firmly and irrevocably

THE DISCOVERY OF SECOND EARTH

under the control of new groups of those highly acquisitive *sapiens*. Europe, consequently, vaulted into the center of wealth, power, and innovation and would now have a big hand in defining what we call modernity.

Compared with, say, the upheaving impact of the Ice Age or photosynthesis, the Great Discoveries may not seem all that significant. Yet the discovery of Second Earth led to big changes not only in global climate and energy flows but also in human production and reproduction, adding up to a world-shaking revolution that left some people with a disproportionate hold over the earth. Whether viewed in ecocentric or anthropocentric terms, it marked truly the beginnings of a worldwide transformation. Earth's continents in effect became reunited and put in communication with one another, reversing millions of years of isolation.

The outcome was a second great transformation brought about by a species voracious for food and sex. Nothing less than a new way of life, a new mode of production, would emerge from it. And all that because of a surplus of babies that forced humans to adapt, migrate, or innovate when all else failed. Historians have written much about the great industrial innovations that began popping up in Britain, including factories, textile machinery, canals, waterpower, and coal mining, along with new global merchants, land companies, and banks. But they have not paid enough attention to what produced so much innovation—the pressure of human reproduction. Just as the cosmic Big Bang occurred at the climax of an intense interaction of matter and energy, so too did the human hunger for food and sex suddenly become very intense, until it burst humanity's boundaries and began to transform the planet. Although the effects of that explosion showed up first in Britain, sitting on the edge of Eurasia, they were not confined there, as *sapiens* dispersed from Europe all across the round earth and, just as striking, begin digging deeper beneath its surface.

Even though it was a rather small segment of humanity that grabbed much of Second Earth for themselves, eventually everyone on the planet was affected, enriched, or impoverished. Humans found new crops that they could feed on—maize, potatoes, tomatoes, and so forth. Their children became heirs to new fortunes. Almost everyone was drawn into expanded networks of trade and commerce, changed by an increase in the silver and gold supply that revolutionized national economies, welcomed many new technologies and learned to use them, and in some cases lost much of their autonomy and self-esteem.

Sometime in 1451 CE, a baby was born to an obscure family in Genoa, Italy, and named Cristoforo Colombo (later anglicized as Christopher Columbus). The baby's parents had been peasant farmers, but faced with declining prospects for that way of life they had migrated to Genoa and found work cleaning wool for clothmakers, a poorly paid occupation but one that they, as people of the land, knew how to do.[11] Genoa, a port on the blue Mediterranean Sea, had for some years been seeking an alternative to farming that involved trade in expensive spices like nutmeg, cloves, and cinnamon. Those commodities were harvested in India or Southeast Asia and sent overland to the Black Sea or to Egypt, where Genoese sailors loaded them on ships and brought them to their homeland for sale. Christopher's family, however, did not want to join the spice trade. Spices offered little to satiate their hunger. They were important mainly to rich urban consumers and could enrich only a few traders. Christopher, like his parents, grew up wanting something other than a place in that crowded, rarefied business. They turned their backs on spices.

In 1453 the Ottoman Empire conquered Constantinople and began blocking European routes to the Black Sea, India, and China, disrupting the spice trade. The busy port of Genoa, on the edge of a declining hinterland of farmers and now facing a blocked market in expensive luxuries, abruptly found itself in trouble. How was a child such as Christopher to make a living? Going to sea seemed promising, but the golden days of trading spices around the Mediterranean were over.

Christopher Columbus seems to have resented the backwardness and poverty of his parents, and that resentment pushed him westward toward the Atlantic shores of Iberia. At age twenty-five, he left Genoa and landed in Lisbon, Portugal's main port on the ocean that would define his future. There he stayed for eight years, during which time he dreamed of new seagoing enterprises that no one else had found feasible. Portugal's head of state was intent on finding an alternative route to the Orient, but it involved sailing down the western coast of Africa, around the Cape of Good Hope, and straight across the Indian Ocean to India's Malabar coast, the center of the world spice market. Columbus was convinced that he could do better. He dreamed that he could sail west across the Atlantic and reach the same destination easily and harvest a wide array of commodities. Discouraged by a lack of local support, he migrated once again, this time to Spain's Atlantic ports, where he went looking again for someone to invest in his watery dreams.

Columbus's basic plan involved sailing due west to reach "the Indies" (a generic term for the eastern end of Eurasia). The Vikings had previously crossed the Atlantic, but their efforts to establish colonies in the Americas dated back five hundred years and were unknown or forgotten. So it was that an enterprising young man from Genoa became the very first person to cross the Atlantic Ocean and find a new kind of fame and fortune. He would be the first, but he was not the last.

Long before Columbus was born, a world map had been drawn up by the Roman-Egyptian scholar Claudius Ptolemy, a map still in use in Columbus's day. Ptolemy was an astronomer-geographer who lived in Alexandria, Egypt, during the second century CE. His map of what he called *Ecumene*, or the known-to-Eurasians world, included only Eurasia and the northern half of Africa, and even then, many of its details were conjectural. Ptolemy's map had long been considered the final authority on the geography of the earth, but that was about to change.

According to Ptolemy, the Atlantic Ocean was nothing more than a narrow riverlike border that circled and framed the continental world. Beyond that terminus, a sailor ran out of cartographic knowledge. Columbus studied Ptolemy's limited geography carefully, but his attention was drawn more to a rival speculation that arrived in Lisbon in 1474, in a letter penned by Paolo dal Pozzo Toscanelli, a Florentine physician and cosmographer. Toscanelli, after meeting a group of Chinese visitors and growing excited by their glowing descriptions of *Zhongguo,* or the Middle Country (China's name for itself), concluded that one might sail west across the Atlantic and reach that glittering civilization, which he called Cathay. Toscanelli had written to a churchman living in Lisbon these excited words that Columbus would absorb and find inspirational: "[China] is worthy to be sought by the Latins not only because immense wealth can be had in the form of gold, silver, gems of every kind, and spices which are never brought to us; but also desirable because of the learned men, wise philosophers, and astrologers by whose genius and arts those mighty and magnificent provinces are governed and even wars are waged."[12]

The visiting Chinese had traveled to Italy by land, but Toscanelli, though no ocean voyager himself, came up with the brilliant notion of sailing westward from Iberia. Why was it a European rather than a Chinese person who saw the possibilities in going to sea? China, of course, faced not the Atlantic Ocean but the much broader Pacific, though no one at the end of the fifteenth century knew just how broad it was. Several decades before Columbus's voyages, the most extraordinary admiral in Chinese naval history, Zheng He, led no fewer than seven expeditions to what he called the "Western Ocean" (that is, the Indian Ocean), all well-funded and grander than anything Columbus ever imagined—but Zhang did not sail eastward into the Pacific. When he returned home to China, his emperor destroyed all his boats and records, shutting down for centuries China's capacity for exploring the Pacific or claiming the western hemisphere. The consequences for that country's future were severe, as China thereafter concentrated on maintaining its agrarian way of life, while Europeans began to dream of creating something new.[13]

Reaching China by sailing westward across the Atlantic Ocean became Columbus's unrelenting ambition. First, he had to open the eyes of Iberians to the possibility and then, in payment for their patronage, bring home some of the wealth and wisdom waiting on the other side. Above all, he dreamed of reaping personal glory, though riches and titles were desirable too, for they might lift him out of poverty and set him forever among the Iberian elite. He was not a crass or evil man, only one consumed with desire, furiously eager, and willing to take big risks. Yet he was also a new type of human being that would soon become quite familiar: the self-made man, the risk-taking entrepreneur seeking abundance.

On August 3, 1492, Captain Columbus set out across the Atlantic Ocean with the goal of reaching Asia. He left from a Spanish port because, after failing to impress Portugal's monarch with his notions, he found backing from the queen and king of Spain, who funded three small wooden vessels and grandly promised to make him "Admiral of the Ocean Seas." Anticipating that title, he had what he wanted most: a promise of honor that he kept tightly pressed to his breast until his death fourteen years later.

According to Toscanelli, the sailing distance to China should be quite short; he calculated that it was eight thousand kilometers closer than it really is. Columbus did his own calculations, but he too grossly underestimated the distance. That they both minimized the span tells us how ignorant all humans then were about the real size of the planet. Sailors then were familiar with latitudes but not with longitudes, so no one could calculate accurately the earth's circumference.[14]

Despite his colossal blunder, Columbus succeeded in crossing the Atlantic. His strategy was simply to go with the wind until he got there. But in fact he ended up in an unexpected and less than glittering place, the Caribbean, unknown to anybody anywhere in Eurasia, although it turned out to be a door to wealth greater than Columbus ever imagined.

Pushed along by strong, steady trade winds, he and his crews arrived on October 12, 1492, after three months aboard ship. They landed on a small, nondescript island in the Bahamas, but Columbus was sure they had reached China, a country that must, he insisted, lie just over the horizon. In

THE DISCOVERY OF SECOND EARTH

truth, he was not even halfway there. Unwittingly, he had run smack into an unknown *hemisphere*—nothing less than Second Earth, an unknown world full of "new" islands, continents, and oceans.

Three more voyages followed, the last of them made along the inner coast of Central America, which was densely inhabited by native people—and there Columbus had to give up his misconceptions. He had not found his way to China. Soon after getting back to Spain, he became bitter and angry about it all. Wealth, honors, fame, and status had come to him, but they proved as unsatisfactory and shaky as Italy's fading peasant life had been for his parents.[15]

In the end it was the planet's nature that undid Columbus. Other Europeans came to explore further what he was not interested in: vast mountain ranges, tall dark forests, intricate river basins, and not one but two large oceans lying between the extremities of Eurasia. On the other side of the Americas lay an even more immense body of water, the Pacific Ocean, some twenty-five thousand kilometers across at its widest point. Only after navigating and surviving all that might others manage to reach China.[16]

Earlier than Columbus, about twelve thousand to fifteen thousand years earlier, bands of migrants had entered and settled the Americas from Eurasia. They did not realize its hemispheric proportions any more than Columbus did; they were as mistaken as he about what they found. What all of them, firstcomers and latecomers alike, discovered was that somewhere between the two ends of the Eurasian supercontinent was a great hemisphere that was almost as big as another planet. All those who came wanted to grab it for themselves. Only the Europeans succeeded because only they collected knowledge of that hemisphere on a grand scale. They made maps, which enabled them to launch many invasions to satisfy their urge to possess. Meanwhile, those indigenes who had arrived much earlier fought to keep their claims intact, even though fatal limitations in their knowledge and technology—as well as a tragic susceptibility to foreign microbes—made them weak and vulnerable. They would lose out in the oldest kind of conflict the planet has known: a competitive war for natural resources.

The full massiveness of Second Earth would not become well known for many centuries after Columbus's death, and its impact on human affairs—from economies, politics, and religion to folklore and fantasy—did not become fully felt until the twentieth century. So far as we know, the first person to grasp the hemisphere as a whole and therefore the first to demonstrate the fundamental truth about our round planet was a brilliant, irascible, and pigheaded man named Ferdinand Magellan, who sailed with a crew under a Spanish flag. Magellan undertook the first circumnavigation of the earth, which he hoped would take him from Iberia across the Atlantic and then, rounding Cape Horn, into the Pacific, the largest ocean of all, and then toward the tip of Africa and back home to Spain. Tragically, he did not complete that plan. Only part of his crew did, and from their reports spread news of many distant lands waiting to be exploited. Out there, mapmakers began to show, was the equivalent of another planet, big enough to satisfy all the natural desires of many generations of Europeans, and more.

Magellan was born in 1480 in Sabrosa, a village in northern Portugal, to a family with ties to the Spanish nobility. Despite his social advantages, he had endured a marginalized, luckless youth that left him, like Columbus, eager to embrace exploration as a way to elevate his status in society. A new monarch on the Spanish throne gave him his chance: King Charles I arranged financial support from Germany's banking giants, giving Magellan enough capital to outfit five ships that he grandly named the Armada de Molucca.

Magellan's fleet left Spain in early August 1519, almost three decades after Columbus's first voyage. He would seek and find a navigable passage around the tip of South America, henceforth known as the Magellan Strait, a safer route for sailing ships than the storm-tossed waters farther south off

Cape Horn. The first European to sail into the South Pacific, he was also the first European to venture across that bigger ocean, sailing straight across its immensity toward Asia.

Only one of his ships would return home, and then only after three years of roaming the seas. It returned without Magellan, who ended up being killed by hostile natives on an island in the Philippines. Rashly, the captain had burned down their village after they refused to become Catholic. After that impetuous act, he tried to punish the natives further. Donning plate armor and brandishing swords, he and his men waded clumsily ashore only to meet a volley of poisoned spears thrown by an army of naked, angry, and defensive men. One of those spears struck Magellan's bare leg. Ignominiously, he bled to death on the beach, still clad in his ridiculous armor—a would-be instrument of God who ended up the victim of his own excesses.[17]

The planetary knowledge that Magellan's crew brought back did little to help Spain with its domestic resource problems, but its leaders became intensely eager to find new wealth, particularly gold and silver, to engage in slave trading, and to do some missionary work, though they had no idea of how the new discoveries might prop up their failing agrarian base at home. Despite extracting much precious ore from the new world and committing many outrages on the native peoples, Spain would one day manage to lose control of its western possessions. Nonetheless, the various Spanish voyages of discovery marked a critical point in planetary history. This fact scholars have long acknowledged, but they still have not fully appreciated that the discoveries rescued a Europe that was reaching the limits of traditional agrarianism.[18]

The most far-sighted explorer of Second Earth, however, was neither Columbus nor Magellan but a rural British lad who became a sea captain and a plunderer. He would turn out to be the shining exemplar of a new capitalism to replace agrarianism. His name was Francis Drake (1540–1596), who with his men became the second expedition of Europeans to circumnavigate

THE DISCOVERY OF SECOND EARTH

the planet. It was Drake who opened the eyes of Queen Elizabeth I and other northern European leaders to the extraordinary potential of Second Earth and who encouraged them to pursue a global market and empire that would become larger and more consequential than any created by ancient Romans, Akkadians, or the rest.

Within a few more centuries, the British, not the Spanish or Portuguese or Chinese, dominated Second Earth. They extended that control into an economic-ecological transformation of the planet that would rock all nations. It was the British who initiated a mass exodus of settlers into North America, the Caribbean, and Down Under, seized the best lands from natives in all those places for growing sugar and cotton, for raising sheep and cattle. It was the British who would invent a new industrial capitalist mode of production to replace the fading agrarian one. And it was a British seaman named Drake who led the way toward that outcome.

Despite his innocent-looking face, his receding hairline, pointed beard, flowing mustache, and natty lace collar that made him look like a choirboy, Drake turned out to be a British lion who roared his way across Second Earth. There were many others in the English pride of lions, including John Cabot, Sir Walter Raleigh, Bartholomew Gosnold, and James Cook (along with their contemporaries who remained back home and built factories, set up banks and corporations, invented machinery, and pursued scientific knowledge). In contrast to the Iberian adventurers, the British adventurers were backed not only by monarchs but also by an aggressive group of capitalists, eager for colonies and profits, eager to add to their assets a world-spanning empire. But above all, the British sought land and natural resources, without which their country might have ended up becoming another Norway or Iceland, small and self-contained. The industrial capitalist way of life might never have gotten off the ground, for without the material reality of American soils, crops, and slave workers, what abundance would there have been for the British to acquire?

THE DISCOVERY OF SECOND EARTH

On his many voyages in and out of the western hemisphere, Drake was awestruck by its magnificent livability. In 1577 as his fleet crossed from the Cape Verde Islands to the coast of Brazil, he challenged a common assumption that the Atlantic was too torrid a zone for British northerners. Not at all, he retorted, for even around the equator the climate was so delightful that it must be called "the Earthly Paradise." Frequent rains produced plenty of fresh water, and the seas were loaded with delicious food, "as if we had been in the storehouse of His blessings, [enjoying all] that princes could have desired." On his voyages, Drake never lacked for ample food. "The sea in God's fatherly Providence did afford us both abundance of change and variety, and that daily, of most wholesome and rare fishes which are not common to the monarchies of the world."[19] If the seas were as bountiful as he reported, how much better must the lands be? Having known poverty and hunger in his life, Drake was delighted to find so much wealth abounding on Second Earth.

Like Magellan, Francis Drake died ignominiously in foreign waters. His death came in the tiny seaport of Porto Bello on Panama's Caribbean coast where he contracted dysentery, an intestinal infection that comes from consuming contaminated food or water. He died a long way from home, but he did not die because of his own intemperate violence or racist attitudes. He was killed by the dangerous microscopic nature of the new world.

The eldest of twelve children, Drake was born to yeoman farmers in Devonshire, England, and grew up on a tenant farm near Tavistock, some thirty kilometers inland from the Atlantic shore, on a farm with patches of good soil but closely bounded by the rocky, unfarmable wastelands of Dartmoor. Drake's father, who at first seemed a promising tenant farmer, turned out to be disreputable and disputatious and had to go into hiding. His wife and children then were forced to move to the nearby seaport of Plymouth and live on the generosity of their ocean-going relatives.[20]

Uprooted from the countryside through no fault of his own, young Drake was quick to seize on a career in oceanic exploration. By going to sea he hoped, like Columbus, to become a self-made man, rich with silver and gold from plundered galleons and from the African slave trade. He followed Magellan's route around South America, sailed up North America's west coast, and then diverted across the Pacific and Indian oceans, cruising around Africa and returning home. Like Magellan, Drake learned little about the Indigenous peoples he met along the way, but he did take home a great deal of wealth for his family and queen. Repeatedly, he risked his life until he ended up a gentleman at last, knighted by Elizabeth I while becoming a ruthless predator in the eyes of the rest of the world.

Much criticized today as agents of western imperialism, as though they were the first and only imperialists in world history, the European explorers tended to come from poor, intelligent, venturesome, and enterprising commoners. They were also benefactors in the eyes of some—their families and nations foremost. Both Columbus and Drake enriched others as they enriched themselves. Neither was a demon out to despoil a pure, noble, Edenic hemisphere. After them came waves of men and women from many countries who likewise traveled with mixed motives. All shared a common desire for self-advancement, a desire not wholly unlike the desires of the people they invaded. The sixteenth century did not mark a grand moral shift on the planet from good to evil, innocence to corruption, kindness to cruelty. Rather, it marked a fresh battleground in the age-old struggle between human desire and the "moral sprouts" that Mencius understood.

Such an assessment might help all of us know our selves better—know what we are and were, why we have changed, and what we have become. Especially it is the historicity of our inborn human nature that we need to understand.

By 1550, when Drake was a boy of eight, Britain's population stood at three million. By the seventeenth century, a time that climatologists include in the Little Ice Age, severely cold temperatures were ruining many harvests, forcing many people to go hungry and die. When warmer temperatures returned, desires returned, until the increasing number of mouths at home made Second Earth seem a paradise of plenty.

Villages tried to deal with their rising numbers by raising the marriage age higher and higher, but to no avail—the babies kept coming. By 1750, although some emigration had begun, the population of England and Wales had doubled to six million, not to mention those conquered people living in Scotland (annexed in 1707) and then Ireland (1801). Almost everyone living in a newly organizing British Empire was a subsistence farmer. Six million people may not seem that many (the western end of Eurasia counted more than a hundred million), but those six million were hungry enough to start Britain down the road to a capitalist revolution. And if they did not all migrate, they had glimpsed a future of plenty.

What the demographer Massimo Livi-Bacci says of Europe in general can be applied to England in particular: "As plague vanished from the continent, industrialization created new energy sources and the means to produce resources, and important openings were made—not only to America in the west but also to the Urals and beyond in the east—which allowed for the departure of human resources and the arrival of material ones."[21]

Squeezed by their own fertility, Britain's people began not only to migrate abroad but also to push beyond the agrarian economy, which they sensed was heading for collapse. In time a flood of migrants would flow to the new world. They would do what humans have always done since the earliest flows out of Africa—first seek new land elsewhere and then adapt one's way of life. Eventually, some eighty million to one hundred million people emigrated from Europe to Second Earth, and then in the twentieth century the migrants would come from any and all countries full of hungry folk.

But in the beginning, those going to the Americas were mainly peasants living in the British Isles, France, the Netherlands, and Iberia. Compared with the tiny bands that had long ago walked out of the motherland of Africa, they were an enormous gang of anxious people—fearing the future and yet embracing it. As much as 25 percent of European residents left their homes for Second Earth, lightening the burden on the neighbors but also depriving Europe of a hard-working, capable pool of laborers.[22]

The British proved most eager to stake out claims on new lands. As their numbers kept on increasing, they came to dominate Europe as well as the planet. Where Italy had once outnumbered them three times over, by 1850 Italy counted 25 million people, compared with England's 16.5 million. Consequently, Italy saw its geopolitical influence wane as Britain's increased, and soon thereafter Britain became the leader of Europe as well as the center of a planet-spanning empire. The English language began to spread abroad, contesting Greek, Latin, Spanish, Portuguese, and Italian as the medium of international communication, becoming, outside of China, the most common language spoken around the planet, with Spanish a close second in popularity. Those outcomes were part of the cultural fallout from the discovery of Second Earth.[23]

As English-speaking men and women proliferated, so too did their herds and flocks—horses, cows, pigs, chickens, ducks. Perhaps the most important animal migrants leaving Britain were flocks of sheep. As Columbus was making his voyages to the new world, sheep were taking over much of the Iberian and British landscape; later sheep imperialists would seize control of Australia, New Zealand, Argentina, and much of the American West. By 1500 Britain counted at home three sheep for every human being—some eight million woolies in all—and they were only beginning their phenomenal increase. Wool shorn from the backs of sheep was highly desired to keep the British warm through their cold, damp winters, but also mutton and lamb became popular sources of protein. The increase in sheep raising came at a steep cost, however, for it meant the overgrazing of far-flung global pastures. Add all the livestock together, and the environmental and agricultural transformation wrought by Britain, Spain, and their overseas colonies was profound.

According to the seventeenth-century statistician Gregory King, who lived in the early years of the great out-migration to Second Earth, the land of Britain contained 3.6 million arable hectares, fully half of which by his day had come under cultivation. King classified 4 million hectares of Britain as wastelands, including much of Francis Drake's home region, with its infertile heaths, moors, and mountains where scanty soils and rock outcroppings defied the farmer's plow but could be good pasture for sheep. Over a million hectares were still covered by native forests, including groves of coppiced trees, which provided fuel and construction timber. But those rich lands in Britain were comparatively small change, compared to what was available in North America.[24]

The future United States covered more than 900 million hectares of land, nearly 162 million of them arable, so that one day it would surpass as a food grower not only Britain but also China, Russia, and India. Canada was even larger in size, though less arable, while Mexico had nearly 200 million hectares. The widespread hope that the Americas could rescue the pinched agrarian way of life explains why Second Earth held so much appeal. A grand rescue seemed possible for a while, but by the twentieth century the United States stopped expanding its arable base, and after that its countryside residents became more and more nervous, fearful, and hostile to immigrants, not unlike the rural districts of Europe or China.

Before that happened, the North American cornucopia attracted a huge rural population, until the most productive parts of the new continent became overpopulated themselves. By 1900 the stock of free land in the United States was shrinking as almost all the best acreage had become private property and was becoming unaffordable for newly arrived immigrants. The declining prospects for agrarianism had also become more painful back in Britain as marginally arable lands there began to be "enclosed," a process of privatization that left common folk with less and less access to soil. They were being wrenched out of their way of life, just as poor farmers in ancient Rome had been, and once more the outcome was very large estates belonging to a very wealthy aristocracy. Until 1730 the project of enclosing the land was accomplished at the local level through private agreements. After that,

THE DISCOVERY OF SECOND EARTH

Parliament took over and proceeded to enclose almost all of England's common land in the name of higher productivity.[25]

Large swaths of terrain came to be the private property of a few rich families, lands made picturesque by stone walls and woody hedgerows lining the market roads, a landscape of fewer but larger commercial farms, while some of their wealthy owners began to manage soils to increase profits. They hoped that innovation would yield even more value. The difference between this development and the land intensification among rural communitarians recommended by Ester Boserup was that in Britain a landowning few insisted on being free of all community oversight. Such was the social outcome of the second great transformation, firmly established by the early 1800s.

Across Second Earth, similar trends toward land concentration and entrepreneurial freedom soon came to rule, bringing pressure on the agrarian mode even in the new world. By 1900 Second Earth, including Australia and New Zealand, all of which had once seemed so naturally abundant, had been taken over by the industrial capitalist mode, as the more successful farmers joined factory owners in a political alliance. Farmers in the United States became a tiny but affluent minority, numbering by the twenty-first century a mere two million out of more than three hundred million citizens. They owned the land, all that they could see in many cases. By that point there were fewer farmers than Native Americans. Ironically, the farmer-business alliance dispossessed poorer white farmers who earlier had dispossessed the aboriginal people.

We will never know for certain how many Native Americans there were at the time Columbus made first contact; we can only make estimates, and those estimates are often tainted by political bias. A persuasive figure comes from the historian Dan Flores: four million Native Americans living in 1492 CE in what became the United States. A more generous, probably inflated estimate comes from the late historian Wilbur Jacobs, who claimed there were forty million to sixty million natives living in the Americas at first contact.[26]

THE DISCOVERY OF SECOND EARTH

Whatever estimates we use, it is clear that before the "new world" discoveries and the first waves of European and African migrants, Second Earth may have been home to 5 to 10 percent of the total human population on earth—nearly matching the population of Europe, though generally the new world people were far less densely clustered. Today, in contrast, the western hemisphere counts one billion people. Since 1500, a massive redistribution of human bodies has gone on among all the continents, all the peoples, all the breeding populations, and a similarly massive ecological effect has been felt on all the continents.

In their first encounters, Native Americans died frequently because of the many deadly diseases brought, quite unwittingly, by the Europeans. According to some estimates, 90 percent of the first Americans died without understanding how or why, their places taken by invaders, some of whom also died as a result of disease, malnutrition, and depleted lands. No doctor at the time could have explained that outcome. Everyone, invaders and invaded alike, tried to explain it in supernatural terms. God, it was said, or powerful spirits dwelling in the land, had for some reason decided to help some of the Europeans, while withdrawing protection from the Indigenous people (although in fact it was invisible microbes carried in the invaders' blood that did the killing). Yet the ruthless invaders did not all escape disease and death as they explored the new world. Drake's death by dysentery was probably caused by microbes transported to Central America by Spanish sailors, priests, pirates, and gold seekers. Thus, he became himself a victim of conquest, as did many other travelers, explorers, and settlers.

Only the Africans imported as slaves enjoyed a relatively high immunity in the transition to a new hemispheric diversity, for their home continent had evolved differently, toward a state of immunity to such deadly killers as malaria and yellow fever, compared with Europe and the Americas. A major reason Africans were brought in chains across the Atlantic was that they were deemed better able to survive the new world's disease-ridden environments and to provide a cheap, permanent labor supply on sugar plantations and in silver mines. But they too could sicken and die from the mixing of microbes.[27]

Europeans, Africans, and the many invisible migrants were not the only organisms to transform Second Earth. Invasive plants played a role too, not only weeds but also long-domesticated plants such as sugar, rice, cotton, and coffee, which became important cash crops in the new world. Also invading the Americas were various bird species, rodents, and insects. As the Europeans destroyed native inhabitants, non-native species were quick to move in and fill the empty niches. Because of what Alfred Crosby has called "the Columbian exchange," the biological changes in the Americas that followed the European discoveries, Second Earth became part of Europe, but also part of and prototype for the whole planet.[28]

No one a few centuries ago could possibly have grasped the full significance of those alterations of the earth. The rejoining of what had long been separate brought cascading changes. It was bound to happen at some point, of course, but it meant unspeakable woe and suffering for organisms that were not ready for the competition. Death rates from invisible microbes brought to the Americas were far worse than those stemming from the plague in fourteenth-century Europe. Overall global fertility, however, did not decline; on the contrary, within three hundred years after its discovery by European explorers, Second Earth was overfilled with people. Like a Chinese firecracker, humans had exploded across the whole planet.

Hot sparks of human passion were another part of the encounter of European invaders with the indigenes, though we can never know how frequently their intimacies occurred. We know that a great mixing of DNA took place in the wake of Columbus, making possible new genetic combinations, redirecting the course of human evolution. As that happened, the question of who was native and who was not became difficult to answer. Genetic mixing became the norm, merging long-separated populations into one common, interbreeding species, a kind of change that had not happened on such a scale since early days in Africa. And as old genes mixed their chromosomes into new patterns, the evolution of the planet gained new vigor.

By 2000 the Americas had become home to the most diversified gathering of *Homo sapiens* anywhere. People had entered the hemisphere from every direction, every inhabited continent. Without Columbus and his fellow trailblazers, without the much earlier migrations from Asia to North and South America, the earth would be a very different place. Our knowledge of the planet as well as our genetic diversity would be much poorer. After thousands of years of seizing resources in both hemispheres, it was astonishing that people could still find a hemisphere so wide open to new migration, allowing its numbers to overshoot what was practical and realistic.

Much new knowledge accumulated because of the Columbian exchange, knowledge that now could be printed in books for all to read. The result proved on the whole liberating and enlightening. Even though America's indigenes had long been learning about their homeland, they could not have said exactly where in the world they came from or where they lived; now everyone, immigrant or native, gained new understanding of the planet. While many indigenes died, others survived and thrived in unexpected ways, as they added new knowledge and new desires to the world pool, a benefit we should not overlook. Columbus, Magellan, and Drake might not be celebrated for their moral enlightenment or intentions, but they might be acknowledged for their revelations of the planet, an outcome that was as important as the news of vast new opportunities for many. Thanks to their exploits, all humans could see that we live on and must share a common home in the cosmos.

Largely because of that gain in knowledge and the pressure of desires that made it possible, Europeans won the competition to possess Second Earth, but the competition and moral evolution are far from over. Immigration continues to this day, and it is hard to see who will end up owning Second Earth in coming centuries. For the Europeans the experience was beneficial, but it was like landing on another planet—luckily, not on the red dust or toxic seas of Mars or Venus but on a hemisphere of unrealized promise, which supported a richness of plant, animal, and microbe life. Hard-pressed Europeans of the Maritimes found their way to one of the most creative and lively habitats in the cosmos. What remains to be discovered is how to live sustainably in both the western and eastern hemispheres.

Excepting the exodus from Africa that began tens of thousands of years ago, there has been no more consequential moment in history than the discovery of Second Earth. It happened once, with Columbus, but it also happened again and again, starting with ancient Asian migrants and continuing with destitute or capital-rich Europeans and many others on the move. As they all gained knowledge of Planet Earth's shape and size, its diverse natures and cultures, the result was an extraordinary breakthrough for humanity. We cannot go back and erase that story or simply condemn it. We can only ask, what are people now supposed to do with what we have discovered?

CHAPTER 5

Dreams of Infinite Wealth

London 1848: an obscure resident with a leonine head of hair and bushy beard has just published one of the greatest political essays of all time, the short but powerful *Communist Manifesto*.[1] He is Karl Marx, a German journalist who regularly faces writer's block, is strongly passionate by nature, and suffers from painful boils on his buttocks. In an essay full of witty, quotable lines, Marx vents his anger at the despised bourgeoisie, without ever admitting how much he shares their hunger for the fruits and pleasures of modern life. As he seeks his own gratification, he skewers the business community's comfortable life. He approaches them as though they were fellow philosophers, and in a way they were—for they were creating, as Robert Heilbroner has written, a worldly philosophy that was new, rational, and coherent but also quite selfish, individualistic, and ultimately unsustainable. They offered an appealing solution to an ecological crisis, appealing even to Marx himself. He lusted after their affluence even as he sought to reject it. But then he did not know himself all that well.[2]

Marx's words flow like red-hot lava across the page, for he wants nothing less than to destroy the emerging power elite of his day. Yet at the same time he admires their intelligence and shares much of their view of the earth, for he too dreams of attaining greater wealth through the conquest of nature. But wealth, he adds, should belong to those who produce it—himself and the workers. Soon, he promises, their full gratification will come to pass, as all wealth will be held in common. Every person will then have everything that is rightly due to him or her. Arise, he tells Europe's underclass; throw off your chains and join the rich. You too can get more material satisfaction out of this planet.

But the chains he has in mind have been forged not only by an elite class but also by the working class: they too have become driven by new wants, while continuing to struggle for food and sex. Their wants are not very different from those of the capitalists at the other end of the social spectrum, for in general human wants have grown larger as the planetary map has grown bigger. The enlargement lay at the very core of the second great transformation in human life, from the agrarian mode to the industrial capitalist mode.

Human desires, partly natural, partly cultural—above all, a new desire to expand wealth—lay at the core of that transformation, inspiring capitalists and communists alike. That desire began rising within almost everyone, even the overwhelmed Indigenous peoples of the Americas. Marx the philosopher did not grasp how powerful those wants had become, although he himself was intensely upwardly mobile.[3] What upset him most was an inequality in the satisfaction of rising desires, old or new. He assured his followers that an economic crisis would occur soon and bring a revolution, ending inequality and giving workers control over the machinery of satisfaction. His predicted revolution, however, did not come to pass; on the contrary, the capitalists continued in power. They even began to assume that they were the permanent masters of humanity.

In the long run it was not class conflict that most threatened the capitalists but their ignorant, unrealistic thinking. Their lack of realism about nature showed up not only in the resource shortages they produced but also in bankruptcies, investment failures, bouts of inflation, booms followed by busts, a rise in environmental degradation, and even an unforeseen fall in fertility rates among women. As the natural sciences would later reveal, the earth, despite its extraordinary life-giving qualities, could never satisfy or fulfill such a sweeping, unrealistic increase in expectations.

Three years before writing the *Manifesto,* Marx called for a new kind of history, which had he practiced it himself might have made him a more credible prophet. "We know only a single science," he wrote, "the science of history. One can look at history from two sides and divide it into the history of nature and the history of men. The two sides are, however, inseparable; the history of nature and the history of men are dependent on each other so long as men exist." So far, so good. He was claiming to be a thorough-going materialist, but despite his call for an integrated science of humans and nonhumans, his brand of materialism was narrowly focused on struggles over the ownership of machines, the distribution of wealth, and the satisfaction of *sapiens'* desires. Unfortunately, he was not interested in seeking the kind of knowledge that could help humans live sustainably on the earth. There was little understanding of the living planet in either Marx or Friedrich Engels, or indeed in Marxist thought until "green Marxism" succeeded them after World War II. Pointedly and without irony, Marx ended further consideration by dismissing the relevance of the history of nature to social analysis: "The history of nature called natural science," Marx wrote, "does not concern us here."[4]

In that bifurcation, he threw away his chance of leading the way toward a critical natural history that included humans. Above all, he dismissed the natural history of his contemporary, the British naturalist Charles Darwin who likewise called for a new science of history that included both nature and human nature. Had Marx embraced Darwinian biology, he might have understood more fully why capitalism had won the hearts and minds of workers. It had done so by accepting the power of their desire, and it would take more than worker resentment or Marxian envy to overcome that power.

Marx wanted to overthrow capitalism, but he also wanted to keep intact a thick wall separating humanity from the rest of nature. He was a dualist at heart: there was nature and there were humans, and they had nothing in common. Evolution would lead humans to see that the old dualism had become untenable on a small planet. Marx too should have admitted that humans are inseparable from the rest of earthly nature and that more modesty in their desires might offer humankind's best hope for long-term survival. He did not do so, however, probably because he was still devoted to the traditional conquest of man over nature.

To be sure, a historical science that would restore humans to the category of nature was nowhere yet realized. Soon, however, it would emerge and would make humans part of nature co-evolving with other species in a unified ecosphere of matter, energy, and life. Such a science would be built on an anti-dualist perspective. From its core of ecological and evolutionary biology would come a new understanding that the rest of nature is not simply an inferior realm to be aggressively manipulated by humans. Human life and institutions would come to be seen as part of the web of life.

Human nature, as Karl Marx knew well, did not originate in some divine brain. But he did not go on to see that evolving out of nature makes humans what we are. He did not recognize that capitalism was part of that evolution, a cultural and material emergent rising and dying as a species does—thriving for a while but then cracking apart as it ran up against limits. Even a planet as fertile as this one could not support forever the infinitely growing desires of one species, and neither could a mode of production based on such desires.

If Marx had tried to understand capitalism as part of natural history, rather than defending a dualistic line between moral, intelligent humans and amoral, stupid nature, he might have realized that capitalism enjoyed power because, following the discovery of Second Earth, it proved able to satisfy a growing population filled with infinite wants. He might have understood that the earth would not be better off with more and more people, all driven by sharp hunger. But then he missed the promise of science.

Capitalism's response to the early modern food-population crisis can be summed up under four imperatives: find new lands, encourage migration, expand world trade, shift to manufacturing. It boarded and commanded a huge treasure ship that ordinary people saw as a bonanza. Their instinct was to seize the treasure like a pirate seizing a vessel loaded with gold bullion. But when the capitalists needed laborers, that turned surplus farmers into factory workers or coal miners, satisfying their wants and organizing a worldwide trading system that made its organizers and the organized all quite rich.

Agrarianism had lasted for ten thousand years, but it was running up against natural limits, and the capitalists were confident that they alone could transcend the limits and discover and exploit the planet more systematically. Marx did not grasp that his enemy might know how to do that better than he did. Nor could he see that capitalism succeeded by knowing humans better than communists could ever do. Furthermore, if Marx had appreciated the role played by capitalist support of science, he might have realized that it was science, including the discoveries made by Columbus, Magellan, Drake, and others, that made capitalism credible.

Second Earth offered a new richness of untapped resources. Capitalists boasted that they were best equipped for "developing" (a synonym for "discovering and exploiting") the wealth of nature. As they went forth to explore and know all the continents, they behaved like a polar bear riding an iceberg down to warmer latitudes. Finding a promising piece of land, the capitalists scrambled ashore and began gobbling up ripe berries and fat seals. Modern humans, however, proved more voracious and smarter than polar bears. They welcomed the capitalists for showing them how to find all the berry patches on earth.

In the past, whenever a new abundance had been discovered, human expectations must have soared, human nature must have changed. The most basic desires remained important, but new wants were added: more children, higher social status, better security, and a lot more stuff. Inevitably, some of the new expectations, which capitalism stoked, had to be disappointed. By Marx's time many people were admitting that even an earth offering two wonderful hemispheres was not unlimited or invulnerable and that once its limits were reached, there might be no more. There could be no Third Earth lying just over the horizon.

Eventually, the natural sciences revealed a bedrock truth: human numbers cannot grow forever on this planet—whether people choose to live under industrial capitalism or industrial communism. As humans learned more about the earth's size and limits, they had to acknowledge the impracticality of infinite demands. Increasingly, they had to accept something less. And then disillusion with capitalism spread.

Before that, capitalism seemed to perform many splendid miracles. Above all, the food supply increased, thanks to the fecundity of Second Earth as much as to farmer innovations. And with more food, human numbers exploded, though eventually the food supply would become expensive and uncertain and a new realism would set in, not so much among capitalists as ordinary people, mainly women of childbearing age who, assessing the economic and ecological realities, began having fewer children. That happened during the nineteenth and twentieth centuries, although the full effects would not be felt until after 2000 CE.

Despite its popularity among a few radicals, Marx's communism did not achieve a world revolution, not because it was wicked or crazy but because it was too unrealistic and unscientific. And too incompetent: few trusted the communists to exploit the planet as fully as Marx hoped. As he turned his back on Darwinian science to focus on matters of reforming resource production and distribution, the man from Germany faded as a seer and philosopher.

Ironically, this failure to grasp the nature of life and limits occurred even though the great revolutionary in biology, Charles Darwin, was living nearby, southward from London in the village of Down. Darwin's *Origin of Species* was published in 1859. Three years later, Marx announced that he was reading that famous work, adding that, "although developed in the crude English fashion, this is the book which in the field of natural history, provides the basis for our views. Darwin's work is most important and suits my purpose in that it provides a basis in natural science for the historical class struggle."[5] Others found nothing of the sort in that work. It did not explain class formation or predict a classless future, which were Marx's main themes. Darwin's focus was not on class dialectics but on "multilectics," the many tangled relationships of plants and animals coexisting on a limited planet.

Compounding his failure to gain a multilectical perspective, Marx ignored Darwin's later book *Descent of Man* (1871), which became the founding text for evolutionary psychology, bringing science to examine sexual reproduction as part of human development. By avoiding the question of reproduction, Marx was left trapped in a quest for human justice, not between women and men but between workers and capital.

In the early twentieth century, when a band of communists in feudal Russia managed to seize power over the state, they followed Marx in trying to outdo the capitalists in environmental conquest. A new revolutionary elite took charge of that country, promising they would make all humans rich. They threw dissenters into prisons or stood them before firing squads. Marx's utopian dream of a dictatorship of the proletariat thus became a dictatorship of party cadres, who even more than the capitalists proved ignorant of and unrealistic about the nature of the planet.

Communism's leaders, like Marx, did not pay enough attention to Darwinian biology, or see how the rise of science was making obsolete the ancient man-nature dualism. Thus, they offered nothing more than merchants and mill owners did in promising endless economic growth. Russia and China were the only major countries where communism gained full control, and in both cases the victors set up authoritarian regimes and regularly made war on nature just as the capitalists were doing, but they never escaped poverty in doing so.

Soon after the *Communist Manifesto* came out, Marx and Engels decided that the only place where they could live the good life while promoting their halfway-critique was in the city of London. There Marx spent long hours reading in the British Museum's magnificent new library, nursing his resentments while sitting in a comfortable chair. There he wrote his masterpiece, *Capital*, the first volume of which was published in 1867. In that book he tried to unfold his philosophical analysis of businessmen. For another decade or so, until his death in 1883, Marx continued to rail against that group, all the while aping them by pursuing his family's desires to rise in society.[6]

Friedrich Engels, Marx's close friend, co-author, and generous patron, similarly sought to enlarge his consumption of resources. He took a position in Manchester, England, as manager of his father's textile mill, though he chose to live in flashier London. Thus, the two most prominent leaders in the communist movement chose bourgeois affluence and "economic progress" over ecological understanding. They became permanent residents of the most prosperous, capitalist-friendly, anti-nature city in the world.

Meanwhile, the discovery of Second Earth was not turning out to be the panacea that many hoped for. British farmers were still unable to produce enough food to support a still growing population. The economic historian Brinley Thomas calls this inability a "Malthusian" crisis. It began around 1500 and deepened through the seventeenth, eighteenth, and nineteenth centuries, as British lands became depleted and poverty and hunger increased, even as a new hemisphere was being explored to the west.[7]

By "Malthusian," Thomas means that excessive reproduction was the root cause of the crisis. (As I noted in the introduction, the Malthusian dogma was based not on scientific but on old religious thinking.) The Cambridge Group for the History of Population and Social Structure, through the study of local parish records, has found that by 1701 the population of England and Wales had grown to more than 5 million. By 1801, it reached 10 million. With the annexation of Scotland, Britain added 1.6 million.[8] And it added much more when it conquered Ireland, where the population had soared from 3 million in 1700 to 8 million in 1841. Those swelling numbers owed little to industrialization or improved health and sanitation. Industrialization did not take off in Britain until the last decades of the eighteenth century, and then it was more a consequence than a cause of population increases. Those numbers are best understood as a continuing optimism regarding the abundance discovered to the west, raising expectations at home that nonetheless could not be sustained.

Later, as the Cambridge Group has documented, Britain's "natural increase" (measured by subtracting deaths from births) amounted to 500,000 people in the 1800–1804 period and then another 1.4 million over the next sixty years—nearly a 300 percent increase in all. By 1870 other countries in Europe were showing similar gains. The human population had begun an upward swing because on the other side of the Atlantic a cornucopia of wealth had been found and some improvement in British living standards ensued, though nothing like what had been promised.

For the fortunate few, big families remained normal. Marx and his wife, Jenny von Westphalen, and his housemaid Helene Demuth together had seven children. Charles Darwin and his wife had a total of ten. Less wealthy couples, working for wages in textile or pottery mills, however, could not do the same; on the contrary, after 1800, they began to restrain their reproduction. Women's fertility rates began to fall, even as Britain's population continued to increase. Many had begun to realize that there were too many babies being born, threatening to exceed the planet's limits. No great mathematician in the sky made those rates fall. The common people thought for themselves. They looked at their fields and crops, they looked abroad to the Americas, and then they decided what was realistic for them.

Thus, among ordinary people, fertility rates began to decline, even as many were choosing to emigrate to America. By the 1870s millions of rural people had sailed off to find their fortunes in a new land, relieving shortages in the British Isles, and yet fertility rates continued to fall. The desire among women for more children, after first soaring out of sight, started a long retreat as women and men began feeling more pinched by rising family expenses and more rigorous competition for jobs in the industrial economy, generating a new set of constraints that has continued right down to the twenty-first century.

According to Ester Boserup, population growth must lead to more innovation that can support an endless number of babies, and she was sometimes right: there were many new textile mills, steam-powered railroads and steamships, paved streets and gas lighting, sewers and indoor privies, more and better dwellings, more schools, and more books and newspapers.[9] All in all, the United Kingdom went through a hyperactive time of innovation. But if those innovations seemed miraculous, and for many families they were indeed so, they led many to worry increasingly about a future of limits.

As Brinley Thomas and others have pointed out, British folk were beginning to realize that a stiff price must be paid for capitalism's undeniable achievements, and the price got higher the more children a couple had. They understood that a booming population would lead to more land shortages, higher rents, and more intense job competition. Overcrowding would become common. More of them would be forced off the land—often by wealthy, profit-seeking entrepreneurs—and there would never be enough jobs or productive fields for the population to secure infinite satisfaction. An impressive string of innovations called "the agricultural revolution," featuring crop rotation and soil amendments, helped fill immediate needs, but they could not make the old agrarian life sustainable. Populations needed to shrink too, although it would take many decades before that began to happen.

One possible reason for the unpredicted decline in fertility rates, despite Second Earth and industrial capitalism, may have been the shift toward imported food and other commodities, which left British consumers dependent on places as far away as the western hemisphere. Importation was necessary to achieve higher satisfaction of wants, but it led to higher shipping costs and supply uncertainties. In response to rural depopulation, British capitalists followed the example of the Roman state: they began buying wheat along with other foodstuffs from foreign producers. First they bought from Ireland and then, as ocean transport expanded, they imported from Pennsylvania or Australia. By 1796, the British were importing 2,515,000 quarters of wheat per year (a "quarter" amounts to twenty-eight pounds), well exceeding their exports of 198,000 quarters.[10]

Ireland for a while supplied nearly half of Britain's wheat, a dependency that persisted even through Ireland's worst years of famine, which began in 1845 (when a fungus devastated the potato crop, a plant that been imported from South America to enhance the food supply). Facing disaster in the potato fields, the Irish watched as their homegrown grain was shipped away to feed English people. After the Irish Hunger finally ended, in 1852, Europe, the Near East, India, Canada, and the United States all competed to supply world markets with grain, with the result that Britain's consumers, in effect, found salvation not by growing their own food supply but by importing it from around the world. By the 1860s fully half of the wheat consumed in Britain was imported, with most of it coming from the United States, including a grain-growing California that was eager to feed Britain and the world.[11] Timber, iron ore, and wool were also sought from distant places, out of sight but not completely out of mind.

Thus, despite a public sense of living in fortunate times and despite the fact that Great Britain outdistanced every other nation in prosperity, there was also a growing private realism about foreign suppliers and global trade networks.

The British social scientist Richard Wilkinson argues that we should not interpret such food importation "as the fruits of a society's search for progress, but as the outcome of a valiant struggle of a society with its back to the ecological wall."[12] According to Boserupian reasoning, a bigger population is a clear sign of progress. But then that population turned out to be more anxious about its survival than ever before. Free trade was supposed to benefit the British people, but it ended up enriching foreign farmers, increasing household expenses, destroying farming villages, and forcing people to earn enough to buy their necessities in expensive markets.

DREAMS OF INFINITE WEALTH

Getting workers to accept the glittering promises of capitalism was not a new challenge. Markets had existed for thousands of years, as the Twice Wise traded goods across Eurasia and up and down the Americas and Africa. But now trade involved such basic commodities as food. The old caravan commerce of silks and spices was replaced by global trade networks, and the change made people less secure.

What was now being bought and sold was, according to an ecological interpretation, nothing less than the vital energy on which all life depends. People were trying to capture and buy more of the sun's output. Wheat, tea, and cotton were all energy commodities for sale in a global economy. And then there were new ways of staying warm in a cold climate. Capitalists, facing an exhausted wood supply at home, began digging up peat and coal, which had been made through the natural innovation of photosynthesis long ago and buried in the ground. Like the Americas, the fossil fuels seemed at first to be a cheap, easy, and boundless means of satisfying family desires in the here and now. But that too was another hope for the infinite that became finite.

Fossil fuel extraction became the trademark innovation in the capitalist way of life, yet it was also a source of new problems and worries, and in the end the mining of coal proved not as cheap or reliable as promised. Burning coal polluted the air, destroyed health, and changed the climate. In Britain's coal-burning cities air pollution far eclipsed what it had been back in Roman times. Both rich and poor suffered from the shift, although the poor suffered more. Much of the new energy produced by coal mining did not go directly to the working class but to mining companies, engineers, and company presidents. Here again was a promise of an infinite earth that at first seemed quite marvelous, but as consumption intensified the promise turned out to be empty, expensive, and life-threatening. Fired by the quest for profit, businessmen had promised nothing less than a *Third* Earth, a Second Earth buried under their feet. The coal fields of Wales and the north country were another America. But they were exhaustible, and so was the American hemisphere.[13]

Coal made British life much more unequal as well as unhealthy, but it gave the capitalists a new justification for holding power. Did a family want to bake a shepherd's pie for dinner? By burning coal they could do that. Even the unfortunate man or child forced to take work mining the coal underground might feel grateful for getting a job with wages to pay for heat and energy, but often it was the women who sensed a trap in that dependency and responded by giving birth to fewer offspring.

Brinley Thomas summarizes the Industrial Revolution as "Britain's response to an energy shortage," but then he adds that it followed "a population explosion."[14] A growing population had been the greatest determinant behind the industrial capitalist transformation. Progeny and desires increased in the wake of Second Earth, but then fertility rates began to decline, even as populations continued growing. The reason was that more and more women of childbearing age existed than ever before, even though they sought to bear fewer children. The chains of causality were complicated, but human nature was altering its desire to reproduce. Besides new energy, trade, and industrialization, there came, quite unexpectedly, the beginning of a shrinkage in family size.

Why did Britain, an impoverished backwater only a few centuries earlier, become the center of so much confusion and ambiguity? Why did it exhibit such contradictory responses to Second Earth? Why did it embrace capitalism even as blackened skies, expensive food, and social inequality resulted? Simply because the British were more desperate than others to discover how to live in the wake of the Great Discoveries. First, they proved quick to follow their explorers into the western hemisphere. During the seventeenth century they were ready to stay home and innovate. By the eighteenth century they were ready for the industrial capitalist revolution. By the nineteenth century they were beginning to curb that most basic of human desires, the urge to multiply and replenish the earth. By the twentieth century they were in a half-hearted retreat from the industrial capitalist way of life.

In the opening paragraphs of his *Manifesto,* Marx offered a brilliant explanation for when and how the transformation to industrial capitalism began, an explanation he later abandoned. Call it his Second Earth story. It acknowledged that merchants had been around for a long time, but that they did not gain much power or standing until the people accepted them as pathfinders to a new hemisphere to the west.

"The discovery of America," Marx wrote in the opening paragraphs of the *Manifesto,* "the rounding of the Cape, opened fresh ground for the rising bourgeoisie. The East-Indian and Chinese markets, the colonisation of America, trade with the colonies, the increase in the means of exchange and in commodities generally, gave to commerce, to navigation, to industry, an impulse never known, and thereby, to the revolutionary element in the tottering feudal society, a rapid development."

Marx borrowed that story from the British economist Adam Smith, an earlier observer of the capitalist transformation. Here is what Smith had written in his book *The Wealth of Nations* (1776), which Marx adapted seven decades later: "The discovery of America and that of a passage to the East Indies by the Cape of Good Hope, are the two greatest and most important events recorded in the history of humankind."[15] Strangely, Smith buried those bold words in the back pages of his book, but a studious Marx found and copied them, for they seemed to explain well the state of things he found in Britain—a natural boost to commerce, then the rise of the bourgeoisie.

The Great Discoveries, Smith (but not Marx) argued, must be ranked above all other events in human history—above the creation of Adam and Eve, the domestication of plants and animals, the incarnation of Jesus, the invention of written languages, the appearance of states and civilizations. Why did Smith believe that Second Earth was so pivotal? Because he sensed that modern capitalism had grown powerful by promising a new, permanent material abundance based on that discovery. Both men understood that the western hemisphere challenged the old agrarian way of life and gave rise to new inventions, new commodities, new desires, new sources of capital, new institutions, and new technologies.

Beyond seeing all that, however, neither Smith nor Marx gave much credit to what was essentially an ecological explanation. Instead, Smith chose to focus in the main part of his book on small, incremental gains in efficiency that came from the inventiveness of ordinary people in factories. Marx became preoccupied with the appropriation of that new wealth by the business class. But if we pay more attention to the natural history of America, if we grant the importance of large, growing populations and declining farms and fisheries in the European Maritimes, we might ask what neither Smith nor Marx asked: might a more ecological approach to the rise of capitalism help us understand how a dynamic material nature, human and nonhuman, has made history, even in modern times?

Neither man was ready to see how profoundly nature can bring about change. Neither was ready to examine how humans might be changed by their environment. And the same could be said for a third man who preceded them both, Guillaume-Thomas Raynal, who provided them with the shell of a better narrative. Raynal was no scientist; he was a defrocked priest in the Catholic Church who became a secular *philosophe* in the French Enlightenment. He was a fierce moral critic of the English and Spanish invasion of the Americas. In 1770, just six years before the American Revolution was declared and *The Wealth of Nations* was published, Monsieur Raynal published a searing indictment of that invasion. He told a rather simplistic tale of "Good" losing out to "Evil," of horrible brutality on the part of the Europeans toward the peace-loving Native Americans. Raynal's chronicle of brutality was so inflammatory that his book had to be brought out in Amsterdam, where the authorities would be less offended.

Before reviewing all the atrocities that had been committed, Raynal offered a sweeping interpretation of what the voyages of Columbus and others meant. Here are his opening words, which inspired both Smith and Marx: "There has never been an event as interesting for the human species in general and for the peoples of Europe in particular as the discovery of the new world and the passage to the Indies by way of the Cape of Good Hope. *Then began a revolution in commerce, in the power of nations, in the way of life, the industry and government of all peoples*" (emphasis added).[16]

Raynal offered in those words a new story of revolution, but he did not add that it was population growth and reproductive desire that had provided the spark for the Great Discoveries. For all three critics, it was moral values that were the main engines of change. Raynal, however, did grasp that a material windfall as large as the western hemisphere could and did reshape human behavior.

All of them accepted that Second Earth hit Europe like a wave train, washing away older relations with the planet. A "wave train" is a phenomenon where one ocean wave follows another, beating on the shore and flooding far inland, sweeping away everything before it. From 1500 to Raynal's own day, such a wave train washed over western Europe, and especially over Great Britain.

Raynal's "revolution in commerce" (that is, capitalism) was the first wave that struck, dashing against western anxiety about growing numbers and shrinking natural resources. Then came a second wave, a revolution "in the power of nations," nothing less than a shift in world leadership from Asia to Europe, freeing the latter from its backwater past, while Asia remained stuck in agrarianism. Raynal's third wave was less easily summed up. He spoke loosely of changes "in the way of life, the industry and government of all peoples," which we can translate as industrialization and democratic politics. The Maritimes of Europe were the first to feel those waves, but every part of the planet would eventually undergo the same.[17]

There was a fourth wave that Raynal ignored: the tsunami we call the scientific revolution. New scientific knowledge began to accumulate with the Great Discoveries, becoming a worldwide wave, crashing against and overwhelming pre-scientific views of nature and humanity. Although Raynal had become a secularist in his native France, he did not know science very well. The English and Scots, in contrast, did. How could their capitalist transformation have succeeded without their enthusiasm for knowledge and science, which taught people to gather facts, verify them, and apply that knowledge to satiate humanity's growing desires?

A key part of the Great Discoveries' entangled legacy, in other words, derived from science, which undermined the authority of traditional knowledge. By the nineteenth century a strong distinction was being made in Great Britain between "knowledge" and "faith." Just as the British way of life was going through a revolutionary shift, so too was Britain's older, Christian-based form of knowledge going through change.[18]

In the aftermath of the Great Discoveries, science was embraced as a reliable, disinterested, and verifiable way to know how nature works. Traditional knowledge was too mixed with faith and fable to help the transformation. Subsequently, science became, according to the *Oxford English Dictionary*, "a branch of study that deals with a body of demonstrated truths or with observed facts systematically classified and more or less comprehended by general laws and incorporating trustworthy methods."[19] The rise of natural science included Charles Darwin's natural history, which was based on the habit of thinking broadly and inclusively, seeking facts, observing carefully, and explaining without the aid of religion the origins of humans and nature. Science delivered not only new knowledge but also new realism about us humans, emphasizing our shaky place on a shifting planet.

In earlier centuries, westerners had depended on the Bible for knowledge as well as identity, while outside the West other peoples created their own pre-science guides in Confucius, Buddha, and Mohammed. After 1500 the West began trusting naturalists and scientists and their kind of knowledge, not the Bible or the Koran. Scientific revelations opened people's eyes to the nature around them, and a new sense of identity and a new ethos followed.

The eighteenth-century French writer Voltaire took note of the growing appeal of the natural sciences across the English Channel. In his book *Letters*

Concerning the English Nation (1733), he claimed that the English were more apt than the French to value scientific knowledge. The historian of science David Wootton writes that "the message of Voltaire's book was that England had a distinctive scientific culture."[20] Voltaire thought scientific culture in Britain was the most advanced in the world. Like Francis Drake, who was attracted to the sea as a way out of poverty, the English were attracted to knowing the green world as a way out of ignorance.

That the British held science in high esteem was due largely to Sir Francis Bacon, a high-ranking British official who promoted the advancement of knowledge among the public, hoping it would prove a savior for the country. It was Bacon who best explained why better knowledge was so valuable. Let us go forth into nature with open, unprejudiced minds, he urged. In doing so Britain would learn how to overcome its perilous condition and make good use of Second Earth.[21]

Bacon's major book, *Novum Organon* (1620), explicitly linked science to the discovery of the western hemisphere. The title page shows a galleon sailing under full canvas, like those that carried European explorers westward. The ship has advanced far into the Atlantic Ocean, while another is following, just clearing the Pillars of Hercules, those rocky promontories that mark where the Mediterranean Sea ends and the Atlantic Ocean begins. In the title page image those natural rocks have become man-made columns marking the advance of knowledge beyond the old world into a new one. At the base of the pillars floats a small banner bearing a Latin inscription, *Multi pertransibunt et augebitur scientia,* which we might translate as "Many will pass through, and knowledge will increase."[22] Bacon's point was that the discovery of Second Earth had opened a new era on the planet that science must lead, opening doors to a new and different relation of humans to the earth. His most famous aphorism captured the ambivalence behind early British science: "Nature to be commanded must be obeyed."[23]

Six years later, Bacon's novel *New Atlantis* was published in London, and once again he used the metaphor of a voyage westward, this time featuring a ship that has sailed all the way to the Pacific Ocean and found there a remote, unknown island. On that island stands a scientific research center called Salomon's House, whose mission is to enlarge "the bounds of human empire, to the effecting of all things possible." In those words, Bacon was telling the British that even their small island, although lying far out on the margins of the known earth, might make a great leap forward to knowledge, wealth, and power.

Unfortunately, science did not turn out to be the blemish-free, cornucopian savior that Bacon hoped for. By the twentieth century, it was accused of bringing devastation to the earth through laboratory-made biocides and weapons of mass destruction. Scientists were often chastised and told to be more virtuous. Some would heed these admonitions and find a new humility, most of them Darwin-influenced ecologists who, by the twentieth century, were asking whether the quest for more wealth and more babies might push people beyond the safe boundaries of the planet. It was natural scientists who led people to adopt more moderate goals in economic development. Thus, science served both as a tool of conquest and as a warning against overweening desire. In addition to wealth and power would come a more realistic, modest view of the planet, envisioning what we now call the sustainable or ecological way of life.

The British people, seeking a way out of their crisis, were not all of one mind. Facing a severe food-population crisis, they initiated a transformation that ranks among the most complicated but also the most consequential in history. They invented the capitalist way of life, which now completely overshadows the agrarian way. But let us not forget that along with becoming colonizers and imperialists, it was scientists who were among the first environmentalists on earth. Capitalism, even as it succeeded, made promises too extravagant to become reality everywhere for everyone. Warnings increasingly came from the natural sciences that we humans are upsetting the earth's climate regimes and depleting fish stocks, arable soils, fresh water, and minerals. Before the late nineteenth and twentieth centuries no one—including Karl Marx and Friedrich Engels—paid much attention to the environmental degradation of the earth. The idea that the earth has limits was usually disregarded. Meanwhile, the old urgent desires kept pushing humans toward new forms of satisfaction. As Second Earth fell into the laps of Maritime Europeans, arousing bigger hungers than ever, those people began to feel more ambivalent, not only primed for individual success but also aware of their interdependence with the earth.

In contrast, the German immigrant Engels, working in his father's textile mill and admiring its rattling machinery, persisted in making an old distinction between nature and humans: "The most that the animal can achieve is to collect; man produces, he prepares the means of subsistence, in the widest sense of the words, which without him nature would not have produced."[24] Engels still was speaking the outmoded language of speciesism, dualism, and anthropocentrism, ignoring what many in Britain were beginning to realize: that humans had in fact spent most of their history doing exactly what other species do—collecting food and energy from the wild—not producing wealth in a factory. The sight of an industrial mill did not fill such people with enthusiasm, while the sight of a wild forest could.

Marx and Engels were too embedded in the old Judeo-Christian tradition to appreciate the radical implications of evolutionary biology. The two communists scorned the nature that spawned them, focusing mainly on redistributing wealth among competing economic classes. They were not bothered by the prospect that doubling or quadrupling the human population might require another planet or two brimming with natural resources to be supported. Missing from the *Communist Manifesto* was any admission that human numbers might have determined the appeal of industrial capitalism. Marx and Engels never realized that the British were becoming more caring about their relations with nature and thinking more critically about their reproduction.

Britain, make no mistake, turned to empire building even as it embraced the natural world. Historians conventionally identify 1583 as the point when the British Empire came into existence by seizing Newfoundland. Among the most important foreign acquisitions that followed was India, where Britain's East India Company in 1601 set up a trading post for spices, tea, sugar, and cotton. Then came the Cape Colony (or South Africa) and then colonial Canada, New Zealand, Australia, Gambia, Nigeria, Egypt, the Sudan, and Uganda, all supplying commodities for sale to British consumers.

By the beginning of World War I, nearly a quarter of the earth's surface belonged to British capitalists and imperialists, and so did a large fraction of the world's labor force. Once a colony, the United States preferred to set up an empire of its own, which eventually stretched across mountain ranges and grasslands to the Pacific Ocean and beyond. Because of that succession in imperialism, the global headquarters of the capitalist transformation moved from London to the United States—particularly to New York City, which in the early 1920s surpassed London in size and, by the next decade, became the first megacity in the world, boasting a population of ten million. Even so, it was Britain and its colonies that gave the world and the United States not only Darwin but a long list of other naturalists and ecologists, along with nature poets and painters like William Wordsworth and J. M. W. Turner, and environmentalists like David Attenborough and Jane Goodall.

The islanders of Britain were beginning to see the natural world in terms of co-evolution and mutualism, and much of the world has followed suit over the past five centuries. All nations are now asking how they can restrain their appetites for oil, foodstuffs, and babies. Many now want to become more sustainable, which may indicate a big crack in the industrial capitalist egg, caused by new knowledge of nature and a new understanding of human nature.

In Britain, the United States, and across the planet the past few centuries of capitalist commodification of land and people allowed an upscaling of human numbers and human desires. The outcome has defined what we call modernity. But now we are all modern, and anti-modern, all wondering whether an insatiable hunger for food and fecundity can be sustained indefinitely on this unique planet.

History does not show that pre-capitalist ways of life were better for people than capitalism or communism have been. What it does show is that all ranks and varieties of humans have been forced by their own appetites to evolve. Whether we be hominins, hominids, *sapiens,* or nonhumans, all of us have tried to make room for our own progeny. Every species has done that, but only our species, because of its innovative brain, has been able to gain more and more knowledge of the earth. Consequently, we alone have come to understand better our drives and desires. We have not reached a state of enlightenment, but we may do so someday.

The Great Discoveries had a powerful but highly complicated impact: enlarging human desires while expanding human knowledge. The result was a second big transformation in humankind and the earth. Five hundred years have passed since that change began, and still we do not understand fully what has happened to us. What comes next? Will one of the two competing versions of the industrial way of life win out, or will both give way to something new? Might we be approaching a third great transformation? If so, will it begin in Mesopotamia or the European Maritimes, or perhaps in Africa or East Asia? Might it be communist China that leads all nations toward a third transformation, the creation of a civilization guided by ecology and sustainability? That possibility is what we must consider next.

CHAPTER 6

The Good Muck

Among the vivid reminders of an older, pre-modern China is the pungent odor of human body wastes (*fenbian*), which one can still smell wafting out of public toilets, sewer manholes, and heavily fertilized fields in the countryside. That gagging, stomach-churning stink comes from gases such as sulfur dioxide and methane generated by creatures with intestines. English speakers call the source of the odor muck, meaning urine and feces or other kinds of dirt and rubbish.[1]

It is the telltale smell of the countryside, the olfactory marker of an ancient agrarian China that was graced by gilded temples and palaces, willows fringing lakes and ponds, and humans getting their living directly from the earth. Peasants generated the smell and then carried it into city *hutongs*—densely packed urban neighborhoods with narrow lanes and squawking chickens—where even the elite could not escape the pall. The smell of muck is not unique to China, no more than are farmers and fields. China has been exceptional only in its zeal for putting human body wastes to good economic use—enriching their crops with muck. "Of all the peoples of the world," writes the British journalist Rose George, "the Chinese are probably the most at home with their own excrement."[2]

An old-style farmer may have perceived muck as a treasure to be gathered and applied to the land, but not so the modern farmer, who prefers to use chemical fertilizer. Not so the modern bourgeoisie in Beijing either, who find the smell of such wastes nauseating and want to avoid all contact with them. Excreta are not part of their notion of treasure or civilization. But rather than turning our noses away from human body wastes as an unsuitable topic for the historian, a sign of an all too natural animality in our nature, we should ask what value muck held in the past and whether China's people, more than most others, once set a good example by seizing on a valuable natural resource and using it wisely, without shame or scruple. We might further wonder where today's communities are supposed to put their body wastes. If not on the land or in privies as China has long done, then is it better to put them untreated into our rivers, lakes, or oceans?

In drawing such comparisons, however, we should be wary of cultural stereotypes. China and the West may *seem* radically different, but in fact they have much in common. Both have polluted their environments—is there any people, community, or ideologue who can say we don't pollute? We may pollute in different ways, for there are different kinds of pollutants and different degrees of pollution, just as there are different forms of evasion and responsibility. We cannot simply flush this subject out of our history.

Poop and pollution make humans alike and make us part of nature, regardless of our economic or cultural differences. Rich or poor, we must all excrete or die. If we think about our bodies and their nature, poop is a major part of our nature, as essential to us as eating, breathing, and reproducing, yet the poop we so naturally produce is a poisonous pollutant to every person and to nonhumans too. Just as each of us must exhale carbon dioxide to stay alive, at very high concentrations (coming out of a tailpipe or smokestack) CO_2 has long been poisonous to life and today is a key cause of global warming. The rich, of course, emit more CO_2 than the poor, along with such industrial poisons as lead, sulfur, plastics, and oil. The rich can also better afford nonpolluting electric cars, composting toilets, and other technological solutions. But rich or poor, we all poop, and we poop a lot. Let the one who has never exhaled or excreted cast the first stone. We all are guilty.

Cultural attitudes toward excrement should be important topics for historians, for those attitudes changed as we moved from country to city, far more than did human digestion or respiration. Attitudinal differences can stem from different levels of economic development, religious teachings, or political identity. Americans may be proud of their flush toilets and bathroom ventilating fans and may feel they live on a different planet from the homeless, blameless beggars of Chongqing or Chicago. But if they go back only a short time in the history of attitudes, they will discover that their ancestors were in closer touch with their body wastes than we are with ours today. Before expensive bathroom technology, all people lived intimately with their excrement. Everyone had to inhale the stench of a family privy or endure the sight and smell of feces daily just as the poorest classes of China or Nigeria still do.

Today's Chinese, however, are not the same people they were fifty years ago. A political and economic revolution that brought Mao Zedong to power set in motion a radical transformation even in excrement, making millions of Chinese as fastidious as middle-class Americans and as eager for a life free of muck. In prosperous Beijing or Shenzhen many are eager to acquire the latest in good plumbing—shiny porcelain fixtures like those made by Japanese exporters—and they demand the removal of human wastes as far as possible from their noses.[3]

Cultural attitudes can have significant environmental consequences, not all of them adding up to simple linear progress. Those who point only to the gains brought by good toilets and civilized sanitation are being highly selective, ignoring such consequences as polluted canals, rivers, and lakes. On the other hand, when we begin to face up to ecological limits, asking how much waste the earth can bear, we may conclude that we should return to those older practices but find we are blocked. We may ask what wisdom has been irretrievably lost through the great transformations we have been through. Did our forebears look on muck differently and therefore treat it more responsibly than we do today? Did they find greater value in muck than we do, and have we wasted that value on our way to modernity?

Learning to appreciate and make good use of our muck, say environmentalists, is part of living sustainably on this planet. Does that mean, as some believe, that we must go back to a simpler time, when supposedly we lived in harmony with the earth? Is that possible when we number eight billion? Going back is an option only if we also go back to earlier population levels. And if that happens, we will certainly want to invent new methods of treating our wastes, and they will bring new attitudes.

A more planet-conscious history is what this book offers, and that includes rethinking human muck—its past production, its future uses, and its historical impact. We cannot rigidly isolate our bodies from the planet or from the laws of matter and energy, and we cannot afford to ignore where our body wastes go when we flush them into dark sewers and expect them to disappear.

So let us admit into the humanistic halls of history the fact, gross to some, that there have always been hungry bellies wanting to be filled and gonads itching for action and intestines straining to be cleared of excrement. Let us acknowledge that those subjects have always been a real, daily concern for humans and other species. With help from science let us try to understand better the significance of food and body wastes and the way they have entangled us in complex flows of matter and energy. As we examine our daily effort to stay alive and reproduce, let us ponder how that effort has brought us to where we are today, how our bodies, like our desires and instincts, have determined the arc of change.

The human belly is directly connected to other parts of our anatomy, including nearly thirty feet of large and small intestines and the human bladder. Historians should pay attention to the whole interconnected "belly-to-bladder" system and its social and environmental impact. The aim of this chapter is to point to a history of China's people that is universal, material, metabolic, and, yes, excremental.

Back in the old, old days of Chinese foraging, we can be sure that bodily effluvia were not considered as valuable as they would later be.

THE GOOD MUCK

Originally, body wastes were considered defiling. Excreta were not welcome inside a home cave or other shelter. They were understood to be dangerous substances that humans should void—and then *avoid* as much as possible. Human excrement was surely the first environmental pollutant emitted by humans. A pollutant is anything foul or toxic that can corrupt and poison its surroundings whenever it surpasses some critical threshold of intensity. All foragers understood that threat, and they took action to minimize it.

Foragers so feared environmental contamination from their own body wastes that they trudged off into woods and bushes to do their business, emptying their bowels at a safe distance from their dwellings and encampments. They understood that excrement could ruin a place, and they tried to avoid that as much as possible. When the woods and bushes became full of human wastes, they moved on, not only to find more food but also to escape their own pollution.

Poop and pee are both dangerous. This has been well understood for a very long time, though the reasons for that danger are better understood today than ever before. Excrement, science tells us, is full of bacteria, viruses, pathogens, and parasites, including helminths (parasitic creatures like hookworm, the Chinese liver fluke, pinworms, or those flatworms called schistosomes that can cause bilharzia, a debilitating disease that can damage livers, kidneys, or bladders). Today, three hundred million people, most of them abysmally poor, carry schistosomes in their bodies and deposit them regularly into the environment. Schistosomes can be acquired by standing in irrigated rice paddies that have been infected by human wastes. Microscopic organisms can invade the human body, causing diarrhea or dysentery, spreading typhus or cholera, or starting an *E. coli* epidemic.[4]

China's agrarian transformation made avoiding human pollutants and parasitic disease a much more complicated challenge. Living densely in fixed locations forced people to put up with a heavier stench around them and to live close to their excreta. They must drink from streams into which someone had voided body wastes. That is another reason why agriculture should not be seen as a great leap forward but rather as a stumbling into disaster. Dung heaps began to appear in the villages, towns, and cities that agriculture created—small, rounded hills made of body wastes concentrated in one place where they festered, steamed, and stank. It was on a village dung heap that the biblical prophet Job went to live, near or on those excremental hills, along with others classified as "untouchables," condemned to the very bottom of society.

At what point did agrarian communities begin to overcome their disgust and learn to gather their excrement and recycle it as fertilizer for their crops? Was there some genius who realized that there was more and better food to be raised by turning muck into a useful natural resource, applying it to crops, making a virtue out of necessity?

Most likely there was no single person who invented fertilizer; many anonymous women and men discovered how to make it in different places and times. Independently, they converged on a strategy of turning their wastes to some practical use. We try to do the same by recycling plastic containers, extracting excess carbon from the air, separating newspapers from the trash before they get into landfills, and turning wastes into profit instead of allowing them to become a threat—causing brain damage, killing fish, changing climates, or piling up in dumps. Today's ambition of transmuting pollution into wealth is not new; it is as old as agricultural intensification.[5]

At some point people began to realize that they could safely reuse their own body wastes—that is, if they stored them until, through fermentation, they became harmless enough to apply as a soil additive. It may well have taken centuries to work out precisely how to do that, and even then the treatment could never have been perfectly reliable or free of risk. Even now, in the twenty-first century, people can die from eating vegetables fertilized with some kind of excrement. But a breakthrough came when farmers began to see how, if they did some careful processing, excrement could be safely used on their crops.

That innovation may not have created much wealth, but it suggested that farmers could create an endless loop of productivity: food in, waste out; waste in, food out. But from that may have come the notion of someday acquiring an endless abundance and inexhaustible wealth, an economy that could feed as many humans as were born and do so forever. Animal wastes, vegetable matter, and household rubbish all became the means to that abundance, and composting became a dream of an infinite, circular economy.[6]

Unfortunately for dreamers, nature puts limits even on the cleverest of human innovations. Agriculture must, like all matter, obey the law of entropy, one of the fundamental physical laws in the universe, which makes the human dream of achieving equilibrium or stasis just as impossible as the dream of endless growth and eternal plenty. Entropy refers to the degradation of the sun's radiant energy to the point where it is too scattered to do any work. No matter how brilliant the sun, its production of energy must end in death, for the energy it emits diffuses throughout the cosmos until it can no longer support life. Each point in the food cycle, whether in traditional or modernized agriculture, entails a net loss of energy, which becomes unavailable to make more food to fuel bodies. That is why no community can ever reach a perfect steady state, a completely closed system, free of all pollution; every system will inevitably leak energy and end in disorder. And that too is why no one has ever figured out how to invent a machine capable of perpetual motion or a method of food production that can satisfy all hungers indefinitely and require little or no work from any of us. Always and inescapably, we must face the reality of entropy.

Putting the stench of muck into human history suggests a long list of new questions. When did farmers begin to get interested in using human excrement as a fertilizer? Did that practice increase over time? What consequences has the use of today's chemical fertilizers had? What can the past tell us about the management of human excrement in older food-producing systems? Should we celebrate China's history as an example of a successful "green" economy, a history of harmony between humans and nature,

THE GOOD MUCK

or should we see it more darkly as a temporary solution for more or less constant overpopulation and agricultural failure? How in general should we look on pre-modern land and water practices when they are suggested as panaceas for today's problems? Should we try to get back to tradition, or is tradition commonly too idealized and impractical? Should we accept scientific modernity as the best hope for finding our way to sustainability?

The first book that many westerners read about China's agriculture was *Farmers of Forty Centuries,* written by the American soil scientist Franklin H. King and published by his widow in 1911. Still in print a century after publication, the book's nearly four hundred pages describe a journey the author made in the early twentieth century along East Asia's shores to learn about what he called "permanent" agriculture. Other editions have followed down to the present.[7]

Sailing from Seattle, Washington, King reached Yokohama, Japan, in early February 1909 and Shanghai, China, in early March. From Shanghai, he steamed south to Hong Kong and Canton; he then retraced his route, spending many idle, frustrating days in Shanghai's Astor House Hotel trying to figure out where to go next. His hotel lay within the fertile and prosperous Yangzi delta, also known as Jiangnan, which long had been the most prosperous agrarian region of China.[8] After much delay King managed to explore Jiangnan, traveling by houseboat through an intricate mosaic of canals, rice paddies, and mulberry groves. At last, he was able to learn how old China had tried to enrich its soils to improve food output. That enrichment was both China's salvation (protecting its agrarian way of life) and its nemesis (preventing an industrial capitalist transformation).

Forty years before the Communist Party came to power, in mid-May 1909, King was sailing northward along the Pacific Coast, arriving after Shanghai and Jiangnan at the German treaty port of Qingdao (then spelled "Tsingtao"). He arrived at the place where the Boxer Rebellion, aimed at

THE GOOD MUCK

expelling European imperialists, had erupted just a decade earlier. Qingdao was then a German colony forced on China, part of a dark history of imperialism that had kept China weak, subservient, and resentful. After briefly seeing Qingdao and its broad bay and hinterland, King crossed Shandong province to Tianjin, another foreign enclave on the Pacific, but he never journeyed inland to the capital city of Beijing or observed China's interior. From Tianjin he proceeded to Korea and Japan before ending his investigations and returning home to the United States.

Professor King's travels lasted nearly six months. During that time his eyes took in a thousand striking scenes and his notebooks were filled with statistical data. Over and over his nostrils caught the sharp tang of human manure. Although previous foreign travelers noted how common the use of human body wastes was in Chinese agriculture, King was the first to examine that practice in detail and to come away convinced that it offered a practical solution to soil problems he saw in modern American farming.

In 1911, King died in his Madison, Wisconsin, home. That was also the year of the Xinhai Revolution in China, which overthrew thousands of years of the agrarian state, replaced authoritarian government with a republic, turned to western industrial capitalism for inspiration, and installed the western-educated, modern-minded Sun Yat-Sen in power. King went home without so much as a glimmer of the political transformation that was beginning, and he never imagined how agricultural practices of China might be among the first things to change, including the widespread abandonment of manuring home gardens. He had left China unaware of the discontent that had been gathering in the countryside, a discontent that went back at least to the Opium Wars of 1839–1842. King came prepared to admire and praise traditional agrarian ways, and nothing he saw during his travels seemed to suggest how vulnerable that way of life was or how heavily overpopulation burdened the land.

Innocently, King believed that he had sailed along stable shores that were completely peaceful, well nourished, and efficient—what we today would call a "green economy." He extolled people there for producing "the highest industrial art of the world," but it was not industrial capitalism that he had in mind. In letters sent home to his wife, Carrie, he showed himself to be an agrarian at heart, describing in detail the careful techniques and ingenious tools that the rural Chinese had invented long, long ago and were still using with skill and precision. Like Joseph Needham, the British scientist who came decades later—"the man who loved China" and who created one of the most impressive publishing projects the world has ever seen, the multivolume series *Science and Civilisation in China*—King was delighted with almost everything he saw on his travels. "China is a strange land in almost every imaginable way," he wrote.

> The more I see of the Chinese the more my admiration for them grows, and the more one realizes that they have really solved their problems along the line of least resistance and of highest economy. Every man and woman seems to be busy and each has put down the bucket where he is and is sustaining life and apparently living in contentment.[9]

In China the most important buckets that farmers were filling and emptying contained human manure—thousands and thousands of buckets filled with poop and carried to the rice paddies, where the poop was carefully ladled on the plants to make them grow.

Although the peasants had to labor hard for a bare pittance—farm workers in Zhejiang province earned about fifty dollars annually—to King they seemed quite happy with their lot. Each one knew his job and did it well. King had formed a positive impression of a self-reliant, agrarian China long before he arrived, and that impression was reinforced each time he ventured from his lodgings.

King did not speak or read the Chinese language, so he had to rely on local assistance to communicate with the people he met along the way, although relatively few of them were farmers or farm laborers. Many of his conversations seem to have been in English with fellow Americans rather than with Chinese farmers working on the land. Did his innocent, uncritical admiration for their initiative and ingenuity obscure his judgment? Was he blind to their hardship, failures, and suffering? How could he miss the long-festering tensions between the country's peasants and their landlords, the dissatisfaction with the Qing emperors, or the clash of foreign and national ideas that imperialism had introduced—ideas coming from Germany, Great Britain, France, Portugal, Japan, and Russia, spreading inland from coastal enclaves, urging new behaviors for an old society?

King was no more blind than other foreign travelers of his time. Even today, looking back on the causes of revolution around the world, we often do not see how worsening ecological conditions lead to weakness, violence, or revolution. Few insiders or outsiders in King's time understood that China had reached an evolutionary dead end, which made further progress in food production doubtful and revolution inevitable. The country was running out of options. Twenty years after King, the American novelist Pearl Buck, a child of missionaries and a fluent speaker of Mandarin, published her popular novel *The Good Earth* (1931), which warned that China's peasant farmers faced a bleak future, but her sobering book came twenty years too late for King to read.[10]

King arrived in China soon after retiring as chief of the soil management division of the U.S. Department of Agriculture. He traveled abroad at his own expense, following a succession of foreign agriculturists who began arriving in the 1890s. They tended to stay in western-style hotels and communicated with each other by telegraph. They were supported by a string of consular officers and buffered by such modern comforts as steamships, hotels, and railroads. Typically, they traveled with the certainty that they had the answers to growing enough food for a dense population that was never far from famine.

Charles Denby, for example, who served as U.S. ambassador to China from 1885 to 1898, simply dismissed the country's impressive history of agrarian successes. Despite "the great antiquity of agriculture among them," he wrote, "the Chinese have failed to make any great progress in it.... They have made no improvements in this line for a thousand years, just as they have stood still in every other art of civilization." Where King came away with a tale of ingenuity, hard work, and wisdom, Denby and other visitors saw only stagnation. Their negative appraisal was echoed by David Fairchild, Seaman Knapp, Frank Meyer, and Pearl Buck's husband, the economist Philip Losing Buck, all of whom agreed that China needed to follow the industrial capitalist model. Perhaps as much as King they were not always well informed, but whether one admired China's peasant ingenuity or rejected it, they found signs of failure mixed with signs of success.[11]

David Fairchild, the son of the president of Kansas Agricultural College, arrived in 1898 and, though intrigued by exotic plants growing in Chinese gardens, he could not regard them as proper foods but only as contemptible weeds, evidence of rural desperation. He was repelled by the stench of the lanes and streets, which came from the muck carried by coolies in earthenware pots suspended from bamboo poles, heavy loads carried on aching shoulders. It was time, he believed, for the Chinese to adopt modern fertilizers instead of manure, whose collection, transportation, and application to crops condemned "many people to lives of disgusting drudgery."[12]

In contrast to most foreign observers, King doubted that the West could provide a better model of change. Before leaving the United States, he had become a skeptic of modern capitalist agriculture, and he came to Asia looking for alternatives. The capitalist model was to his mind wasteful, destructive, and unable to feed a growing population. Growing up on a family farm near Whitewater, Wisconsin, he had earned a Ph.D. in agriculture at Cornell University, studying with the famed horticulturalist Liberty Hyde Bailey. Perhaps it was Bailey who turned him against modern farming and made him such an admirer of the old ways. After graduation, King was hired as professor of agricultural physics at the University of Wisconsin, where he wrote one of the first textbooks on soil science. Then he left his state for a career in Washington as a government researcher. Along the way he seems to have taken up the cause of natural resource conservation, which echoed his worries about America's diminishing bounty. Like other conservationists, but unlike most of his fellow agriculturalists, King feared that the United States was heading toward a crisis of too many people trying to derive sustenance from a deteriorating soil base.

"If the United States is to endure," Professor King wrote, "if we are to project our history even through four or five thousand years as the Mongolian nations have done, and if that history is to be written in continuous peace, free from periods of widespread famine or pestilence, this nation must re-orient itself."[13] The United States, he argued, must stop wasting its abundance. Compared to China, the United States could seem a source of hope for humanity. But King did not share that optimism and, arriving more humbly than most, he asked what China, Korea, or Japan might offer to western farmers. During his travels he concluded that all those East Asian countries were and had long been models of sustainability from which much could be learned.

By 1910 the U.S. population stood at one hundred million, while China's was five times larger.[14] Throughout much of human history, fully a quarter of humanity had lived under Chinese rule, more than 90 percent of them living directly on the land, raising just enough surplus to send grain as taxes to the imperial capital or to other towns and cities as saleable commodities. Both the United States and China occupied about the same amount of acreage on the world map, but the Chinese had to sustain themselves on far less arable land per person than North Americans. King calculated that his country's farmers possessed more than twenty acres per capita, including nonarable and arable soils, while China's farmers had only two acres per capita, more than half of which was mountain terrain, difficult or even impossible to farm.[15]

But even if in 1909 Americans enjoyed a big advantage in good land, their prospects among conservationists had begun to look less bountiful. King assumed that his country's population might one day rise as high as 1.2 billion, making the United States about as crowded as China. (So far, that dire prediction has not come to pass; after more than another century the U.S. population stands at only 350 million, while China's has risen to 1.4 billion.) A huge growth in American numbers was imminent, some agricultural conservationists warned, an increase that could not be prevented and that many patriots seemed to welcome out of nationalist pride. How could such a future behemoth feed itself, King worried, and what lessons might China teach the farmers of Wisconsin or Iowa so they would be better prepared to farm a more and more crowded land?

Everywhere he journeyed King recorded an astonishing diversity of crops growing on very small plots, presenting more biodiversity than did farms in the United States, where huge, expansive monocultures of corn or wheat were becoming the norm. He saw diversity-rich agroecosystems of grass carp swimming in rice paddies, pigs fattening in muddy yards, silkworms feeding on mulberry trees planted along paddy dikes, tea growing on nearby hillsides, and among all that the major cereal crops of rice, millet, and wheat sprouting in rich green carpets. He found Second Earth plants like corn and potatoes growing in Chinese fields. The typical farmstead, however, included far fewer domesticated animals than in America. A Shandong farmer, for example, kept only a single donkey for farm labor and a single cow and two pigs for meat and manure to support twelve humans per household—altogether sixteen creatures struggling to survive on a single hectare of soil. Such intensively managed farms, in contrast to those of meat- and milk-producing Wisconsin, were more like gardens than American-style farms, but their per-hectare yields were often higher.[16]

That astonishing productivity would not have been possible, King realized, if the peasants had not become used to brutal work schedules, which they imposed on themselves and their animal domesticates. He did not overlook the whip hand of traditional farming, but rather than seeing it as cruel or domineering he lauded its moral effects. China's hard work ethos, he declared, was the source of its national strength and virtue. "This marvelous heritage of economy, industry and thrift, bred of the stress of centuries," he solemnized, "must not be permitted to lose virility through contact with western wasteful practices, now exalted to seeming virtues through the dazzling brilliancy of mechanical achievements. More and more labor must be celebrated in all homes, and economy, industry and thrift become valued impulses, compelling and satisfying."[17] North America, with its new bounty, encouraged too much laziness and wastefulness, while in China farmers could succeed only by following a rigorous work regime, practicing thoughtful, patient thrift, and whipping everyone and everything in sight. King was repelled by the contrasting lazy and conspicuous consumption that industrial capitalism had brought.

King's enthusiasm for rigorous discipline and small-scale efficiency blinded him to the full costs of China's farm production: tired muscles, long work hours for man and beast, and the distasteful but inescapable chore of collecting all the excreta possible, a task that entailed many health risks. To collect such vile stuff required the efforts of everyone in the household. Even small children were given buckets to fill with excrement. After collection, the wastes had to be stored on-site until it was time to spread them over fields or paddies.

King had come to a China caught in what the historian Mark Elvin has called a "high equilibrium trap." As early as the eighteenth century, Elvin points out, yields per acre were "very nearly as high as possible without the use of advanced industrial-scientific inputs," including improved seeds, pesticides, and chemical fertilizers. From that point onward yields in wheat cropping remained high by European and American standards, but also they remained static, no longer keeping up with population growth. Yields for rice were much better than those for wheat, but rice production had become stagnant even as China's human numbers continued swelling. Here, in

THE GOOD MUCK

Elvin's words, was "a system working near the limit of what was possible by pre-modern means."[18] It did not help that traditional population restraints such as epidemics, which had long left many victims, were no longer so frequent because people were acquiring better immunity and medicine. Despite a high level of knowledge, rationality, and intelligent management, China's farmers were failing to keep pace with their own fertility. The facts suggested that their style of agriculture offered no model for the United States or other western nations, not without some moderation in fertility rates. For centuries the Chinese had birthed five children per married couple on average.

Despite the beauty and grace in that old style of farming, there was also severe hardship and insecurity. David Fairchild may have been too condescending toward Chinese agriculture, but he was surely right that the peasants had to put up with a great deal of "disgusting drudgery," forced on them by the need to extract more and more output from the same piece of land. King, on the other hand, was also accurate when he saw in the peasant way of life an "almost religious fidelity [to work] . . . which may well cause western nations to pause and reflect."[19]

Data gathered by King, not from China but from Japan and Europe, indicated that a single ton of human excrement contained more than twelve pounds of nitrogen (symbolized by N on the periodic chart), about two pounds of phosphorus (P), and four pounds of potassium (K), the three elements identified by the nineteenth-century German chemist Justus Liebig as the essentials of soil health. The total amount of those nutrients lurking in the excreta of China's five hundred million people was substantial, totaling around forty ounces per person per day. A wealth of NPK was literally lying at their feet.[20]

But note that it took a lot of human waste to get a small improvement in production. To produce twelve pounds of nitrogen would take eight hundred people voiding their bowels and bladders. Using King's numbers, we can calculate that in 1909 the body wastes across China roughly added up to 7,500 tons (6,800 metric tons) each day. Scanty though it was for such an immense country, nothing like that resource was being recycled in the United States. America's much smaller population, if it matched the Chinese results, would have produced only about 1,500 tons (1,360 metric tons) of N per day. Instead of being recycled into the soil, those tons were washing away into rivers and seas. It was not being used to restore fertility on crop fields. The usually placid King became furious at the thought of so much biological richness not being put to productive improvement: "Man is the most extravagant accelerator of waste the world has ever endured."[21]

But it was not humans in general that King criticized: he exempted the Chinese from his indignation. He recalled the sight of one farmer walking down his crop rows, buckets of muck swinging from the pole he carried across his shoulder. With a long-handled dipper he carefully ladled precious wastes onto his cucumbers and other vegetables, treating each plant individually with intelligent care because he had twenty people to feed at his table.[22]

At the same time, King excused China's farmers from any responsibility for widespread soil erosion—yet here too natural wealth was being wasted. Soil was washing down from plateaus and mountains, clogging rivers and canals with eroded silt and sand, and eventually ending up in the sea. Conservationists of the day pointed out that such erosion was caused by farmers, as they cleared away native vegetation and plowed highly erodible ground. Undeniably, a lot of fertility had been washing into the Yellow River over centuries. The result was that a silt-loaded river flooded again and again. In 1855, after much shifting erosion and deposition, the Yellow River unexpectedly cut a new course across Shandong province and began pouring its silt-heavy waters into the Bohai Sea instead of the Yellow Sea.[23]

King, as he traveled along the coast, sailed right across the mouth of the Yellow River and must have witnessed its heavily soil-laden waters staining the ocean. He was familiar, as were other American conservationists in the days of President Theodore Roosevelt (he left office in the year of King's journey), with the long history of Chinese soil erosion and heavy flooding. But that part of the standard conservationist lament King resisted. To his wife he wrote that a plausible explanation for the heavy silt load carried by rivers "cannot be that man has ruthlessly cut away the forests and thus brought ruin upon the land as foresters are all the time talking."[24] The silt must be caused, he believed, by nature—the scantiness of mountain vegetation in an arid climate. China's farmers were not guilty, he argued; rather, they should be praised for having appreciated the compensatory power of muck.

Franklin King was, despite his erroneous views about the causes of soil erosion, on to something important. Careful soil stewardship is essential for all societies, and it stems from a popular appreciation of the soil's foundational role in human welfare. Justus Liebig's contribution to knowledge was identifying the three major chemical elements in soil fertility; however, such success in the laboratory encouraged oversimplification and overconfidence in human ingenuity. Liebig and his reductive approach ignored what traditional farmers of Asia knew from long experience, that good soil is more than a three-element problem. Farmers should approach soil conservation with the concern they would have for their own health or that of any complex organism.

Both King and Liebig should have realized that modern agriculture needed more than antique folk methods or chemical panaceas, distorted as they often were by superstition, bad habits, and unreliable data. Maintaining good soil conditions required a science of soil ecology that was holistic in understanding and respectful toward nature's ways. It also required a society that not only discouraged soil depletion or erosion but at the same time understood that soil is a living ecosystem with complex interrelationships among plants, animals, and inorganic matter.

THE GOOD MUCK

For a more holistic and critical science than Liebig's we can turn to one of the most remarkable men of the twentieth century, Sir Albert Howard. Born in 1873, Howard grew up on a Shropshire farm not far from Charles Darwin's birthplace. Like Darwin, he grew up in rural English culture and had become a natural historian. He adopted an evolutionary view of farming; where Darwin had spoken of "the web of life," the intricately woven fabric of nature, Howard preferred "the wheel of life," emphasizing that nature flows in circles. Plants, both men understood, are interdependent parts of that ever spinning, ever turning web/wheel, and so is the soil.

We can call both Howard and Darwin ecologists, for they anticipated twentieth-century challenges to old, reductive science and emphasized the relatedness of all life on earth.[25] Ecology would not fully emerge as a science until the twentieth century, but like Albert Howard it did so by appreciating the intricate relationships among soils, plants, and animals and asking how they might determine a farmer's success or failure. Like Darwin in his study of the role of earthworms in soil formation, a modern classic in agricultural ecology, Howard and Darwin approached farming in terms of evolutionary science, believing that agriculture should be regarded not merely as the cultivation of crops, or as injection of NKP into the soil, but as the nurturing of an organic, interdependent community in which many kinds of beings were netted together for mutual benefit.[26]

In 1905 Howard was hired to work in the town of Pusa to discover how to raise more food for famine-plagued India. Howard's wife (née Gabrielle Matthaei, also a trained scientist) joined him in the work, and it was Gabrielle who pushed him to realize that a mechanistic, reductive science could never fully solve India's food problem.[27] The Howards, at the very moment when Franklin King was inspecting China's rice paddies, had begun looking for a better strategy.

In 1924 the husband-wife team moved to the city of Indore, located in the heavily populated Narmada River valley of Madhya Pradesh. There they took over a small government-owned farm of seventy-five acres and made

THE GOOD MUCK

it their laboratory for a new but traditional-thinking agriculture. Gabrielle died in 1931, whereupon Albert married her younger sister Louise. In 1940, with Louise's help, he published his most important book, *An Agricultural Testament*, which set forth in lucid prose an ecological model for farming. It started with the importance of building humus—the living, organic component of the soil—through frequent additions of muck. Along with Franklin King's book of three decades earlier, *An Agricultural Testament* became an influential scripture for what we now call "organic" or "regenerative" farming.[28]

Here are the opening words of Howard's *Agricultural Testament:* "The maintenance of the fertility of the soil is the first condition of any permanent system of agriculture." Echoing King, Howard called for more attention to soil quality before the farmer planted seeds in the ground. Unfarmed nature shows us how to begin building and restoring soils, he asserted, for nature is "the supreme farmer." The human farmer must learn from natural examples how to take care of the soil through better practices: "Mother earth never attempts to farm without livestock; she always raises mixed crops; great pains are taken to preserve the soil and to prevent erosion; the mixed vegetable and animal wastes are converted into humus; there is no waste; the processes of growth and the processes of decay balance one another; ample provision is made to maintain large reserves of fertility; the greatest care is taken to store the rainfall; both plants and animals are left to protect themselves against disease."[29]

Can a farmer learn to think ecologically? He can if he is observant, Howard believed, and then countries like India might achieve an abundant and sustainable supply of food and fiber.

But where and how, Howard asked, could one learn from "Nature's farm"? Go to any old-growth forest where a diversity of trees and other plants could be observed, along with animals and microorganisms, all living as one community. Walk through that forest and learn what permanence required. "The [mature] forest," Howard wrote, "manures itself." Get down on your knees and examine the forest floor. See how animal and vegetable residues mix, how fungi and bacteria decompose those residues and turn them into humus. All is sanitary, clean, and pleasant to the nose. "There is no nuisance of any kind—no smell, no flies, no dustbins, no incinerators, no artificial sewage system, no water-borne diseases, no town councils, and no rates. On the contrary, the forest affords a place for the ideal summer holiday: sufficient shade and an abundance of pure fresh air."[30]

Why was the same sustainability more difficult under human management? Simply because farmers did not pay careful, respectful attention to how the natural world works. For them nature was not a model to be emulated, but an enemy to be defeated.

Howard's laudatory view of nature (a word he always capitalized), ironically, owed much to traditional farming cultures, particularly the old belief that a divine and intelligent power had made the world and pronounced it good. Call that power "God" or "Nature," it amounted to the same thing. But the transformation to industrial capitalism had been hard on that ecological view of the world. It had become less possible to approach nature reverently as the nurturing mother of life or to argue that God had organized the earth for the good of all creatures, not when so many of them died so cruelly and soils could be so easily depleted.

But then Howard's counter-model of a wild forest's evolving complexity over millions of years, his notion of the forest as a kind of "farm," was also hard to teach to a modern society. How could one think of a forest, with its many species competing to reproduce themselves and take possession of the land, as a farm? Was there no difference between an evolving ecosystem and a man-made crop of rice or maize? Those were not questions that Howard asked. Instead, he made heavy use of nostalgic metaphors and images, some of which had begun to lose their cultural power.

The depiction of nature as a "supreme farmer," for example, was nothing but an anthropomorphism. In trying to straddle past and present, Howard overlooked or minimized the fact that in a forest there are no overall goals and no designs either; rather, there is fierce competition going on across the land. A real forest, Darwin had explained, encompassed much that might seem bad as well as good by human moral standards: a profusion of flies, odors, and diseases, along with truly dangerous creatures like tigers and wild elephants who could take a person's life. The agrarian way had long sought to gain control over that dark wildness. How could one simply turn to "Nature" as an ideal model, forgetting its darker side as known to farmers?

It was a conundrum that Albert Howard did not try to resolve. We can give him credit for at least seeking to find a balance between science and tradition. At the same time, we must ask whether evolution, so different from the farmer's selective hand, was a good model for feeding so many people. A great deal of adjustment had to be made in older, pre-Darwinian rural knowledge, to be sure, as science described a post-Darwinian knowledge. Nature as the sum of material things, nature as the world that humans did not create, nature as an evolving set of patterns based on fine-tuned adaptation—all these were Darwinian themes, and they were not easily reconciled with the old agrarian way of life. By mimicking natural processes, Howard argued, farmers might learn important new ways to farm more successfully. A biologically trained agriculturist, he would have said, should not approach the land with an unquestioning faith in whatever is new and profitable.

With the advent of factories and the market economy, Howard feared, had come increasing hubris and overconfidence in human reason that ignored the wisdom of tradition. Modernity was for him both threat and panacea. "Since the Industrial Revolution," he declared, "the processes of growth have been speeded up to produce the food and raw materials needed by the population and the factory. Nothing effective has been done to replace the loss of fertility involved in this vast increase in crop and animal production. The consequences have been disastrous. Agriculture has become unbalanced: the land is in revolt: diseases of all kinds are on the increase: in many parts of the world Nature is removing the worn-out soil by means of erosion."[31]

The cotton being grown in Howard's India, a practice he was trying to end, was one of the biggest commodities produced and traded internationally. Manufacturing nations like Great Britain were unable grow it at home, so they began importing it in great quantities and then spinning and weaving the cotton fibers into cloth in their textile mills. Along with other mass-produced crops such as wheat, maize, sugar, jute, oil seeds, dyes, opium, tobacco, tea, and coffee, cotton had become a "money crop," raised to sell on world markets with as much profit as possible. To grow such a crop, capitalists had turned India and other countries into exporters, taking over vast acreages that had traditionally been devoted to raising food for local consumption. Cotton came to be grown under a new economic philosophy that aimed at quick extraction of resources, big profits through mass sales, and the realization of infinite wealth. Although the older subsistence farmer could be ruthless in raising food, he still considered land a valuable asset to be safeguarded; the capitalist farmer, on the other hand, tended to see land as capital to earn a profit, not as part of a natural community to be protected.[32]

Albert Howard and his spouses were sharp critics of modern cotton farming—its overreliance on chemical fertilizers, its oversimplified monocropping, and its devotion to mechanization and profit. By the 1930s and 1940s it was apparent to them that much of Asia was being overtaken by a far less ecological kind of farming. Under British power India's food production system seemed to be losing whatever sustainability it once had—and the Howards were there to fight that change. In reaction, like King, they came to see China as a viable, pre-modern, but science-friendly alternative to western modernity.

To understand that alternative, Howard turned to King's *Farmers of Forty Centuries,* writing that "the peasants of China, who pay great attention to the return of all wastes to the land, come nearest to the ideal set by Nature. They have maintained a large population on the land without any falling off in fertility."[33] China, Howard hoped, could help colonies like

India throw off the influence of western industrial capitalism and its approach to raising food. At the same time, he looked to science as his teacher, even though that science did not lie easily alongside traditional agrarianism.

One must ask whether in fact an agrarian China, more than western capitalist farming, could withstand scientific criticism. After all, China's farmers had failed to keep pace with population growth. What other problems might condemn that old way of using land? Had it been good for people, domesticated animals, or the land? The answer was more complicated than either King or Howard supposed.

A planetary history that takes science seriously should ask critical questions about traditional ways, while paying attention to the high social and ecological costs that modernity has brought. It must apply the best available knowledge to soil loss or depletion, the use of human excrement, and its efficacy as a soil amendment. Above all, it should never deny that muck is a dangerous pollutant, no matter how "natural" it may be. Its repulsiveness to humans is not a mere cultural fashion among fastidious, overcivilized minds but a biological truth deeply wired into our senses and brains. Few people have ever willingly wanted to handle it. Acknowledging its dangers should lead us to ask how and why muck ever became a valued soil additive in the first place, collected and handled by vulnerable children and adults, what its adoption as part of agriculture required of humans, and why it proved unable to keep up with the demands of a growing population.

Unquestionably, China was among the earliest and most successful places in the world to collect human body wastes and use them to renew soil and increase food production. In contrast to feces-avoiding hunters and gatherers, China's peasants began at some point to embrace poop for its utility, treating it with care and intelligence, even to the point of making it a commodity to sell and buy. Thus, what had been considered "unclean" became a vital resource with material value, deposited regularly in the farmer's

THE GOOD MUCK

bank account. Traditional agrarians were not completely opposed to an economic way of calculating, for they too aimed to make all nature serve their material interests.

Before there was any collecting of muck, there had first to be the innovation called agriculture. China, which became the greatest agrarian civilization of all, had been preceded, as we have seen, only by Mesopotamia. Its history was remarkable, as King observed, for longevity, continuity, and productivity.[34] From the Qin dynasty (221–206 BCE) to the Qing (1644–1911 CE), a span that ended in Franklin King's time, farming dominated the country. Wheat replaced millet because of its higher protein content, but in the south rice endured as the favorite domesticate. Fortunately, the south had many natural waterways, coursing through its hills and deltas, providing ample water. When tapped for irrigation, the streams brought to the farmer's crops loads and loads of aromatic mud. That sediment was rich in nutrients, and the growing season was long enough to support more than one crop per year, but even under such favored conditions, China's agriculture could not be sustained forever. Farmers had to add nutrients. But nonhuman animal manure was in short supply because farmers kept comparatively few livestock—a water buffalo for plowing, a few chickens and ducks, a pig or two for pork. Thus, it was not so much ingenuity as hunger that brought them to capture and use their own urine and feces.

The soil scientist King had set himself the goal of learning how it was possible, "after twenty and perhaps thirty or even forty centuries, for [China's] soils to be made to produce sufficiently for the maintenance of such dense populations." He first spoke of "twenty and perhaps thirty" centuries and then rounded up to a full four thousand years. The alliterative roll of "farmers of forty centuries" would stick in people's minds and get repeated by agrarian boosters around the world.

So, when precisely was human muck first used on Chinese farms? Did this practice really go back as far as King claimed, or did it appear later—perhaps as a common practice only a few centuries ago? The evidence for any date remains shaky and imprecise. Some scholars believe that human excrement was used as fertilizer as far back as the Shang dynasty, 3,000–3,600 years before the present. That would fall almost a millennium short of King's book title. In any case, we have only a few inscriptions on "oracle bones" as evidence. During the Shang dynasty, diviners began inscribing, with a knife or brush, small pictographs on the shoulder blades of oxen or on the belly shells of tortoises, and it is those inscriptions that may confirm the point when human excrement was first used as a fertilizer.

After careful examination of ancient evidence, Wang Lihua has concluded that "Chinese farmers began using human excrement, along with the stool of livestock and poultry, a variety of weeds, burned animal bones, and ashes for fertilization more than 2,000 years ago."[35] Two millennia, he says, not four. But then we still must ask, which farmers, how many of them, and what quantities of excrement and other supplements did they apply to the land? A scratching here or there on a shell or bone cannot tell us what the average peasant did and how often he did it.

There is another important clue from the later Zhou and Han dynasties (1045 BCE to 220 CE), consisting of small clay models of pigsties unearthed in the rice-growing area of China. They are charming models of buildings that housed pigs but also human toilets, where pig and human wastes mixed together, and the mix could be saved as fertilizer. Those structures look elegant, with solid masonry walls enclosing a yard on the ground level where pigs were kept and a stairway that curves down gracefully from a second-story toilet where people could sit and drop their excrement on the animals below.

Not surprisingly, the elegant models have found their way into Chinese museums, for their architecture could grace a palace. But were such integrated human toilet/pig yards in use by common farmers? They must have required considerable capital and labor to build and maintain. Would a farmer struggling to raise food on only a few *mu* (an old Chinese measurement, equal to 0.165 acre) have been able to invest in such a common

THE GOOD MUCK

man-animal toilet? Or were they limited to the largest estates, used only by the richer classes? Until we can say with certainty how common such buildings were in the landscape, we remain in the dark about when or how commonly human waste became a fertilizer.[36]

Other soil additives appeared throughout China and Eurasia during early times, including many kinds of biodegradable trash—ashes from stoves and fireplaces, a wide array of animal droppings, urine-soaked straw bedding from stables and barns, and so-called green manure, crops that were grown not for food but for soil improvement, to be turned under by the plow. We also know that as late as 1400 CE farmers in China, presumably the well-to-do, were adding "fertilizer cake" made of soybean oil to their soil amendments.[37]

Books on agriculture include such long, diverse lists of fertilizers that we must conclude there was a widespread demand for soil treatments. But there also can be no doubt that in more recent times, a mere five hundred to a thousand years ago, China's demand for food reached a point of crisis and farmers began to hold their noses, add human wastes to their lists, and put them into regular, widespread use.

The agricultural historian Li Bozhong has argued that a more systematic use of human fertilizer began with what he calls "ecological agriculture," a new, integrated system of farming that began in the early modern period, featuring a diversity of crops and heavy doses of human manure to maintain soil fertility. That system first emerged in the Song dynasty, he says, which lasted from the tenth century to the thirteenth century CE. But, Li argues, it was during the Ming and Qing periods that the use of human muck became the common practice, and it did so in that most progressive region called Jiangnan. This was the densely populated and agriculturally productive region that Franklin King visited in 1909.[38]

Li tracked the excremental revolution in farming to Changshu County, near Suzhou, and a pair of brothers named Tan. They created a farm consisting of a linked set of agroecosystems, including dry land crop fields, irrigated paddies, and fishponds, from which they harvested cereals, fruit, vegetables, chicken, fish, and other edibles. They were pioneers in integrated management. Their tight nutrient loops, including the recycling of wastes, yielded more food and fiber, including silk, all of which could be sold on the market. The result for the Tan brothers was a substantial jump in family income. A key part of their success came from their willingness to make greater use of human manure. Every ounce of the stuff was like money to them.

During the Ming and Qing dynasties, which lasted from 1368 to 1911 CE, Li believes, "ecological agriculture" spread throughout Jiangnan, becoming more and more popular and essential to that region's economy. With more intense application of human wastes came not only abundant food but also a cleaner, more sanitized landscape. Farmers collected all the excrement on their own farm, while at the same time they began buying the wastes of towns and cities and spreading them on their fields. The air became redolent with the stench of muck. Was this, then, what Professor King was seeing, not a common practice going back forty centuries, but a relatively modern one?

We know that during the past five hundred or six hundred years, a late point in the agrarian way of life, a brisk trade in human wastes developed. Excrement became part of an intensified commercialization overspreading the region, responding to population increase. Muck markets emerged for almost every commodity produced on the farm. More than ever before, the use of excrement expanded, uniting city and countryside into a single web of natural resource conservation, and excrement came to smell like money.[39]

This new agriculture seems to have been far less prominent north of the Yangzi than in Jiangnan. An imperial treatise published in 1737, during the early Qing dynasty, complained that while southerners "treasure[d] night soil as if it were gold," northerners remained quite indifferent. The author of the treatise noted that "the streets in the north are not clean. The land is filthy. . . . The northerners should follow Jiangnan's example. Every household should collect night soil."[40]

Why didn't northerners see the potential for wealth in human excrement that southerners did? In the opinion of the treatise's author, they were less intelligent or enterprising. Might it have been, however, that northern urban workers were less eager to take on the grubby task of making city life more pleasant by removing human wastes? Or perhaps they were less impelled to increase the farmer's agricultural productivity because they did not feel the same population pressure for change. Perhaps their soils had not been so thoroughly depleted, and their numbers were not so severely pressing on the land.

Undoubtedly, the cities of the Yangzi delta became central to a new feces-based economy. Those cities were for a time the largest, fastest growing, and richest in all of China. Hangzhou (formerly known as Hangchow), a seaport sitting at the head of a deep bay, was the leader. It began exploding in numbers and importance after becoming the southern terminus of the Grand Canal, a man-made waterway for commerce that by 609 CE reached all the way to Beijing. By 1820 Hangzhou's population exceeded three million; by the mid-nineteenth century it had become one of the largest urban conglomerations on earth. Similarly, the city of Suzhou (or Soochow), also located within the Yangzi delta, counted 6.5 million inhabitants by 1851, while in the same year its sister city, Nanjing, located just south of the Yangzi, had increased to 6.2 million residents. All those expanding cities required a lot of food, and they produced in return a lot of body wastes.[41]

China's cities grew big very quickly because people from rural districts were flooding into them, abandoning the agrarian way of life and looking for urban work, just as they were doing in early modern Europe. It had been common to void one's wastes along the streets or alleyways, but as the feces piled up, shrewd minds saw an opportunity to make a profit by collecting from house to house and selling the excrement to farmers in the countryside, eager to increase their farm production. Among the leaders in that new business were some who had fled the countryside, who began collecting manure from the streets, private homes, and businesses. They called

THE GOOD MUCK

that waste by the euphemism "night soil" because it was collected before dawn. The collectors figured out which neighborhoods to visit for the best manure and which routes out of town led most directly to farmers. This unprecedented market became the core of a new excrement-based agrarianism, unprecedented in profitability. The determining factor behind that market was a growing population.

Marxist scholars have coined a phrase they have applied to the industrial capitalist transformation, "metabolic rift," suggesting a fracturing of human ecology, as body wastes were produced in growing cities, interrupting the natural recycling of excrement. Metabolism refers to the matter and energy exchange that goes on within any organism to keep it from dying. Humans must practice metabolic exchange as all organisms do. For thousands of years when almost everyone was a farmer, humans derived whatever nutrients they needed from their own farm. But with increasing numbers came fewer but larger farms, outmigration, urban growth, trade, and commercialization—and then it was that a rift opened between city and country, leaving both places impoverished, depleted, and polluted. But this condition did not originate with modern industrial capitalism; it was there in China by the Ming period, long before industrialization, and it continued into the Qing period. Food was raised on farms and transported to cities, where former rural people were congregating and body wastes were piling up, becoming a deadly pollutant and an offense to the senses.

The phrase "metabolic rift" comes not from Marx but from the American sociologist John Bellamy Foster, who was inspired by a short section of Marx's *Capital,* volume one. Both teacher and student blamed western capitalism for this serious breakdown in human metabolism. Capitalist investment in agriculture, Marx argued, pushed people from the land—remember those infamous eighteenth-century enclosure acts in Britain that put so many tenant farmers off their fields and forced them into towns and cities. Capitalist relations, Marx declared, disturb "the metabolic interaction between man and the earth, i.e., it prevents the return to the soil of its constituent elements consumed by man in the form of food and clothing; hence it hinders the operation of the eternal natural condition for the lasting fertility of the soil." Marx summed up this history in a pithy phrase: "All progress in capitalist agriculture is a progress in the art, not only of robbing the worker, but of robbing the soil."[42]

But a Marxist explanation risks oversimplifying the course of history, exaggerating the uniqueness of the capitalist West, and perpetuating the myth of a pre-capitalist harmony on the land. China in fact began to experience metabolic rift wherever it built cities, long before capitalism began taking form in western Europe and peasants were flocking to cities. Not until the late twentieth century did China become highly influenced by industrial capitalism, in government policies and in waste generation and reuse.

Before the twentieth century, businessmen did not rule China. A merchant class existed there, of course, and had existed for many centuries, though it was not highly esteemed or honored. Traditionally, merchants ranked below farmers, laborers, and government officials. Merchants did not become emperors in China's agrarian state. The pre-capitalist state, nonetheless, was often eager to promote "development," that is, encourage technological innovation and expand income and wealth. The agrarian way in China had long pushed for a conquest over nature, and it was farmers who carried the spears in that conquest. In Jiangnan, farmers and state together pursued an intensification of agriculture and urbanization. They did so because they had many babies that must be fed and made secure.

Today, we might try to rejoin what has been sundered, but to be successful any modern state must value innovation. Li Bozhong offers a telling example of how Jiangnan villagers tried to overcome metabolic rift by adopting new strategies. He focuses on a village located far from urban centers and lacking sufficient fertilizer to meet its needs. Desperate for bigger crops, the adults and children learned to go along the roads collecting the feces of travelers who, while passing through, heeded the call of nature.

THE GOOD MUCK

Then someone came up with a bright idea: build a clean, comfortable public toilet for travelers. Make it a three-room palace and paint it in glistening white. Offer free use of the facility with free toilet paper. The traveler would pay with his excrement. Thus, the town could collect poop from a bigger population, importing new resources.[43]

When farmers lived close to a town or city, they had easier access to a bonanza of fertilizer. All that was needed was a group of middlemen, called the *fenfu*, to transport the muck to farmers. By the Qing dynasty (which began in 1644 CE) much of the feces being spread on farms in Jiangnan came from China's urban centers. Men driving "honey wagons" became a familiar sight, combing the main avenues and byways for human wastes. A typical cart transported six to ten wooden barrels, each covered and holding as much as sixty pounds of excrement. Or where barrels and carts were in short supply, men with buckets and yokes could be hired at very low wages to fill their buckets with feces and carry them to collection centers.

Human workers and their animals brought all the buckets and barrels of human muck to those centers located outside the city, selling their contents by the pailful, usually for a low price. In the suburbs the muck was spread out, dried, and sanitized. Nearby were special docks designated for a fleet of poop gondolas to load their cargo on board. "The boats," King wrote in a letter, "are carefully washed outside and covered before leaving the city and the offensiveness of the practice is not nearly so great as you might think."[44] Each year the city of Suzhou, from its foreign-resident districts alone, shipped out many tons of excrement, reaping a benefit from the European imperialists.

The poop gondolas—long narrow boats devoted exclusively to muck transportation—were a common sight. In the early twentieth century Franklin King saw them in Suzhou, their crews collecting urban wastes from the cities, taking them to the farmers, singing lustily as they floated through the network of canals that crisscrossed the countryside. King was impressed by the gondolier's cheery attitudes. In his pages we can almost hear the

THE GOOD MUCK

boatmen poling their gondolas through rural districts and shouting enthusiastically, "Here comes your muck!" Along the way they may also have sung a few popular romantic tunes about willow trees swaying over the water or a maiden's dark eyes inviting a lover, just like the gondoliers of Italy's Venice who floated on canals likewise redolent with human excrement. Did the farmers who received all the muck from the cities also sing lovely songs as they ladled the purchased fertilizer onto their growing plants, carefully feeding each new sprig of rice with the body wastes of strangers? This was how "metabolic rift" worked.

To treat human poop as a valuable commodity, bought and sold in markets, returning to the soil what had been separated by urbanization, marked a major change in China's use of the natural environment, perhaps a native equivalent to western capitalism. It required farmers who were eager to get the most profit out of feces. It required too a class of laborers who formed a human drainpipe from water closets and privies to agricultural fields. And then it required an elaborate scaling of prices paid for different grades of excrement. The body wastes of Hangzhou's rich folks, because of their better health and nutrition, fetched the highest prices. Even in excrement markets there was hierarchy. Pig manure was highly ranked too, but not so highly as human manure; usually pig poop was applied to a special set of crops, whereas sheep manure was esteemed best for different crops. Urine had its own special market, black river mud (another kind of muck) merited a different price and use, and old bones and slaughterhouse blood and offal found still other market values and farm uses.

By the time of King's visit, the Jiangnan region had become very skilled in extracting a profit-seeking order out of a nauseating chaos. It had created a system of waste recycling for the agrarian way of life, which enhanced the output of farmers and the revenues of the state. Not everyone shared fully in the labor or in the wealth that made this system function well. In the city as on the farm humble workers were expected to collect the crap while others gathered most of the profit.

THE GOOD MUCK

This country-city network did not come from the West, but by the nineteenth century western imperialists were influencing it. The historian Cao Mu has probed the archives of the great coastal city of Tianjin and uncovered fascinating insights into the anti-rift movement that went on there in the early twentieth century.[45] Tianjin was a treaty port, a cluster of territorial possessions owned by the imperial powers Britain, France, Italy, Japan, and Germany. There were nine concessions in all, creating a multinational commingling of peoples unlike the rest of China. Still, its residents had to defecate as others did, on the streets or in backyards. But such behavior became intolerable with denser settlement. Cleaning up the unsanitary conditions became one of the Tianjin government's main projects, especially after western traders and residents began demanding better sanitation.

The foreign quarters of Tianjin urged the city to construct elaborate sewers that could collect and carry all the wastes to the sea, as many cities in Europe and North America were doing. But before such an expensive investment in infrastructure was taken on, Tianjin began licensing and constructing public lavatories to save money. By the late 1940s almost five hundred neighborhood lavatories existed. They were not equal in size, comfort, or accessibility, but generally every neighborhood had its own public toilet—avoiding further street pollution, providing facilities not too far for anyone to reach in case of urgent need, requiring only a short walk on a cold morning. Some residents never visited the public lavatories, either because they were too rich to tolerate a commoner's facility or too weak to walk there. But most citizens learned to visit regularly, paying a small fee for access and feeling better off than ever before. No longer were they forced to dwell among their own or others' muck in the *hutongs* or alleyways.

The quality of Tianjin's public lavatories improved steadily as people came to use them more habitually. At first, they were often no more than straw shelters, with grass-matted walls and tattered roofs, open to gusty winds and peeping toms. New or old, however, those facilities required one to lower one's bum over a dark and stinky cesspool—squatting down on one's haunches while swatting away the buzzing flies. And in those very public places people moved their bowels while visiting with neighbors or listening to fights. Privacy was impossible.

So horrible were the first such structures that in 1937, according to Cao Mu, Tianjin's Public Health Bureau had to pass regulations specifying that "each lavatory [must] have a red brick wall, a lead roof, a screen door and windows, concrete floor and squat pits, and a seeping pit to discharge urine." The exterior wall must be coated with cement one meter thick, while the clay tanks installed below the ground were left to local standards. But better regulation alone could not assure a high degree of cleanliness or teach people better habits of use, and neither did it end all controversy over who had the right to collect or sell the public's excreta.[46]

One especially fierce battle occurred between a publicly licensed lavatory owner named Ma and an unlicensed competitor, a man named Wu. The latter acted quite aggressively—boldly seizing space on the street and putting up an outdoor privy for the use of his restaurant patrons, while hoping to get a government license too. Ma and Wu accused each other of endangering the public health. The battle went on until mediators intervened and backed Ma, but only on the condition that he must first clean up his own squalid facility to keep his license. Irresponsibility was not to be tolerated in this business. Yet always there were aggressive entrepreneurs like Wu who tried to grab control of the lavatory business across the city and perhaps control the entire urban fertilizer market. They wanted to pocket all the gain that came from selling muck beyond the city.

None of the muck markets that appeared in Tianjin, Suzhou, Beijing, or Shanghai lasted for long. Already by the mid-twentieth century forces were at work breaking up the muck market, reopening China's metabolic rift, and allowing human feces once more to be wasted, poisoning the air and robbing the land.

THE GOOD MUCK

Before we go further into the twentieth-century collapse of China's centuries-old excremental economy, we need to ask why it ever came into existence. Why did China's peasants come to rely so heavily on human excrement to grow food? Farmers in other parts of the planet often scorned the practice as too "dirty," as they still do in parts of China. The explanation for this turn in business can be linked to another, larger question: Why over many centuries did China's pre-capitalist farmers devour so much of what was natural around them—forests, grasslands, wetlands, mountain slopes, all ecosystems needed by other species? Why did the peasants push into extinction the country's once numerous elephants, tigers, and rhinos, along with birds, fishes, and insects of many dazzling colors and shapes?[47] The answer to those questions, like the answer as to why excrement became a marketable commodity, is the same: because there were many human bellies desiring to be filled, too many for the fields to support without more and more excreta being recycled to boost production. That is the simple, obvious answer, but explaining why there were so many people crowding onto China's lands is more complicated.

Peasants larded their lands with their own excrement not because they were motivated by modern capitalist greed. They were still agrarians until well into the twentieth century. They continued to believe that nature was the home of many in-dwelling spirits that must be revered or at least feared. Kowtowing to the spirits within nature, they did not ask themselves the question Albert Howard thought all farmers should ask: What practical lessons can we learn from nature to live sustainably in this place? How does land remain fertile where there are no people?

The peasants devoured almost every piece of land that could serve them as an alternative teaching resource. In place of the wild they constructed an increasingly human-made and human-centered landscape, though it was more "artificial" in some places than others. If Jiangnan's farms could be called "ecological," as Li Bozhong does, they were never ecological in terms of carefully preserving the natural environment and regarding it as a model for humans. "Ecological" when used as a label for agrarian societies usually means only that they recycle their wastes, using fish carcasses or mud or feces to fertilize their crops, and so forth. Peasants were not ecological in a modern scientific sense; they did not investigate systematically the evolution of ecosystems in nature. They were, instead, *economical* in their behavior—thrifty and careful with nutrients, but all the same intent on exterminating or appropriating.

All over the planet, from the earliest invention of agriculture, it was peasants, not urban businessmen, who destroyed the wild nature that had developed over millions of years. They did so to feed their growing number of children, even when it might not have been clearly wise or just to do so. Long before the rise of consumer societies, in which needs have become infinite and unsatisfiable, peasant societies have felt many pressing needs and wants of their own, especially an urge to eat and have sexual intercourse.

Why should we view human nature among peasants as more pure than that modern human nature to which shopping malls cater? From the perspective of the planet, one human "need" is not necessarily better than another. In the face of peasant desires, the elephants, tigers, birds, and rodents had to flee and find safer, less populated places where people were not so numerous—until finally they ran out of places to go.

China has, to be sure, historically practiced some restraint in sex and food, but it did so mainly to cope with famine, not to achieve a long-term ecological balance. If peasants ever tried to prevent pregnancy or manage their family size, it was not because they desired to find harmony or equilibrium with the land. Moreover, their halting, poorly understood, and sometimes violent methods (like infanticide) did not prevent them from making a relentless assault on ecosystems.

By choosing lots of children over observing environmental limits, China's peasants and emperors sought their own self-interest, hoping to demonstrate their virility or to acquire male children to depend on in old age.

After all, who but one's sons would be there to help at the end of life? For thousands of years neither the village nor the state offered any old-age assistance, leaving male children as the only kind of pension. So children kept sprouting like cabbages in the field: they were fed by their parents with nutrients and stocked for the rough days ahead.

Trying to satisfy the most fundamental of human desires, the survival of oneself and one's offspring, has led us all to increase the output of food. According to Dwight Perkins, in the period from 1368 to 1968 China increased its agricultural output by no less than 400 percent, with the conquest of new lands explaining half of that increase, while "the other half was the result of a doubling in the average output per unit area, which was again a development powered by the population growth."[48] In other words, Chinese farmers figured out how to produce more foodstuffs on the same plot of land, even as that increase became insufficient after a few centuries. If China fell into a "high equilibrium trap," one important reason was its increasing reliance on excrement. Poop kept China agrarian until the twentieth century, when it could no longer keep pace with the nation's demography, and then came crisis and revolution.

Today the lands of China, which once supported only a few thousand humans, support 1.4 billion mouths and bellies, making it after India the most populous nation on earth. One can laud that achievement and see it as a refutation of all Malthusian pessimism, or one can see it as a tragedy for the earth, nothing less than the wholesale destruction of a big part of the earth's evolutionary legacy. In any case, such huge population increases have become nearly impossible to sustain further.

Perhaps the most reliable overview of China's demographic history comes from Judith Banister, a specialist in Chinese population history who makes clear just what the Chinese have been through over the past six-hundred-plus years: "From the early years of the Ming Dynasty in the late fourteenth century, China experienced six centuries of population growth. Only twice was this growth checked, once because of the fall of the Ming Dynasty in the early seventeenth century, and once during the Taiping Rebellion that hastened the decline of the Qing (Ch'ing) Dynasty in the late nineteenth century. . . . The period of most rapid population growth (1749–1851) saw more than a doubling of China's population in a century."[49]

Banister's summary ends in the mid-nineteenth century—when 432 million inhabitants were fighting for food where once there had been only 60 million. The pressure did not end there. After 1851 the numbers kept on increasing exponentially, until demographic curves were bending almost vertically upward. Surely that extraordinary increase in human beings has been one of China's most distinctive features and, for visitors like King, its most impressive achievement. Nothing else competes with reproduction as a determinant of the country's social and environmental change.

Change never stops in this long story of population growth and social upheaval. In very recent times China's farmers, like those elsewhere, have turned to using modern chemical fertilizers instead of human manure. Environmentalists often decry that turn, pointing to the heavy ecological costs it has levied on the health of people and the planet, but there are powerful hungers deeply felt in China as in other countries that have been pushing such innovation forward.

Back in 1940 Albert Howard was fearful that modern chemistry would make his organic farming model harder to create and put into common practice: "What may be conveniently described as the NPK mentality dominates farming alike in the experimental stations and the countryside. . . . For the moment farming has been made to pay. But there is another side to this picture. These chemicals and these machines can do nothing to keep the soil in good heart. By their use the processes of growth can never be balanced by the processes of decay. All that they can accomplish is the transfer of the soil's capital to current account."[50] Howard saw change coming and protested, but millions of farmers disagreed, and even before World War II artificial fertilizer began to come into widespread use. It did so by promising to increase agricultural production beyond all limits.

THE GOOD MUCK

During World War I, the German chemist Fritz Haber discovered how to convert atmospheric nitrogen, a gas, into liquid ammonia by bonding that gas to hydrogen, which he derived from fossil fuel. Nitrogen was abundant in the air; it was not a limiting factor. Germany and other nations first wanted to extract it for use in armaments manufacture. To aid Germany's military defense, the chemical company BASF gave one of its top scientists, Carl Bosch, the job of collecting nitrogen to make explosives. Then after the war ended came the Haber-Bosch process of nitrogen extraction, which instead of making bombs could produce chemical fertilizers. Again, liquid ammonia became the base for that fertilizer. Combine it with phosphorus and potash—chemicals that were easily mined in various parts of the world—and a new generation of "multi-nutrient" fertilizers resulted. The new products dramatically altered the world farming economy, making fertilizer not only cheaper than it had ever been but also far easier and more pleasant to handle.[51]

All over the world, farmers began buying N in the form of liquid ammonia or dry-powder urea, along with P and K, to restore their depleted soils. New seed varieties designed by plant breeders to absorb those elements efficiently also became available, and the result was a much higher crop yield in the countryside—more vegetables, grains, cotton, and cabbages.

That enhanced production came at a cost, not in terms of money but in soil quality and the ecosphere. Muck quickly dropped out of the farmer's list of vital "resources" and became once more, as it had been in a forager's environment, a "waste" product, dismissed and unused. Without a socially valuable role to play, muck became once again a pollutant, although now it was being generated in prodigious quantities because there were far more people crowding the planet. Muck that was no longer part of agricultural production became dangerous once again, fouling streams and lakes, creating algal blooms, and killing other species.

At first China had to purchase chemical fertilizers from other countries. But then it started building its own supplies, starting with nitrogen factories, the biggest of which was built in the early days of the Chinese Republic—a factory named Yongli, constructed in Nanjing in 1933 and for a while the biggest in East Asia. Then it was destroyed by the Japanese war machine during its invasion of China. But in 1975, just one year before Mao Zedong died, a new national facility began production, symbolizing China's great leap forward into the agrochemical age. As communism began to break down the old land ownership patterns, it turned farmers into customers for chemical fertilizers. Eventually China was producing and consuming more of the miraculous man-made granules than any other nation on earth.[52] Today its factories turn out some fifty million metric tons a year, about half of the world's total. Those two numbers may be among the most important data for understanding recent world history.

Cheap mass production of man-made fertilizers began to revolutionize practices on even the smallest Chinese farms, allowing their owners to keep working the land for a few more years until their farms were worn out and ready to be sold to housing developers. The *National Geographic* writer Dan Charles tells the story of an elderly farmer near Nanjing who had worked the same 1.3-acre parcel his whole life. In pre-chemical days he would annually spread on his rice paddy some 130 pounds (60 kilograms) of nitrogen—all of it coming from natural sources. Manure-based farming, however, was hard work for an old man, as it required much stooping and ladling poop onto rice sprouts in a paddy. Then there was planting, harvesting, and threshing of the crop. Weary of so much labor, the old man decided to make his life easier by substituting a bag of urea for muck. He could buy manufactured urea in the form of pellets packed into large bags. It proved so easy and inexpensive, and so effective in results, that he soon escalated his purchases to 500 pounds (227 kilograms) of chemical fertilizer per year. Happily, his crop yields more than doubled. Never mind that most of the fertilizer he spread was wasted, running off into ditches, streams, and rivers or lakes before it could be taken up by plant roots. But what this aching, aging farmer saw and cared about was not the impact his fertilizer runoff was having on the water supply, but the bounteous crops he harvested from his paddy and the painful labor he avoided.[53]

Today many Chinese producers have become completely dependent on raising rice and other foods with chemical fertilizers. Whether they are farmers or city folk, whether they purchase food in supermarkets or raise it for their own consumption, they (and all of us) are in effect growing and eating laboratory chemicals. Astonishingly, some 80 percent of the nitrogen in Chinese bodies now comes from food containing traces of chemical fertilizers. What does that mean for human health? When does such a wholesale substitution become damaging?[54]

As fear and concern have spread about the health consequences of modern food and the industrial capitalist mode of production, China's corporate supermarkets, like those elsewhere, have begun to promote organically raised fruits and vegetables, which claim to be produced with little or no commercial fertilizers or pesticides. It remains to be seen whether a nation the size of China can be fed an all-organic diet, whether it must go back to recycling the good muck, or whether all of us are piling up health and environmental dangers as agricultural innovation continues.

Night soil has not completely disappeared from Chinese farms—here and there it is still part of food production. Around Tai Lake (*Taihu*) in the Yangzi Delta, a few farmers continue to store their bathroom wastes and use them on highly profitable crops. Large ceramic tanks or concrete pits are in plain view around their houses. A sluice may connect the bathroom to a storage tank, mixing animal with human manure and urine. But these days such demand for organic fertilizer is quite small. Where excreta are still used, it is almost exclusively to fertilize vegetables like Bok choy (Chinese cabbage).

The supermarket price for that organic produce is high, so perhaps we should not squander much pity on the old-fashioned vegetable farmer who is still ladling smelly stuff out of a bucket and spreading it over cabbage or broccoli. She or he may be making a better income than ever before. Among supermarket consumers it is a common view that vegetables grown with human excrement taste better than other kinds, and therefore they cost more.[55]

But in general, over a span of four decades, China's agriculture has shifted (though not completely) from using human muck to using industrial chemicals. There are strong economic and humanitarian reasons for promoting that shift. It has brought greater abundance for a larger population and a more nutritious, balanced diet for consumers. Not least, working the land has become physically easier than it was in the old days. Modern methods have allowed millions of surplus, exhausted farmers to abandon their fields and paddies and relocate to cities, many of them now raking through overflowing garbage bins outside restaurants and dining halls or, in a few ideal cases, teaching university courses about the history of agriculture.

Besides the steady decline in rural population, with its hidden toll on mental health, and besides the acceleration of economic inequality, China has gone through a host of environmental calamities resulting from chemical fertilizers, including the growing eutrophication of waterways. The new fertilizers leach from paddies and fields into lakes and rivers, causing algal blooms that deplete suspended oxygen and kill natural ecosystems. Along the China seacoast the chemical fertilizer industry has created a series of "dead zones," similar to those found at the mouth of every major river in the world—zones where toxic runoff accumulates in the sea, allowing almost nothing to live under new anaerobic conditions. These areas are fatal not only to marine species but also to the fishermen who depend on them.

Many decades ago, the western scientists Francis King and Albert Howard came to Asia seeking new ideas and inspiration from an ancient agrarian way of life. But since then, the effect of population pressures, recurrent famines, the economic imperatives of industrialization, urbanization, and Asia's own versions of capitalism, along with many new technologies, have wiped out the lessons in permanency that those western visitors once sought. Not completely so, for awareness of the multi-threats that body wastes or excessive chemical fertilizers can bring has spread across Asia and, by the twenty-first century, that awareness has begun to be articulated with sophistication and reason. But by the time Howard died in 1947, the writing was already on the wall. Even China, which for a long time stood fast as a holdout for traditional methods of maintaining soil fertility, would go through the modern transformation.

King and Howard valued tradition, for good reason. Traditions in farming and elsewhere can offer hard-won, much tested wisdom. With that rich treasury of experience, a lot of field-testing has already been done that cannot be replicated in a laboratory. Tradition can offer guidance on how to lower a harmful impact on society and the environment. In agriculture as elsewhere, we would do well to consider seriously how and whether the old way was or was not better than our way today.

Yet any tradition, no matter how wise or tested, can become a dead end, a trap from which there is no escape. It can lead to what we call social or biological involution. Instead of evolving, the agrarian way of life can become stagnant, turning in on itself, failing to adapt sufficiently to growing demand, and then it can fall apart abruptly. This seems to have happened in China. Fixed on following traditions, farmers failed to innovate or to restrain themselves and their progeny. Their communities found themselves in a downward spiral until they began to crumble into the soils they were exploiting. Tradition can carry seeds of destruction, especially when a preference for large families and high fertility continues unrelentingly, until the traditionalist is drowned in a violent whirlpool of upheaval and revolution.

For a long time, the use of human muck solved two problems: a dangerous pollutant for foragers was turned into a natural resource for farmers, and the latter used that resource to feed their ever growing populations. Mark one up for the agrarian way of life. But then the innovation lost its efficacy. China could not continue forever on that road. It could not support any further population growth on excrement alone. More than increased production was necessary. But because the farmers could not depart from tradition, they ended up farming on an endless production treadmill, suffering anxiety and degradation.

When tradition fails, science and technology may try to come to the rescue—or at least that is a common hope. With the aid of natural sciences like ecology, humans may discover how to recycle their wastes in new ways and continue turning them into golden treasure. We may learn how to raise our food with more sustainable perennials rather than annuals. Nonetheless, relying on modern science and technology is never without drawbacks. Every innovation, including the latest sewage treatment plant designed to meet the highest engineering standards, may experience operating difficulties and unwanted consequences. We can only press forward in hope, tempered by a realism about the usefulness of tradition.

The earth is a planet of limits as well as human desires. The limits are real, and they tell us not to turn up our noses at the odor of muck-covered fields and gardens. Don't run away from any stink or foulness. At the same time, don't idealize other ages, other people, or the earth or knowledge, as some have done, and don't idealize the traditional agriculture of a country like China or sentimentalize its poor overworked people, who have been forced by their own fecundity to make use of their body's wastes simply to survive year after year.

No people are so aware of their past humiliations as the Chinese. They know how difficult it can be to survive on this fertile planet. For them especially, and for all of us, utopias vanish when we stare down at our own excrement.

CHAPTER 7

The Empty Cradle of Hope

In the twentieth century the rule of industrial capitalism over the planet experienced many severe shocks, but somehow it survived, just as we humans have survived and spread. Warning signs have long indicated that industrial capitalism cannot last forever, that, like its predecessors, it is unsustainable. Extinction seemed imminent during the Great Depression in the 1930s, coinciding with fears of war and militarism spreading across the globe. Many countries, from the relatively new United States to the very old China, were rocked to their core. Yet capitalism survived, though it became more regulated and scrutinized, and it has continued to face skepticism about its future.

Since that time of world depression and war, we have added the specter of planetary destruction—anthropogenic climate change, Covid-like epidemics, ecospheric destabilization, increasing human migration and inequality, all traceable to the industrial capitalist way of life.

Surely at some point our relations with the earth will not only rise toward destruction but also shift toward caregiving. We should not be overly fearful about that shift. The earth has, for more than three billion years, gone through immense changes, yet the miracle of life has continued to flourish and need protection. When species become extinct, new ones find an opportunity. And when one great transformation has run its course, we can be sure that another will take its place.

One indicator of a major transformation would be any change in human reproduction—that's how it starts. In the past the prevailing pattern has been one of excessive births bringing pressure on food production, stimulating innovation in technology and values. Now, contrary to that pattern, it appears that population growth is reversing and a *shrinking* in human numbers has begun globally. If that pattern holds, we can expect profound but unpredictable consequences to follow for people and planet.

About two centuries ago, as we saw earlier, fertility rates among women started to decline. Many have loudly decried the trend, but no one has yet figured out how to stop it. Whether we like it or not, we should be prepared for a future characterized by much lower human numbers and, as a consequence, a future that rejects the ferocious pace of innovation and the dream of infinite wealth that have been so prominent under industrial capitalism, even its raison d'être.

All over the world, regardless of wealth or cultural values, women and men have recently become aware of this slowdown. We don't altogether know why it is happening; the mysteries of outer nature and inner nature continue to baffle us. We know only that fertility rates are going down and that a new era characterized by slower growth, smaller families, and increasing disinterest in marriage and procreation has arrived. More people are saying that sex is fine but having hordes of children is not.

One plausible explanation for the turnabout might be an increase in female education and a desire to be liberated from patriarchy. But there are other possible factors, including the sheer pressure of so many other people around us, competing for resources. There are now eight billion of us, with a few more billion coming before the numbers start going down appreciably. Whatever explains this turnabout, we are seeing that the old human propensity to reproduce is now becoming something new.

As late as the 1930s and the Great Depression, procreation was still a strong human motivation. Take the Chicago poet Carl Sandburg, for example. In 1936 he published his epic poem *The People, Yes.*[1] As long as a book, the poem suggested that the Great Depression would end when ordinary people recovered their self-confidence and began reproducing again. For a short time that is indeed what seemed to be happening; women began having lots of babies again. But that brief baby boom did not last.

The people, in Sandburg's eyes, were supposed to be just like the rest of nature—programmed to be highly fertile. The poet took for granted that no form of life could cease being fruitful and multiplying. In the last words of his poem, Sandburg found hope in a return to fertility: "The people take the earth / As a tomb of rest and a cradle of hope."[2] Death, he was saying, was part of nature, but so also was birth, and with a return to birthing we need not worry. More babies would mark a recovery and should be encouraged and celebrated.

Sandburg was right about the people's capacity for recovering from hardship, but he failed to grasp that reproduction might change. He was unaware that the people had decided that childbearing was not always good for them or the planet. The fertility rate kept falling after the Depression into the twenty-first century. Far from wanting more babies to fill their cradles, women and men were happy with fewer. Sandburg should have asked ordinary people what they wanted. He might have been shocked to hear their answers.

At first, fertility rates in the most advanced industrial economies seemed to be in step with the stock market and employment. But the relationship was temporary: markets had been cycling up and down for more than a hundred years, but not fertility or family size.[3] Well before the Great Depression, the average fertility rate of women had begun sliding downward. In 1800 it stood at 7.0 children per woman during her reproductive years, reflecting the patterns of an agrarian way of life. It continued down to 2.0 children in 1940. In the 1950s, anomalously, there was a short-lived "baby boom" that confused the signals. Then that boom fizzled, and fertility rates resumed falling, slowly but persistently.[4] Similar declines could be found all over the world, regardless of affluence, ideology, or culture.

Carl Sandburg himself should have realized that cradles would be emptier in the future. His wife gave birth to three children, not the seven that had been the norm in 1800. Those three Sandburg babies would grow up to produce only a single baby among them. Shrinkage was the future of the Sandburg line as it was for the nation and the world. Families began packing away their cradles as their reproduction waned. Wives, if not always their husbands, continued to feel that high fertility was *not* the way to happiness, fulfillment, prosperity, or security. That was the hope in agrarian days, but under industrial capitalism it was not.

Fertility in the United States and almost all other nations have continued to fall right down to the present. Yet for several decades *populations* went on increasing, and the doubling time for human numbers got shorter and shorter. But that phenomenon was due largely to decreasing mortality, especially among the elderly and children, and to the large number of women of childbearing age.

Long before the time of humans, whenever the earth seemed to expand with new opportunities—across Africa and Eurasia, up and down the Americas—people had modified their fertility. The modifications took centuries to unfold. So it should not have been surprising that fertility began to shrink as people experienced not an enlarging but a crowded planet, even a crowded new world. No person needed to be told by others to change. This time no amount of discovery or innovation seemed to make any difference.

In earlier centuries, as populations increased, people first tried innovations that commonly required more intensive use and management of the earth. *Sapiens* spread out to new environments or found new ways to exploit resources. But after the discovery of Second Earth and despite industrial capitalism's innovations in transportation and manufacturing, fertility rates did not go even higher. Within three hundred years of the Great Discoveries, fertility rates had fallen to replacement level.

A key reason for that extraordinary decline was the modernization of birth control, which began in the first half of the nineteenth century. It happened as women assumed control over their bodies, which in turn happened as they found themselves in more crowded environments. Overall, industrial capitalism may have increased the wealth of nations, but that wealth did not lead to more pregnancies.

At the same time as birth control came the modern environmental conservation movement, as people felt nature's limits closing in. The history of that movement has been well told for North America, but it has other beginnings around the world. The historian Richard Grove, for example, has argued that conservation was a consequence of the British Empire's encounter with environmental limits, when some imperial agents found themselves in new but highly vulnerable lands, especially oceanic islands. They acquired a sense of limits that spread across the United States too, starting with New England naturalists such as Henry David Thoreau and George Perkins Marsh, who in the first half of the nineteenth century began calling for the protection of American minerals, water, forests, and wilderness. That reaction continued into the late nineteenth century and all the way down to the first Earth Day in 1970, when the planet seemed suddenly to be shrinking rapidly in carrying capacity.[5]

Some culture-focused scholars may insist that both movements occurred simply because of the ideas being published by social or environmental reformers, but that would be too simple an explanation. Although ideas, books, and manifestos were important counters in the struggles against both patriarchy and ecological destruction, books were not the only determinants. The human body, male or female, had a role to play too, deeper than ideas or books. Ordinary people, then as now, did not have to rely on some writer to tell them how to think and behave. Their inner nature was doing that.

Common sense told women and men that they could not continue expanding their numbers infinitely on a finite earth. Nature's fertility could not support an infinitude of human bellies without endangering the intricate web of life that supports us. As those facts became more intensely felt, owing little to the likes of Thomas Malthus, human desires changed and so also did human behavior.

This much seems clear: about two hundred years ago, as human numbers reached one billion worldwide (demographers calculate that happened in 1804 CE), fertility began to change. Despite the promise of Second Earth, some began to feel more crowded than ever in the places where they lived.[6] One response was that women started to exercise more control over their fertility. What they lacked, however, was reliable knowledge about their bodies, reproduction, and fertility, knowledge that they began seeking from doctors and scientists who listened and offered help.[7]

We can see this pattern in the Berkshire Hills of western Massachusetts, where in the late eighteenth and early nineteenth centuries, a once heavily forested land had been extensively cleared by farmers. By 1850 most of the state's rivers had been harnessed to generate waterpower for textile mills producing cheap cotton clothing.[8] Wild though the Berkshires still could be, in this place remote from Boston, lacking much affluence or higher institutions of learning, reproduction took a new turn.

The Berkshires were a microcosm of shrinking desires that would characterize much of North America and other parts of Second Earth over the next century or two. As agriculture expanded to raise more food, as the possibilities for further expansion in the Berkshires decreased, the children of farmers were forced to migrate into upper New England, New York, Ohio, and farther west, reaching the Great Plains after the Civil War and then running hard against an arid West. In a matter of decades, what had been a wide-open continent seemed settled, and then the residents began to talk of achieving sustainability, permanence, and fewer offspring.

Living in the Berkshires at that time was a medical doctor, Charles Knowlton (1800–1850), a contemporary of Thoreau in Concord and Emily Dickinson in Amherst, Massachusetts. Knowlton's female patients began asking him for advice about birth control. We know little about the doctor or his patients, except that women complained to him about their unwanted pregnancies.[9] Tired of giving birth so often, they feared that excessive childbearing was damaging their health and hurting their family's prospects. They were not the only women in the world who were seeking help, but fortunately they had in their doctor a sympathetic, knowledgeable listener who gave them the information they sought.

In 1829 Knowlton published a small guide to birth control, *The Fruits of Philosophy: The Private Companion of Young Married People by a Physician*. Selling for twenty-five cents, it was the first popularly written manual in the English language for couples seeking to prevent conception. *The Fruits of Philosophy* appeared just two years after a biologist in Estonia, by using a microscope, discovered that female bodies produce eggs.[10] He was the first person ever to establish such a basic and vital fact. More research into how females reproduce followed, revealing that women like men are indeed organisms, producing eggs as mammals do, and those eggs need male sperm to produce embryos.

A new science of reproductive biology began taking form to help people understand and control their fertility. Of course, it had many opponents. By writing his little book, Knowlton was challenging long-established doctrine emanating from the many churches in his region.[11] Massachusetts had outlawed contraception as an interference with God's mandate for the world. Knowlton, a free thinker in religion, accepted that women have natural sexual desires and agreed to help them prevent what were becoming unacceptable consequences.

Even though it was locally denounced as a "dirty" and "filthy" book, Knowlton's little guide found an audience in far-off London. Published there in 1833, it ended up selling more than forty thousand copies. In 1877 a second British edition came out, in which for the first time the name Thomas Robert Malthus appeared in the book—and it did so in a very positive light. Malthus's much disputed warnings about too many children had first appeared in 1798, at the peak of the British population boom, and had gone through six editions by 1826.

Knowlton's British editors, Charles Bradlaugh and Annie Besant, were liberal reformers who felt some concern about overpopulation, although they did not blame the working class, as Malthus did, for increasing the nation's poverty.[12] The two editors added these prefatory words to Knowlton's text:

> We believe, with the Rev. Mr. Malthus, that population has a tendency to increase faster than the means of existence, and that some checks must therefore exercise control over population. The checks now exercised are semi-starvation and preventable disease; the enormous mortality among the infants of the poor is one of the checks which now keep down the population. The checks that ought to control population are scientific, and it is these we advocate. We think it more moral to prevent the conception of children than, after they are born, to murder them by want of food, air, and clothing. We advocate scientific checks to population, because so long as poor men have large families, pauperism is a necessity, and from pauperism grow crime and disease. The wages which would support the parents and two or three children in comfort is [sic] utterly insufficient to maintain a family of twelve or fourteen, and we consider it a crime to bring into the world human beings doomed to misery or to premature death. It is not only the hard-working classes which are concerned in this question. The poor preacher, the struggling man of business, the young professional man, are often made wretched for life by their inordinately large families, and their years are passed in one long battle to live; meanwhile the woman's health is sacrificed, and her life embittered from the same cause.[13]

Malthus was often criticized, and rightly so, for his failure to see that land could produce more food, but Bradlaugh and Besant argued that merely growing more food was not a solution. What was needed was helping women control their fertility. Pronatalist views had to be challenged and replaced by a more factual, open-minded, pragmatic, and scientific attitude.

Consider the book's prefatory words: "We advocate scientific checks to population." They point to a turning point in human history, as important as the agrarian separation of humans from other species or taking possession of Second Earth. Human urges, the editors were saying, should not go unquestioned; rather, women and men should be less restrained in their sexuality. A new freedom to control oneself—here was a powerful desire that now looked to science for support.

Back in the United States, another change was brewing that would likewise affect the status of women everywhere. It began with Susan B. Anthony, the leader of a national movement to secure women's political and economic rights. Anthony lived only a few hundred miles west of Knowlton and his patients, but she seemed less interested than they in challenging the fixity of women's nature or in restraining the number of babies. Born in the Berkshires in 1829, Anthony had grown up in New York state, the daughter of a man who once owned a farm in Massachusetts but left it to run a textile mill, which she rightly connected to the enslavement of African Americans on Southern cotton plantations. Fearlessly, she began to agitate for black slaves' freedom and women's rights as linked social issues.[14]

In 1848, when Anthony was not yet twenty years old, she inspired the world's first women's rights convention, held in Seneca Falls, New York. From that gathering emerged a coalition to secure the freedom of slaves, industrial workers, and women of all races and classes. By the 1860s Anthony and her followers had added the goal of acquiring voting rights for women, although it took until 1920 for women's voting rights to be established in American national elections, almost half a century after the abolition of slavery. Following those victories, the feminist movement entered a post-Anthony, post-suffragette phase that included the sexual liberation of women through birth control.

Thus, the movements for birth control and other women's rights grew in the same seedbed but had different roots. For Knowlton's patients, the most pressing need was to avoid unwanted babies. They sought to control their reproductive nature and were less vocal than Anthony about challenging patriarchy. The contemporaneous women's movement, in contrast, emphasized freedom from patriarchy and human slavery, but decades later it added freedom to practice birth control and seek an abortion.[15]

"Civilized life [had been] one continued battle against nature," writes Sripati Chandrasekhar, a demographer of India and historian of Knowlton and his work. The battle to which he refers began long before Susan Anthony began organizing for change. The women addressed in Knowlton's book preferred to seek a new fit for their nature in the face of new circumstances. In the words of Chandrasekhar, they would try to "prevent overpopulation; mitigate the evil of prostitution by making early marriage possible; reduce poverty, ignorance, and crime; help prevent hereditary diseases, and preserve and improve the species; reduce the number of artificial abortions and diminish infanticide; and prevent the ill-health caused to women by excessive childbearing or habitual abortion."[16]

Chandrasekhar writes that the advent of modern birth control depended on a "democratization" of knowledge. Perhaps so, but the change started with material and behavioral changes. Female fertility rates dropped from 3.6 babies in the early nineteenth century to fewer than 2.0 babies (the replacement fertility rate is 2.1 children per couple) by 2000 CE. The decline brought new hope for fully half the human species, even though its significance was long ignored and little noted by what have been predominately male experts.[17]

Control over reproduction was, in short, a private, practical response to a changing environment. For a long time in western society, people had taken fertility for granted, regarding it as God-decreed and seldom questioning its impact on society or the land. But then such thinking gave way, and new attitudes and behavior began to spread that would one day have planetary consequences.

After 1800, opposition to birth control began to soften, first in the United States and Europe, later in Asia and the Middle East, and finally in Africa. New knowledge helped by setting people free from culturally imposed roles. Knowledge helped people adapt and change. By gaining self-control over reproduction, women sought freedom from old desires and the beginnings of new ones, including a desire for freedom, prosperity, health, and a sustainable environment.

In 1877, Knowlton's book and its British editors were put on trial in London for violating Christian morality. "Not guilty" was the court decision. An equally surprising outcome was that the book boomed in sales and inspired many competing guides. In the second half of the twentieth century, the dissemination of contraceptives and birth control information went on almost everywhere, leading to the decriminalization of birth control practices and an even greater demand for scientific help. Conquering the biology of human conception and self-limiting of family size won nearly universal approval, becoming a desire articulated in every country on earth, rich or poor, Muslim, Confucian, or Christian.[18]

Which of the available contraceptives worked best? The most popular methods in the early nineteenth century were all ancient in origin, crude in design, and not very reliable. Charles Knowlton recommended only two of them, each aimed at preventing male sperm from entering a woman's fallopian tubes and fertilizing an egg. He advised women to insert a small sponge moistened with water, which was supposed to block a man's sperm, or to kill the sperm using a syringe filled with sulfate of zinc. The doctor recommended either method over such primitive solutions as cervical caps made of lemons and diaphragms cut out of silk or the practice of coitus interruptus, abortion, or infanticide, all of which dated back to the time of hunters and gatherers. More and better contraceptives would be developed, he promised, through scientific research.[19] To establish a right to practice contraception, however, would require more than knowledge. Birth control must be formally supported in the legal code. That too happened as the demand for control became louder, but it took more than a century.

From Knowlton's day on, a change began in the two natures, inner and outer, each flowing strongly until they merged and became a powerful torrent. The most controversial of the new currents was the "eugenics" movement, which emerged in the late nineteenth and early twentieth centuries. It was an old idea given a new name by the British scientist Francis Galton, who believed that the right of reproduction should be allowed only to the mentally and physically fit. The right to bear children should not be granted to everyone. If the species was to improve biologically, he argued, the state must decide who was permitted to reproduce and who was not.

Galton's views derived from "artificial selection," which Galton's cousin Charles Darwin had identified as a special kind of evolution practiced by farmers and breeders. Out of this hallowed practice had come the agrarian conquest of nature. Hardly anyone had ever objected to that conquest when the aim was to breed better dogs, horses, roses, or wheat, for such interference was considered necessary to satisfy human wants. Similarly, people had not objected when marriages were arranged by parents, for that kind of control over the young was supposed to lead to better grandchildren. But Galton's proposal to make government the breeder-in-chief ran into fierce resistance from both liberals and conservatives. Clearly, it would mean giving the state a lot of power. Governments might decide to go beyond deciding who was "fit" or "unfit" and try to force sterilization on women or men, an idea that proved quite unpopular. By the 1940s the eugenics movement had become discredited and had nearly dried up in European circles, where it had become further tainted by "racial purification" doctrines preached by the Nazis. Decisions over reproduction, it was commonly held, should be left to women and the men they selected as their mates.[20]

Another branch of the intricately braided stream leading to birth control was the international pacifist movement, which appeared in the early twentieth century as the scale of modern warfare increased. Some began to argue that war had become outmoded or that it was getting too violent because of overpopulation and mounting competition for natural resources.

Some began to argue that peace was best pursued by having fewer children. The first World Population Conference (WPC) was held in Geneva, Switzerland, in 1927, and in that same year demographers announced the planet was now home to two billion people, the number having doubled since 1804. After that, the WPC became a meeting ground for biologists, food experts, and others who looked to science to deal with overpopulation.

Humans, according to one of the WPC's most prominent leaders, the American biogerontologist Raymond Pearl, resemble bacteria reproducing in a petri dish—too many organisms fighting for room, seeking to expand their food supplies through aggression. The WPC, however, proved to be another ignored elite group and never attracted many followers.[21]

A third contributing stream was an expanding women's movement. Women protested more and more fiercely against patriarchy, which they saw as arrayed against them on many levels. Although some men supported that movement along with birth control, most men had been, for many centuries, trying to restrain female freedom, not enlarge it. Now as their own wives and daughters demanded birth control as a human right, men feared that they might be losing all control over female bodies.

Active in all three streams was one of the most effective advocates for birth control in modern times, Margaret Sanger (1879–1966), who like Susan B. Anthony hailed from upstate New York. Unlike her predecessor, who was unmarried and childless, Sanger married three times and had three children.[22] She became a powerful opponent of all restrictions imposed on women's sexuality; she wanted them removed not only in the United States but across the earth. During the 1920s, Sanger journeyed to Asia where she concluded that "the only method of family limitation known to the poor Chinese [is] infanticide of girl babies by suffocation or drowning."[23] That was oversimplifying, but she was right that women in China faced heavy restrictions on their nature. Back home, Sanger became the chief organizer of the WPC in 1927 and of a health clinic in New York City that offered birthing advice to women of all classes and races.

Seeking to persuade both elite and common people, Sanger recruited a wealthy friend, Katharine McCormick (1875–1967), one of the first female graduates of the Massachusetts Institute of Technology. McCormick had become rich through marriage, inheriting a fortune from a family that manufactured agricultural machinery, a fortune she used to fund Sanger's crusade. Together, the two women decided to find and fund scientists and capitalists who seemed ready to see women freed from their shackles.[24]

The modern birth control movement had diverse streams of thought, pioneers, heroes, and promoters, but Sanger and McCormick were the most prominent and practical. Both would be widely ignored by men, including male academics and intellectuals who failed to acknowledge the vital interest among women in managing their own fertility. All the same, the two leaders showed that women could become a powerful social and cultural force, able to influence and even change the nature of human desire.

By the 1950s Sanger and McCormick at last found what they were looking for—a team of scientists, doctors, and businessmen who were willing to help them develop a practical, effective contraceptive. All of them were men intent on bringing science and capital to women's aid. Two of the most important were Dr. Gregory Pincus and Dr. Min Chueh Chang (or Zhang Mingjue), both specialists in mammalian reproduction. Pincus, nicknamed Goody, was the son of Jewish immigrants from the Ukrainian port city of Odessa, who had settled in New Jersey. Goody Pincus had earned a Ph.D. in biology at Harvard University and had worked for that institution for several years until he was dismissed because of fears he was playing God by stirring up interest in *in vitro* fertilization. Boasting that he could create life in a test tube, Pincus seemed to some the incarnation of Dr. Frankenstein, a dangerous meddler in the secrets of life. The dark circles around his eyes and his wild bushy hair gave him the look of a mad scientist, but in fact he was a benevolent pioneer in reproductive science who was convinced that effective birth control was possible and necessary.[25]

Working quietly with Pincus was Dr. Chang, who avoided controversy by focusing mainly on reproduction among laboratory rats and rabbits. He had been born in a small, impoverished village in the loess region of Shanxi province in China, not far from Taiyuan; he studied biology at Tsinghua University, the University of Edinburgh, and the University of Cambridge—a remarkable example of an internationally mobile, self-made man. After settling in the United States, he too became a leading researcher in human reproduction, focusing mainly on the critical role of newly discovered hormones in the animal body.

Joining their research team was Dr. John Rock, a well-spoken gynecologist who like the others was active in reproductive science. Rock was director of Boston's Free Hospital for Women and, despite being a Roman Catholic, he held liberal views about women's sexuality. He defended Pincus and Chang's work against the fulminations of the Catholic Church, which remained implacably opposed to birth control as an interference with the Genesis mandate. The Church would accept only sexual abstinence or the rhythm method as "natural" methods of birth control.[26]

In 1944 the two women and the three men joined forces at the Worcester (Massachusetts) Foundation for Experimental Biology. They sought a better way of preventing unwanted pregnancies, which they were convinced would come through mimicking the natural hormones that regulate the body. Hormones are a big part of human nature—complex chemicals produced by internal glands, evolving over time, and moving through the blood stream to regulate desires, including those for food and reproduction. Hormones tell the body how to function—when to start and stop the menses cycle, for example, or when to ovulate.[27] The challenge for the Worcester scientists was to determine how to use those natural chemicals to stop ovulation without endangering women's health.

Progesterone was the most important hormone they investigated. Once an egg has been fertilized, progesterone shuts down any competition in the womb, allowing a single fertilized egg to develop into an embryo. To become practical for birth control, the chemical had to be synthesized and sold in pharmacies. The synthesized version was called "progestin," a chemical developed from wild yams.[28] Progestin was then combined with another female hormone, estrogen, to manage human reproduction.

Progestin was synthesized in 1951 by Carl Djerassi, another scientific immigrant from Europe, in a Mexico City laboratory.[29] But a more useful synthetic hormone was developed by Pincus, Chang, and Rock, who then licensed the G. D. Searle company of Skokie, Illinois, to mass-produce and distribute it under the trade name Enovid (popularly known as "the Pill") in 1960. Little capital, it must be said, came from Searle; the biggest investor was Katherine McCormick, who put up nearly $20 million of her private wealth, as American corporate investors proved skittish about funding birth control research and development.

Pincus and team were required by federal law to prove their pill was safe, although the safety standards at the time were rather low. They carried out tests on some two hundred women in Puerto Rico and then added more tests in Australia, Britain, Ceylon, Haiti, Hong Kong, Japan, and the United States. A drug that could change women's reproduction was bound to become controversial, especially in a time of such controversial technologies as the atomic bomb and DDT; however, neither Enovid's supporters nor its critics paid attention to those other technologies. The Protestant and Catholic churches also tended to overlook those other interventions into nature, but they did not overlook the birth control pill, which, they argued, represented disobedience and defiance of God. But the Food and Drug Administration, after doing its own testing, approved the new contraceptive in 1961, launching modern birth control and the sexual revolution.

There remained only the imposing obstacle of the laws of the land. In 1965, by a vote of 7–2 in *Griswold v. Connecticut,* the U.S. Supreme Court struck down a Connecticut law that prohibited birth control. The Court declared that the old law violated a couple's right to privacy. After that, the pill could be purchased by any woman, married or not, for whatever use she wanted, though each container of Enovid included a warning list of possible side effects.

Criticism of the pill continued throughout the 1960s and 1970s, some of it coming from radical feminists who argued that the control of fertility constituted another male assault on women. Some warned that the pill was dangerous to women's health. The critics, however, did not include the most influential feminist of all, Betty Friedan, author of *The Feminine Mystique* (1963). Friedan blamed the high number of youthful brides and large families in the United States on the "problem that has no name." Women, she said, felt discouraged from pursuing "unfeminine" careers, college degrees, or political positions; they married early, stayed home, and got pregnant. Oddly, Friedan said nothing about the pill, which had been released just three years before her book, or about its promise for women's liberation.[30]

In contrast, another leading feminist, the Australian writer Germaine Greer, was emphatically opposed to birth control, charging in her book *The Female Eunuch* (1970) that "the devisers of the pill worried so little about the female psyche that it was years before they discovered that one woman in three who was on the pill was chronically depressed." The claim that the pill led to mental depression turned out to be bogus, although a small number of women did sicken and even die before the high level of estrogen in the early mix was reduced to a safer level.[31]

Still other feminists charged that birth control was part of a male conspiracy to control and enslave women. One of them, a radical activist from the Science for the People alliance, seeking to defend women against patriarchy, denounced birth control as the tool of "the whole power-penis-potency complex." In that critic's view the "PPP complex" had falsely hyped the pill as a "great new wonder drug."[32] Somehow forgotten in the mêlée in the United States was the important fact that it was women who originally called for the drug and provided funding for its development. Another controversial innovation in those years was the ill-fated Dalkon shield, an intrauterine device created in a scientific lab, and this one truly did injure many people and had little backing from women.[33]

The birth control and sexual revolution is now more than a half century old, and its long-term effects are still not fully known. It is clear, however, that the results of the scientific turn in birth control have been more significant, sweeping, and popular than anyone, even the most radical feminists, expected. "The Pill" altered the personal lives of women and their relations to men, but also it altered nations, ecosystems, and the state of the earth. This iconic symbol of human contraception may even have been the first step toward a third great transformation, to a sustainable way of life.

After approval from the Food and Drug Administration and the U.S. Supreme Court, the pill and similar contraceptives came into daily use by more than 6 million American women. By 2019, oral contraceptives were being taken worldwide by 151 million. Another 74 million were injecting synthetic hormones into their veins, a riskier practice popular in Asia. Those various means of reproductive control encouraged other innovations, including mass-produced male condoms. (There is no *male* contraceptive pill, however, as men have proved far less ready to tolerate restraints on their bodies.) In Asia, female and male sterilization became common, although sterilization was not always freely chosen but sometimes was imposed on people, especially on women, by the state. In all, one billion women would begin practicing some form of birth control, nine out of ten of them using modern, scientific methods.

Contraceptive use has been lowest in Africa, only half as common as in Europe, Latin America, or the Caribbean, but even Africa saw rapid adoption. In North America 70 percent of women and girls in their fertile years began practicing some form of birth control. In planetary terms, the birth control pill has become the most important technology of our time, and its impact, though often taken for granted, has shown no signs of slowing.[34]

The reason for such rapid, overwhelming acceptance of the pill was simply that it was easy to use, not very expensive, and yet effective in results.[35] Because it put control in the hands of women, it proved liberating. It gave women more self-control over their bodies than ever before, and that control brought major gains in family planning. Women secured more freedom to go to school and college, to study for the professions, to get hired for what traditionally had been male jobs, to run for political office, to serve in the military, to earn an income, and to become something other than baby producers.

As for problems like global warming or biodiversity loss, the results have been more positive than many environmentalists realized, for there are fewer people polluting and consuming the earth. According to one estimate, more than one third of global warming has been caused by population increase, so a decline in fertility would over time diminish that threat significantly.[36] We can be sure that, as female fertility declines, other forms of pollution and fossil fuel consumption will also be lessened, helping the planet's atmosphere and oceans recover from their dangerous levels. Polar bears, lemurs, tigers, and coral reefs will no longer be so endangered and will even find a reprieve from their march to extinction. As for humans, the pill's effects might become as big and important as the discovery of Second Earth.

Remember that at the end of the foraging era, the human population stood between 5 million and 15 million. By 1960, when Enovid began to be marketed, the world total had soared to 3 billion. By 1999 it reached 6 billion and kept climbing. According to the Worldometer's Population Clock, here is where we stand now: there are 8.2 billion humans in all. Since humans first emerged, there have been 117 billion of us born. The most populous nation is now India at 1.44 billion, followed closely by China at 1.43 billion. Then come the United States at 345 million and Indonesia at 280 million, followed by Pakistan, Nigeria, Brazil, Bangladesh, Russia, Mexico, Ethiopia, Japan, the Philippines, Egypt, and the Democratic Republic of the Congo, each of them counting more than 100 million inhabitants, while Vietnam is growing so fast it will soon enter their circle.[37]

How has it been possible for humans to add so many billions while fertility rates have been going down? This is a confusing picture that might seem contradictory. As late as 2023, the annual population increase was about 75 million.[38] As noted before, this was due to improvements in health conditions, which allowed more babies to survive infancy, more seniors to live longer, and more women to grow up and become sexually active. The age pyramid explains the apparent contradiction. Population increase and fertility decline have been yoked. At some point, however, as the difference between fertility and population disappears, there will be fewer and fewer of us on every continent.

But the largest nations in this year's population rankings may not be ranked so high tomorrow. Projections say that in a few years Nigeria will replace the United States as the third most populated country, and other African nations will also move into the higher ranks. Africans will continue for several decades to have lots of babies. In contrast, some of the lowest fertility rates in the world will be found in the West, creating an unprecedented kind of gap between those with wealth and global influence and those without. The very lowest nations in fertility have become some of the most prosperous: for example, South Korea, Japan, China, and Singapore. Korea's fertility has now fallen to .07, a mere third of the replacement level, the lowest in the world. The People's Republic of China has a low current birthrate too—less than one child per family. Because of that low rate China fears losing influence and status in a world where "more" of everything is often admired and "fewer" is regarded as a curse.

Average population density worldwide has reached sixty people per square kilometer. One person is added on average to every square kilometer per year, though most of the increase is concentrated in less developed countries. More crowding and more density may, however, slow reproduction further. Right now Africa, the poorest continent of all and the most densely settled, is showing higher fertility rates than average. In fact, the African fertility rate has been dropping far more quickly than most experts expected. Already in Ghana, Kenya, and Libya, there are fewer than four children per woman and in South Africa, Mauritius, and Tunisia, there are fewer than two.[39] Africa will likely cut its fertility rates much more quickly than anyone expects, freeing women from heavy burdens and demonstrating that even the poorest people can change quickly when they are supported and enabled.

Much of the world's increase in fertility is occurring in just eight African countries, among them Niger, which now has the highest fertility rate in the world—6.82 children per woman on average, suggesting a society that is still caught in the agrarian way of life. Yet Ghana, Kenya, and Libya now produce fewer than four children per woman, while in the Republic of South Africa, Mauritius, and Tunisia there are fewer than two.[40] It seems possible that all African countries will soon lower their fertility rates further, demonstrating that a rich economy and full pockets, the usual determinants according to economists, are not required to slow fertility.

Recent forecasts of falling population levels do not suggest that there will come a sudden catastrophic collapse within this century. Overall numbers will keep on increasing for a while, until we reach a peak of some 9 billion to 12 billion worldwide. The highly trusted United Nations Population Division says that the world may peak at 10.4 billion by the mid-2080s. After that, the predictors say, the overall numbers will start going down, whether gradually or quickly—perhaps going down as fast as they have gone up. How far the numbers will fall, no one can say for sure.[41]

To grasp what our planet may look like over the next century or two, one must begin by admitting that just about anything is possible. This is the message coming from demographers like Wolfgang Lutz and his colleagues at Vienna's International Institute for Applied Systems, who have tried to project what the human population might be as far off as 2100 or 2200 CE. They assume that human fertility will continue falling through the rest of this century and into the next, perhaps falling for several hundred years. In the *Journal of the Royal Statistical Society,* they made this spacious estimate: a future population of between 2 billion and 6 billion.

We face a wide spectrum of possible outcomes, but all of them would be lower than today's numbers. Would that be so bad? Six billion was the number of humans living on earth as late as 1999. Two billion was the level back in 1927, less than a century ago. Was life so hideous at those levels? One might call such loose estimates cautiously realistic—observant of current trends, open to unanticipated events, and assuming that humans will manage to adjust smoothly on the way down as well as on the way up.

The Vienna demographers have chosen Shanghai, China, as the key city to watch, with perhaps twenty-five million inhabitants. In 1979, women there had an average of 2.1 children during their fertile years. (More on China's birth policies will appear in the next chapter.) At that point, the city's fertility had dipped below replacement level. If that level holds, Shanghai will grow smaller and smaller, and the dense crowds that go strolling nightly along the Bund, watching the extravagant neon displays along the Huangpu River, will become thinner and thinner and so will the number of automobiles jamming the streets. The overheated real estate market will cool off. If a massive city like Shanghai is heading for such change, other cities will follow. It is even possible that the global pattern of red-hot urbanization might reverse direction, retreating to what it was in 1980—or 1950 or 1900 or 1800.

What happens in cities can also happen in nations and across the planet. The total human population might drop as low as 1.0–1.5 billion, a level not seen since 1800 when the modern fertility decline began. If current trends persist for the next two centuries, our modern way of life, which has been based on constant growth in everything, will surely be shaken to its roots and we will experience a sweeping revolution in values and the social order.

Some experts, who have gotten used to populations that only increase, are finding these downward trends threatening. They warn that humans are heading in the wrong direction and need to get back to producing more children and believing in such goals as economic growth, rapid innovation, and an expanding welfare state.[42] Seniors may soon make up a quarter of the world's population, all of them wanting a secure, comfortable retirement with access to health care. Economists warn that there may not be enough young people to support with tax revenues all those seniors. The young who must pay for senior benefits like low bus fares or free health care may complain that such burdens are unfair. The outcome will be more social conflict, pitting the young and healthy against the sick and elderly.

Yet more and more the industrial capitalist way of life seems like a Ponzi scheme, taking money from a few initial investors and paying them high dividends by stealing from a horde of new investors. Must we keep on reproducing more of our kind merely because it is the only way we have so far imagined for supporting the old? Surely, if nations could reinvent themselves as welfare states, they can find new ways of raising revenue. Surely it is not beyond our capacity to adapt to big changes in demography. We may see shocks and adjustments ahead, but future decades will find ways to cope.

Not so long ago an age-distribution diagram for most countries looked like an Egyptian pyramid, with large numbers of young at the bottom while small numbers of old people made a pyramid at the top with a very narrow peak. Now the pyramid is looking more like an older man with a bulging stomach. Instead of being pyramidal, young and old groups are growing thicker all the way up the pyramid, making a society shaped like a square block.

Policy makers exaggerate the problem posed by having fewer young workers to support retirees. Governments complain that they will have to come up with new ideas about taxes and income redistribution, but they should consider there may be benefits to reap. A larger senior cohort might mean quieter, less violent communities with diminished crime, fewer drugs, and more wisdom. Swollen military budgets might be slashed, for international conflicts over natural resources might become less common. All nations might look more like Denmark or Japan, where populations have been aging rapidly for a long while but the old are still getting their needs satisfied. And then governments and companies might fill the needs with more robots and immigrants for the workforce.

There will be, for many decades yet, people looking to move to find better job prospects. A country like China could respond by opening its doors to its poorer neighbors, letting in millions of young immigrant workers from South Asia and other regions. In the past, millions have left what they experienced as an overcrowded China to find work elsewhere; now why not allow the world's poor to migrate into China? It could relieve the economic problems of that country, bring in new talent and energy, and keep tax revenues high. As its numbers drop, China could erect its own Statue of Liberty and encourage newcomers to enter and take important jobs. China and Japan could become more multicultural societies.

Societies with an ethnically homogeneous citizenry and few young workers risk becoming less innovative and more traditional if they don't adapt and change. In the West, for several centuries now, taking risks to gain wealth has encouraged a migrant, competitive, individualistic ethos. If a future China or Japan finds itself with fewer capitalists, inventors, or patent applicants, then they might follow the pattern of the United States or Canada.

Alternatively, people could begin to buy less stuff. As cradles get emptier, as the earth and its people get older, citizens may turn away from shopping. Malls may close their doors or be turned into senior health centers where the old get their daily exercise by strolling along empty corridors. In a future with dropping populations fewer kids will need schools, colleges, universities, or vocational training centers, and teachers will be happy to see smaller classrooms. Social needs and policies are bound to alter over time, as they always have.[43]

Perhaps a declining population will even prompt humankind to reassess its place on earth and question its role as masters and conquerors of life. We may all tend to see ourselves, as foragers do, as one form of life among many. The environmental consequences, if that happens, could be quite astonishing, and such a change would not be bad for the planet. Great stretches of continents and seas might revert to wildness. The Green Revolution in agriculture, which involves forcing more and more food out of the soil, might be declared over. Fish stocks might be less intensely exploited and begin to recover. Many other species and ecosystems might rebound, with savannahs given back to the elephants and northern islands to seals and polar bears. Already in Europe, as populations have begun to shrink, a wilder nature has begun returning. In Italy and Switzerland, for example, wolves are returning to the mountains, just as deer, puma, and coyotes are repopulating North America. Someday we may have no trouble meeting the goal sought by some conservationists of allowing at least a half of the earth to revert to other species.[44]

The consumption of all natural resources in future decades will surely be lower than now, including fossil fuel consumption, with positive implications for the planet's atmosphere. Economies could shrink, and industrialization could slow its pace or become easier to sustain. A hundred years from now, humanity might be asking not what additional lands or natural resources must be found or how capitalism can be saved but whether humans can find contentment where they once faced disappointment.

We cannot predict what people will want or value fifty years from now, let alone one or two hundred years, but we can suppose that our ancestors felt similar anxiety as they shifted from farming to seagoing. They had no choice but to change without knowing what kind of future they were creating, and so might we. So might all species. Life has not finished adapting and evolving.

If we have learned anything important from the recent past, it is how changeable not only human ideas and philosophies but also human nature can be. The future may see a very different human nature—with new desires and appetites, new sexuality, new gender identities and roles. Women have long been demanding more autonomy from men, starting with more freedom to determine when and how they will bear children. As women gain more power over such matters, there will be unprecedented ramifications for men, children, and the earth.

This is why the modern turn to birth control should be so interesting to historians. The change is affecting not only marriages, families, schools, and governments but also countries, species, and the earth. More than ever, it may be women rather than men who determine the course of history, and from that change in power may come a better world.

Of course, it is unlikely that *Homo sapiens* will go extinct in this new millennium. What they will have to do is accept change and not try to go back. The urge to increase our numbers will not likely disappear, for it is too deeply embedded in our nature and in that of every species. Has any species ever vanished because it failed to reproduce?

One remaining question needs attention: why have so many of us, including many historians, been caught unaware that our numbers are starting to decline? Perhaps because men were in charge who did not take women and their fertility seriously. Male agronomists, for example, have been so determined to show how much food can be grown that they have paid little attention to the history of fertility. They have seen themselves as heroes fighting against the evil of hunger. But that hunger was largely due to high fertility rates. Too long ignored were the women who realized that the way to decrease hunger is to limit family size.

In recent years, an aggressive agronomy has rolled across the earth like an armored tank on a battlefield, with the cry of "feed the world" heard above the din. The loss in biodiversity due to agricultural expansion has been nothing short of catastrophic. Agronomy has also added to the practice of applying excessive fertilizer, augmenting greenhouse gas emissions and air and water pollution. An army that seeks to feed all of the hungry forever must rely heavily on chemical fertilizers, pesticides, and genetic engineering, weapons that have not only caused biological damage but also undermined many rural communities.[45] Yet if agronomists have been blind to the downward trends in human fertility of the past two centuries, they are not alone.

THE EMPTY CRADLE OF HOPE

There are also the environmentalists who have tended to embrace too quickly a message of gloom and doom. They have spread fear and anxiety. They have warned, misleadingly, that a ticking "population bomb" might soon detonate across Asia and elsewhere.[46] Yet even as they have been sounding an alarm, fellow scientists have been creating contraceptives that would give women what they sought and diminish human fertility. A crisis was being defused faster than many realized.

Then there were the demographers, who likewise missed the turnaround in fertility and the role of women in making that happen. Founded in the seventeenth century, demography began with enthusiastic cheers for more population and economic growth, including contributions from John Graunt, Benjamin Franklin, and Thomas Malthus (the latter was for growth before he was against it).[47] Because of indifference to women, demographers may have failed to notice that women were turning to birth control.

Among those who did not appreciate fully the effort being made by women to modify their fertility rates were those population experts who talked about a coming "demographic transition." That theory originated in the 1930s and 1940s as Frank Notestein and others tried to explain how capitalist prosperity determined fertility and population.[48] They forecast a natural transition to smaller families as the rich got richer. They were thinking not as Darwinian biologists but rather as economists and engineers trying to get the most out of earth's physical systems, ignoring the law of entropy. Families would stop growing, they prophesied, as parents made more money, until at some point everyone became rich. Then they would stop having so many children. It was the old dream of wealth becoming infinite, solving all problems.

After World War II, demographic transition theory identified with "modernization" theory and its predictions of universal capitalist prosperity and social equilibrium. If nations got on the path to economic growth, becoming richer and richer, fertility rates would drop until they reached a steady state. Some were sure the earth could then go on forever in a state of equilibrium. Such a happy day was coming, it was said, though by then the planet might be so densely populated there would be standing room only for those enjoying their prosperity.[49]

Equilibrium theories were popular after two world wars, as demographers promised that such turmoil was coming to an end. In Kingsley Davis's words, "The next century will see the peak of the population reached and demographic balance spread throughout the world."[50] Well, 2045 has not yet arrived, but a happy stability is no nearer than ever, certainly not in the United States. Davis was not wrong that a big transition lay ahead, but he was too optimistic that the United States would lead it. Davis and many other predominately male theorists did not ask women what they wanted and why. Demographic theories became conservative, in effect, promoting the United States as a model for all while paying no attention to the women's movement or the deteriorating state of the earth.

Here is what really happened. After the birth control pill came out, average fertility rates in the United States began falling quickly. By 2017 they had fallen as low as 1.77 among native-born women and were only slightly higher among immigrants. But they were falling among all social groups, poor as well as rich. We cannot explain that decline as the inevitable outcome of a higher GDP. It came after upheaval and rebellion. No one could predict where it would end, although it would not likely end in a prosperous steady state run by modernizers or capitalists.

The experts paid no attention to women seeking a more socially conscious, just, balanced relationship with the earth. As they had done in nineteenth-century Massachusetts, women after 1950 were asking for two things: more power over their bodies and more balance and stability for their families. Feeling thwarted in both, they set out to make their voices heard and their communities safer.

History is made not by abstract models but by ordinary people confronting the everyday realities of real estate, food prices, childcare, education, inflation, pollution, the state of soils, birds, and the nonhuman environment.

If women in particular feel that there are too many people populating the planet, their fertility will fall, regardless of their prosperity. Experts would be well advised to listen to what women like Grø Brundtland, Margaret Sanger, and Rachel Carson wanted. Set your theories aside, they hinted, and listen to us women, for we are good at sensing when living things have been broken or hurt, and we should be put in charge of decisions.[51]

Here is Carl Sandburg again, reminding us of what all elites and experts, all agronomists, environmentalists, demographers, and all men and women should never forget.

> The people have come far and can look back
> and say, "We will go farther yet."[52]

It is the inner nature of the people, and on the matter of reproduction it is the nature of women, long repressed but now freer to speak and act, that has been pushing us to limit fertility and save the earth. It is those same women who will go farther yet.

CHAPTER 8

Building the Ecological Civilization

The most important event of the twentieth century may be Mao Zedong's accession to power in 1949 through a takeover of the Chinese Republic, which was renamed the People's Republic. Life across the planet has been in turmoil since that event. We will never know all of its ramifications, but they have been many and profound, not only within China but everywhere, from the plains of Kansas to the savannahs of Africa.

A disciple of Karl Marx, Mao and his mostly male followers were less interested in the Marxian theory of dialectical materialism than in China's long, bitter humiliation by the West. The son of a rural landowner, Mao was determined to restore greatness to his homeland by collectivizing its agriculture and urbanizing its peasants. Those achievements, he hoped, would bring back the lost grandeur of an ancient civilization. He wanted his country to become a distinctly *non-western* great power, independent of western capitalism, but he began exactly as Britain had a few centuries earlier by destroying the old agrarian relationship of people to land.

And where does China stand seventy-five years later? In Mao's terms, it is a roaring success, but it has become so by concentrating more and more power at the center, which has meant putting an old Humpty Dumpty back together again. Officially, China is an industrial *communist* nation, but under that banner it is a nation that includes many capitalists and many nostalgic nationalists. Marx has become largely a mythic figure. All the same, China seeks not really a return to the past but a new, bigger vision of itself that can shake the world, and its leaders now hope they have found that vision with the slogan of "building an ecological civilization."

What that requires is leaders who merge communist, progressive, and technocratic inclinations with nostalgia, all working together in harmony to create a sustainable China. No doubt some in China aspire to lead a third great transformation, one that reflects China's ancient traditions yet provides a new, greener model for all humanity. At its core would be a Chinese relationship with the earth, based on the science of ecology, which ironically was created by the West. There has never been anything like Mao's China for scale or ambition or ambiguity. But so far, a full ecological civilization has not materialized in the production of food or the birthing of children, or in making houses, moving about the planet, relating to other species, or incorporating women into the ruling hierarchy. We are left with a bookish concept, good and necessary perhaps, but without clarity until it becomes material.

Meanwhile, the earth as a whole mostly remains stuck in the industrial capitalist way of life, where the means of production are privately owned, where farmers seek bundles of capital to invest in land and machinery, where food comes from supermarket chains, where entertainment comes from movie moguls, where aircraft and computers and cities are made by a handful of economic planners. China has, with astonishing speed, become one of the principal participants in that modernity, as its factories send a flood of exports to world consumers. Each month some $300 billion worth of goods leave China for markets abroad, generating one trillion dollars a year in trade surpluses. Within China, huge new cities have appeared, linked together by high-speed trains, highways, and airlines, all of which, we are told, will soon run on renewable, climate-neutral energy. Perhaps so, but China has by now become deeply enmeshed in the capitalist economy of fossil fuels, corporations, coffee shops, and shopping malls. It is impossible to predict what will happen next, but at this point what is most clear is that a country that was among the poorest in the world has made itself rich in terms that westerners can appreciate but ecologists criticize from afar. At the same time, China is eager for new ideas and cultural memes that it hopes will become an alternative to the West. It's early days, to be sure, but right now the idea of a third transformation remains exceedingly vague.

Perhaps the phrase "ecological civilization" will someday materialize as a blueprint. But that will take more than words and slogans; it will require a change in production, but also changes in reproduction and consumption. China's leaders seem unsure, as well they might be, on what they want to see for their country and the rest of the world. For now, what matters is whether their powerful state can, by harmonizing all the conflicting ideas and interest groups, move confidently forward.

In the quest for harmony, China seeks to define a new imaginary—a unifying vision or social ideal. In the past that was not how transformations proceeded. Instead, ordinary people found themselves in a crisis and cobbled together a new mode of life, a process that required many centuries to unfold. Choosing an imaginary, on the other hand, means putting the cart before the horse. The Chinese state wants to build that cart and take the place of the horse.

Chairman Mao was a master of creating imaginaries, which he used to mobilize his downtrodden rural laborers and peasant farmers into an army of change. What that army wanted was really nothing new: more personal security, more freedom, plenty of children and food, shiny automobiles . . . all made possible without the western bourgeoisie. China's leaders waved red flags and lifted little books of slogans into the air, but they represented no post-capitalist alternative to the West, only a more aggressive, powerful state. The state sought control over nature and promised the wealth that concentrated power would produce.

Mao's signature program, according to the historian Judith Shapiro, became making war on nature—poisoning birds, slaughtering rats, killing flies.[1] Late in his life, however, he began wondering whether his people could ever succeed in that war without the state restraining their reproductive appetites. China began turning toward ecological thinking, but how could any state be enlightened enough to create from science a new top-down civilization?

China's masses were content to become richer, even as some of Mao's reforms turned out badly. State capitalism created millions of factory jobs but also led to many failures in environmental health and safety and a spreading alienation among workers. It was Mao's successor, Deng Xiaoping (1904–1997), who, by opening China's doors to western business methods, achieved a more widespread prosperity, although power became even more concentrated in the state than ever before. Together, Mao and Deng prepared the way for the current party boss, Xi Jinping, who in turn has emphasized building splendid infrastructure. Is this then what ecological civilization means—a bigger, more powerful government, whose technocrats and state companies manage food and reproduction, based on ecology? Few dared to ask that question publicly.

The most indisputable gains in postwar China have come in population. After Mao took command, and despite a massive famine he caused, the country grew from 554 million (1950) to 654 million (1960)—a gain of 100 million in ten years. Then by 1970 the population jumped to 823 million and a few years later to one billion. By 1990 China counted 1.3 billion inhabitants, nearly triple what it had been at the founding of the People's Republic.[2] Could such an impressive increase go on indefinitely, or was some restriction needed too? The growth in numbers gave China the world's biggest labor pool, the source of its trade success, but in creating that pool there was little ecology or greening of the earth.

The Great Steersman, in fact, watched population growth overwhelm his goals of rejuvenation and grandeur. It threatened to absorb China's gains in productivity and family prosperity. A cloud of frustration hung over Mao's final years. In the mid-1970s, after nearly three decades in power, he decided it was necessary to take more radical action and curb Chinese sexual reproduction.

Addressing the population issue required a heretical departure from Marxist ideology, which had long held that population growth could never be a danger and that population control was an abomination.[3] An account (perhaps apocryphal) of Mao's early thinking comes from the Russian leader Nikita Khrushchev, who heard Mao declare at a 1957 meeting in Moscow that if war with the West ever came, China could not lose. Half of its people might die from atomic bombs, but that would not be a tragedy. The West would collapse and die, leaving most of China standing. Such demographic calculation may have sounded like a callous factory owner in a capitalist country, pronatalist in views and indifferent toward the human costs. But Mao soon came to rue his words and to see that his country could not become truly great unless the government curbed women's fertility rate.[4]

A crack in Marxist orthodoxy began in the late 1950s, when the economist and president of Peking University Ma Yinchu (Ph.D., Columbia University, 1914) called for the Chinese Communist Party to make family planning and birth control a priority. Professor Ma, although opposed to the practice of abortion, believed that a high fertility rate was a threat to women's health as well as general living standards. He gained Mao's ear, though he was ostracized by the party for his nonconforming views.

Professor Ma's most powerful ally, besides Chairman Mao, was the second-in-command lieutenant Zhou Enlai, who, in a widely publicized interview with the American journalist Edgar Snow, argued that birth control had become necessary for China. Zhou admitted that his government had sent people to Japan to observe its fertility slowdown and that China was seeking to reduce its own numbers through "planned parenthood," adding, "this is a matter of fundamental importance."[5] At the very top, then, a turnabout had begun. Just before his death in 1976, Mao issued a directive that became known as the "one-child policy," which decreed that families should have only one child. But it was not Mao who implemented the policy; that job fell to Deng Xiaoping, who became China's ruler just two years after Mao's death.

Strangely, the Mao-Deng one-child policy was viewed in the West not as a repudiation of Marxism, but as evidence of the low value placed on human life in China. Over and over, the policy was denounced by westerners as "draconian." Western religious groups were especially prone to call it immoral and to portray China as a country where human life did not matter (which was not true) and where Christian views about the sacredness of human life were not welcome (which was true). Despite foreign criticism, Chinese state power over fertility began and increased.

In truth, China's one-child policy was carried out less rigidly than outsiders realized. From day one, the policy exempted all of China's fifty-five ethnic minorities. Then for majority Han couples, the policy was rewritten as a "one-*or-two*-child policy," as it tried to accommodate the desires of peasants seeking many sons. If a couple's first child was a girl (an outcome much feared by farmers), the couple could try again for a boy. Sometimes the zeal of local officials went beyond what Mao or Deng had in mind, becoming brutal, though in most cases noncompliant families were merely fined rather than forced to have an abortion or vasectomy. But then, in 2016, the policy was changed once again. This time the state, following such countries as Iran, Vietnam, and Singapore, decided to allow all couples to have two children per family. Later the maximum would be raised to three, a modification which, if enforced, would sabotage the building of an ecological civilization.

Critics of government birth control have asserted that any state intervention in reproduction was unnecessary. If leaders had been more patient, they say, fertility rates would have come down in China just as they were doing in Japan or South Korea, a consequence of women demanding control over their reproduction. But for a while, leaders like Mao, Ma, Zhou, and Deng all thought that women could not be trusted to do as they desired. In China, it was said, the women were more backward than their East Asian neighbors. Japan, for example, had become a modernized country as far back as the nineteenth century, so its female fertility rates did not require state intervention. Japan was not in the same mode of life as China, which had not yet shaken off its agrarian past. Therefore, China's leaders were convinced they must act—their situation had become critical.

Eventually, China's fertility rates did begin to fall, just as those of its neighbors did, and they fell more precipitously than anyone predicted. By the 1990s, those rates were almost as low as Japan's, although that was a consequence of the one-child edict. Daniel Goodkind of the U.S. Census Bureau has estimated that China's policy averted 360–520 million births.[6] The power of the state was huge, enough to keep the numbers much lower than they might otherwise have been. But without strong government support for lower fertility rates, would the country's population keep growing or not?

Seldom noted is that birth policies of any kind, whether pro- or anti-natalist, elevate state power and planning. That was true not only in China but also in Japan, Korea, and the West, where a variety of governments all set out to influence women's reproduction, either to stop births or to encourage them.

China, shrouding itself in a communist red curtain, had more in common with the West and Japan than its leaders wanted to admit. That became even clearer when a few Chinese leaders began taking notice of the deteriorating state of the earth, an awareness that began even before they made their country a manufacturing center for western consumers. In 1972 China sent a delegation to the United Nations Conference on the Human Environment, held in Stockholm, Sweden. Out of that meeting came a new imaginary called "sustainable development," which acknowledged that further population growth was incompatible with sustainability. Government, the delegates agreed, must take the lead in curbing their populations. As the new imaginary spread, China agreed with other countries that an ecological crisis was raging, though like everyone else the state seemed confused over how to respond.

BUILDING THE ECOLOGICAL CIVILIZATION

In 1987, the new "sustainable development" imaginary became the core theme in a United Nations report prepared by Grø Harlem Brundtland, the former prime minister of Norway. Her commission issued a report, *Our Common Future,* which called for merging economic growth, social justice, and environmental protection. The subtitle read *From One Earth to One World.* The phrase "One World" meant that the whole planet should come under human responsibility. The report suggested that the "One Earth" of environmentalists was not enough. One Worlders, unlike "One Earthists," would seek to overcome national differences by addressing "the needs of the present [world population] without compromising the ability of future generations to meet their own needs." It was environmentalism with social welfare state values that Brundtland promoted.[7]

The Brundtland report stressed two objectives. First, all humans, particularly the poorest, should be helped toward a better life. Second, the satisfaction of humanity must not ignore "the limitations imposed by the state of technology and social organization or the environment's ability to meet present and future needs." The commissioners did not try to identify what those limitations might be, saying only that "a commonly accepted definition" of sustainability "remains a challenge for all the actors in the development process."[8] But sustainability was, above all, about resource sharing, even if it meant more exploitation of the earth by humans. The sustainability imaginary quickly gained support from humanitarians, for it supplanted old cutthroat schemes of economic growth and old north-south rivalries with maternal values of sharing and inclusion.

China was among the nations that adopted Brundtland's sustainability imaginary, with its maternal spirit of generosity, but very soon China became excited by an even more appealing vision, which an overwhelmingly male leadership preferred. China, they said, should go beyond the maternal spirit of the Brundtland Report, with its emphasis on inclusiveness and family values, and embrace what they called *shengtai wenming,* or ecological civilization. Perhaps that alternative seemed more scientific, masculine, and somehow Chinese.

The first word in that alternative was a manly sounding emphasis on "building," suggesting that anything truly important requires an act of material construction by muscular workers, whether it be a dam, railroad line, recycling center, wind farm, or national park. Protecting the planet became a construction project, requiring state power to create a brand-new infrastructure in the name of the people. Capitalism may have been good at generating wealth, but Chinese communist leaders wanted to emphasize how it took their leadership, expertise, and money to build infrastructure efficiently and to build it green.

In the alternative imaginary, the word "building" was followed by the science of ecology, a science focused on ecosystem modeling, a technical integration of knowledge and theory that was appealing to the Chinese Communist Party. In effect, ecologists would be added to the state's technocratic team and given the job of healing the planet, making it produce more wealth, and taking charge of human-nature relations.

The final word in the new imaginary was "civilization," a word that had long referred to an advanced stage of economic and social development, based on the noble idea of reason guiding human nature, leading, as Cicero had long ago put it, to a new second nature. By including civilization in the alternative imaginary, China was reminding other countries that it had standing as one of the oldest countries embracing civilization and therefore was well equipped to lead the world in constructing a second nature to replace the original.

Taken together, those three words became for many Chinese a fresh and appealing vision. It promised harmony among social classes but not maternal values, a harmony under state rules, blending modernity and tradition.[9] College educators, environmentalists, and bureaucrats were quick to take it up. Among them was the deputy director of the State Environmental Protection Agency, Pan Yue. The public had begun calling him "Hurricane Pan" after he battled against some of the worst corporate polluters in the country. Here again, enforcement of political mandates had been left largely to local officials, many of whom were more or less zealous than Pan in protecting the environment.[10]

By the first decade of the twenty-first century Pan was getting frustrated by the persistence of China's environmental problems. The people themselves, he complained, were ultimately the cause of that frustration, for they lacked an appropriate ethic. They must be led by government agencies, he concluded, if they were going to achieve a higher civilization. One great advantage for China, Pan and others grasped, was that the party held ownership over all the land and water, rivers and mountains, all the grasslands, forests, and croplands across China, a power that allows it to act freely to stop pollution or save habitat or build missiles or bullet trains. But now it must do more, Pan implied; it must put the state in charge of reaching a new level of civilization.

How much Pan searched beyond China's borders in pursuit of his program is unclear. He believed that an adequate capacity for civilizational greatness was missing elsewhere in the world, a failing he blamed on capitalism. But it was not simply individualistic greed that was at fault. It was western dualistic attitudes, he added, that separated humans from the rest of nature. Here was where China could offer leadership—toward a non-dualistic ethic in which the state enforced new moral values on both humans and nature. Pan looked to an ancient agrarian model whose Confucian values he supposed could help China and other nations overcome the moral failures of western modernity. A people rooted in the land, believing in an authoritarian moral hierarchy, as represented by Pan, need not go abroad to find an environmental ethic. Henceforth, he began advocating for government adoption of old agrarian traditions to heal current ills.

Pan overlooked the dualism lurking in China's agrarian past and could not see that, in any case, the agrarian way of life could offer little help because it was nearly gone. Peasants may once have loved the land, but they were compelled by their own fertility to devour it. If the rural past offered such an ideal model of human-nature relations, why had it failed? How could anyone expect an aging peasantry, worshipping at animistic roadside shrines, to become the practical core of a new science-based ecological civilization?

Along with Pan, a leading historian at Nankai University, Wang Lihua, also called for an ecological civilization that was "distinctly Chinese" and rooted in the idea of a traditional agrarian civilization. He too sought to bring back "the fine traditions and historical achievements of the Chinese nation based on respecting, conforming to, and protecting nature." Nonetheless, Wang, an authority on Chinese agriculture, admitted that those "fine traditions" might have atrophied at the village level. He pointed out that it would not be the first time that people abandoned or forgot their values. Are not westerners, he asked, also prone to forget the values they once knew and practiced? With some qualifications, Wang promoted the state's vision of an ecological civilization as a shining path into the future.[11]

Pan and Wang were right to say that China had unique cultural resources for healing the environmental effects of rapid economic development. Back in the Tang and Song dynasties (628–1279 CE), for example, the country went through an efflorescence of nature-affirming poetry and painting as China's sages, poets, painters, and philosophers hiked into the mountains and found unspoiled natural habitats. They included artists like Wang Wei, Meng Haoran, Ouyang Xiu, and Su Shi, who ventured beyond cities to find a more natural China. In their minds, as they floated in small boats across mist-covered lakes or climbed steep hills, seeking a life beyond city dust and disorder, they too rejected human-nature dualism.

Besides those voices from the old days, there were even more ancient ideas that could help heal the earth, but not perhaps in the way that the state wanted. As far back as the Warring States period (476–221 BCE), a wave of nature loving had swept China. One much admired product of that time was a popular collection of fables and allegories, the *Zhuangzi,* which appeared in the fourth century BCE. Their author, Zhuang Zhou, challenged the dualism that separated humans from nature. His story "Zhuang Zhou Dreams of Being a Butterfly" asked, if a man can dream of being a butterfly, can a butterfly dream of being a man? Unlike dualistic philosophers and writers, Zhuang would not draw a rigid line between *sapiens* and other species.[12]

Anti-dualism became one of the main themes of China's early philosophy, most brilliantly represented by the *Dao De Qing* (The Book of the Way and Virtue), written around 400 BCE, one of the most important contributions China has made to human philosophy. It is profoundly antithetical to any state. Repeatedly, the Dao has been offered as an alternative to modern thinking—an "ecological philosophy" before its time.[13] Unlike the state planners, however, Daoists taught that humans could never gain sufficient knowledge of the earth to manage it. Humans, they believed, should kowtow before the ultimate unknowability of everything. Precisely because we will never be able to know nature fully, we will never be able to civilize and control it. Instead of assuming that we humans can know enough to manage the world, the Daoists said, we should try to let it flow freely and be itself.

Zhuang Zhou and the Daoists were not the only voices from the past who offered lessons that might civilize a tumultuous new China. Pan Yue nominated Confucius as a guide to a new environmental ethic. Confucius, he claimed, could teach heads of state and government officials to show more respect toward authority of all kinds. He could show modern technocrats how to save the earth from degradation without giving them too much power.

In 2007, President Hu Jintao, serving both as chairman of the Chinese Communist Party (CCP) and as head of the Chinese government, officially endorsed the idea of an ecological civilization. Five years later, in 2012, the National Congress of the party amended the nation's constitution by adding the mission of building an ecological civilization. The next year, Xi Jinping took over as general secretary of the CCP. A year later he was named president of the People's Republic, becoming one of the most powerful men to rule China in centuries. A sixty-year-old male, with a pudgy face, dark confident eyes, and a tall, robust frame, Xi would remain officially committed to the Maoist revolution, but he persisted mainly in Mao's demand that other nations respect China's self-determination. At the same time, Xi aspired to a Confucian-like leadership, spreading wisdom among the masses but now extending that wisdom across the planet, especially to Asia and Africa.

A rather private, inaccessible man, Xi seemed sincerely committed to improving his nation and the planetary environment. To do that he wanted to extend state power over the land because he believed that the state alone could effectively balance the extraction of wealth with the preservation of beauty, health, and longevity. Only the state could be nature's protector, overcoming ugliness and toxicity, creating a happy home for a more civilized people. But along the way Xi showed little concern for the autonomy of nature, insisting that the earth should become a human-made and human-managed infrastructure.

Infrastructure refers to the underlying physical structure and facilities needed for the development of a civilization: dams and irrigation systems, highways, airports, railroads, campuses, housing, cities, waterworks, and power grids. Extending that list to include land, geology, and ecosystems might seem hubristic, but it made plenty of sense to an ardent civilizer, and Xi was just that. For him a river was not a free and natural force to be admired or respected but a primitive thing that should be made to irrigate crops, transport goods, provide health and sanitation, or serve as an amenity for the community. In all those ways nature could be remade to improve human life.

In 2013, after becoming head of state, Xi Jinping introduced his conservation agenda as part of the "Chinese Dream of National Rejuvenation" (*zhongguo meng*). "Protecting the environment," he explained, "equates to protecting productivity, and improving the environment also equates to developing productivity." Civilizations seek to raise productivity and yet also protect nature. In that same year Xi decreed that China should "leave to our future generations a working and living environment of blue skies, green fields and clean water" and that China should work with other countries to "make the earth an environmentally sound homeland." What he was proposing was not so much a revolution as a higher level of civilization based on economic development (*luse fazhan*).[14]

After becoming president, Xi continued to pursue the uplifting of his country. After four years in office, he was ready to boast: "We have made notable progress in building the ecological civilization." His primary commitment, he made clear, was not to protect nature for nature's sake but "to sustain the Chinese nation's development." Then he added a softer, more aesthetic and ethical tone: "[We must] cherish the environment as we cherish our own lives. We will adopt a holistic approach to conserving our mountains, rivers, forests, farmlands, lakes, and grasslands, implement the strictest possible systems for environmental protection, and develop eco-friendly growth models and ways of life."[15]

Now elected for life, Xi seeks to civilize nature through exercising state power. He spreads his vision through his Belt and Road Initiative, a Chinese program in which states across Asia, Africa, and even the West are helped with infrastructure funding. The whole planet must be managed, urges the government of China. Adding credibility is the undeniable fact that China is in better shape today than it has ever been—richer, more civilized, more environmentally conscious. Xi and other party visionaries offer to use their success to show other nations how to escape their backwardness. But only China and the Chinese state, Xi suggests, have the skills and capacity to lead the way to a new ecological civilization.

Implied in the new imaginary is that nature is an object to be used and exploited or to be restructured by technocrats, an old and familiar doctrine. Was that what Pan Yue meant in calling for an end to dualism? There is no duality where everything on earth is ruled by the state. Perhaps Pan was unaware that states and technocratic experts have long had trouble rising above dualism. They prefer total victory, fighting only for what expertise wants. If Pan missed that tendency, he was naive.

The technocratic side of the ecological civilization was fully on display in 2013, when President Xi Jinping laid his agenda before the National Congress of the Communist Party. He still was sure that government and its experts must be organizers of a new earth. Government must manage China's lands and turn its territory into a kind of infrastructure, including water transfers, national parks, wildlife refuges, and restored forests. Building or maintaining all kinds of infrastructure depended on putting the CCP, which is to say the Chinese state, in charge of everything.

Revolutionary Marxists in the nineteenth century were not free of the same ambition of state control. But in contrast to the post-Marxists of China, the old-school radicals promised that the communist state, after securing control by the people, would fade away. In contrast, the new Chinese state has not been so self-effacing. Now it intends to stay around indefinitely, doing for the people what they will not or cannot do for themselves. Xi's infrastructure program turns the earth over to engineers, scientists, health experts, and environmental planners. Just as rivers are impounded and diverted, so too must people be managed, moved around, and utilized efficiently. The fertility of the earth must also come under state control.[16]

Thus, China has undertaken many huge construction projects—new public highways, coal-fired plants, and gated apartment complexes and boulevards that replace farming villages on the urban fringe. The state has assumed command over the food supply, soils, and agroecosystems, as well as fertilizers and other chemical compounds. But the infrastructure-building state, for all its material achievements, seems likely to repeat the same environmental problems generated by western capitalism.[17]

BUILDING THE ECOLOGICAL CIVILIZATION

Strikingly, the Chinese state has not acknowledged that its ecological civilization imaginary has scant roots in China's history; it had to be imported from the West, specifically from postwar Germany and critics of fascism and the Third Reich. The imaginary was first introduced by Iring Fetscher, a Green Marxist philosopher in Germany's Frankfurt Institute for Social Research, which was founded in 1923 as a center for updating Marxism. Even before the United Nations conference in Stockholm, Fetscher pointed to the planet's deteriorating environment and expressed disenchantment with Marxism and its worldview, which dated back to coal-burning factories and workers arrayed against bosses. Fetscher's most influential book, *Überlebensbedingungen der Menschheit* (Conditions for the Survival of Humanity), published in 1976, warned against an old-fashioned Marxist faith in machines, economic growth, and reductive, instrumentalized thinking about people and nature.

Fetscher called on the holistic science of ecology for guidance. The science got its name in 1866 from the German biologist Ernst Haeckel. But even as he seized on it, Fetscher cautioned that a new dictatorship might lie ahead as that science took command of the environmental crisis.[18] Ecology is needed to deal with the crisis, he believed, but it should not be given too much power. Fetscher feared that elevating ecological science might end by repressing dissent and making the state more paramount than ever. There were other questions that needed resolution. Did creating an ecological civilization require a drop in the world population? And if it did, what power, if any, should the state exercise over fertility? Should the people be free to govern themselves in this and other matters?

From Fetscher and the Frankfurt School the philosophically complex imaginary traveled to communist Russia and then to such capitalist countries as the United States, Canada, Great Britain, and Australia, though nowhere did it have the pervasive impact it had on China.[19] But generally left behind in that transit of ideas were the perspectives developed by other, more widely read critics of modernity. There was Max Horkheimer, for instance, and the Black Forest philosopher Martin Heidegger and his students, especially Hans Jonas, Herbert Marcuse, and Hannah Arendt. Any of them might have offered China and other nations a far less optimistic appraisal of a state-led ecological civilization.

Then in the United States, where many of those writers took refuge from Hitler, there were the likes of Rachel Carson and Aldo Leopold, both active from the 1930s on. Rachel Carson (1907–1964) echoed those European critics of modern civilization. Here are the dark words she quoted from Dr. Albert Schweitzer: "Man has lost the capacity to foresee and to forestall. He will end by destroying the earth." Similarly, the American forester Aldo Leopold (1887–1948) offered a skeptical appraisal of any civilization in his "Land Ethic" essay. But who among China's environmental leaders turned to those western skeptics for insight?[20]

Aldo Leopold, a trained forester who for many years taught wildlife ecology at the University of Wisconsin, could have warned China's leaders that protecting nature and promoting civilization could not be easily yoked. Although he was translated into Mandarin and published in student textbooks, Leopold was known mainly as an American nature writer, not as a moral philosopher. Yet decades before Pan Yue, Leopold called for a "land ethic" based on the community concept in ecology. The extension of ethics to the whole planet, he maintained, was "an evolutionary possibility and an ecological necessity." Sounding much like the old Daoist philosophers but writing in modern America, Leopold called for a change within humans "from conqueror of the land-community to plain member and citizen of it."[21]

By an ethic, Leopold meant a limitation on "freedom of action in the struggle for existence," which can be translated as the evolving of moral sprouts in the human organism. He called his land ethic "a kind of community-instinct in the making."[22] "Only the most superficial student of history," he cautioned himself and all philosophers, "supposes that Moses wrote the Decalogue. It evolved in the minds of a thinking community, and Moses wrote a tentative summary of it for a seminar."[23] Leopold had as little confidence in a civilizing state as he did in Moses. A land ethic, he argued, must come from ordinary people who are close to the land and whose future depends on finding a better way.

If Leopold had little hope in the state as moral leader, so did Fetscher, Arendt, or Jonas, for they had all suffered severely from Hitler's state. "If we do not succeed in establishing an ecologically balanced 'alternative civilization,'" warned Fetscher, "we face not only the danger of 'nuclear destruction' but also the possibility of an authoritarian and autarkic 'ecological dictatorship'" that could spread everywhere on the earth.[24] But how to succeed without creating a new dictatorship? It was a question that went unasked in the state corridors of China.

A similar warning about the dangers of environmentalist fascism came from the American economist Robert Heilbroner, who in 1974 published *The Human Prospect*. "The rise of 'iron' governments, probably of a military-socialist cast," he warned, might emerge in response to an environmental crisis brought on by runaway technology, adding that "the pressure of political movement in times of war, civil commotion, or general anxiety pushes in the direction of authority, not away from it."[25]

Perhaps the most provocative voice among the anti-fascist, anti-authoritarian, anti-technology critics of the past century was Hans Jonas. Born in Germany to a Jewish family, he ended up teaching philosophy at the New School for Social Research in New York City. Jonas's most important book was *The Phenomenon of Life*, which advocated the embrace of biology by humanists. Jonas wanted not only to break down academic walls but also to challenge what he, like Pan, thought was the root problem of any civilization: an ontological dualism separating humans from nature, a dualism that led to humans trying to take command over nature. From that dualism, Jonas believed, stemmed environmental degradation and all forms of human or animal enslavement. Dualism deified that magnificent brain sitting atop the human spine, regal and autonomous, manipulating the passions, a would-be dictator who should, in Jonas's view, be feared and defeated.[26]

BUILDING THE ECOLOGICAL CIVILIZATION

Jonas ended *The Phenomenon of Life* with an essay on "Nature and Ethics." A rejection of the war on nature, he avowed, should be the first step toward a new environmental ethic and a new planet-centered civilization. Bad ontology, he believed, had produced bad states, including fascism, nationalism, and authoritarianism. To prevent that from happening again would require restoring humans to the rest of nature, extending moral feelings beyond one's species toward the protection of all forms of life, and seeing human nature as more trustworthy than a big brain.

After publishing *The Phenomenon of Life,* Jonas went on to write a companion book, *The Imperative of Responsibility* (1984), which includes these words about ethics: "Man's inroads into nature, as seen by himself, [until now have been] essentially superficial and powerless to upset its appointed balance.... Nature was not an object of human responsibility—she taking care of herself and, with some coaxing and worrying, also of man; not ethics, only cleverness was applied to her."[27] For Jonas, that old attitude toward nature was a flaw in all previous civilizations. If the flaw persisted, then new fascists would rise on the earth, claiming more understanding than their subjects and seeking total power over nature. Humans must resist that trend, Jonas argued, by taking a different view of the earth. "An object of an entirely new order—not less than the whole biosphere of the planet," he wrote, "has been added to what we must be responsible for because of our power over it."[28]

Past civilizations, Jonas granted, preached ethics, but they extended no further than the "neighborly virtues"—tolerance, honesty, fair treatment of other humans, good citizenship—all desirable but insufficient in a time of environmental vulnerability. With the spread of human power came an unprecedented tilt toward global disaster. Without new inner checks on their desires, humans would end up under the thumb of a fascist technocracy, wearing uniforms, business suits, and white coats, where people could not tell the difference between what was natural and what was not. Of course, we should attend ethically to the welfare of our neighbors, Jonas said, but we should also attend to "the good of things extra human . . . beyond the sphere of man and make the human good include the care for them." "Power conjoined with reason," Jonas concluded, "carries responsibility with it."[29]

The point of this digression is that, in recent times, there have been important western as well as eastern advisers on how to overcome the ills of modernity. The leaders in Beijing were not interested in listening to advisers. They gained control over a powerful state and felt confident that they knew what to do next. They had big wads of export earnings to spend. They were eager to bring about a third transformation with Chinese characteristics. They were not interested in an open, planet-wide conversation; on the contrary, they built new walls against public conversation and outside advice.

The Chinese state must be credited with the most impressive economic miracle ever, perhaps the greatest feat of modernization in history, lifting hundreds of millions of humans out of severe poverty in mere decades. In 2024 the gross domestic product of China reached $18.5 trillion a year, the second highest in the world (compared with the United States at $28.8 trillion).[30] But what will happen to that country when its growth comes to an end? As it becomes a money-driven state like others, as its state officials successfully compete against western capitalism, China covers itself with slogans of ecology and civilization. Dreams of infinite growth continue to motivate its leaders, and all they offer the public is a new and better conquest of the earth.

Xi has repeatedly insisted that his party's first goal must be to sustain the Chinese nation's economic development. Far from being a new kind of visionary, he has followed a familiar, if now aging, agenda. In the United States, for example, such a goal animated Theodore Roosevelt, who in 1901 became the American president and served until 1908. Roosevelt, like Xi, defined the state as a great engine for economic development, which started with nationalizing the forests and went on to state-funded dams, land reclamation, and power generation. Xi has done the same, and like Roosevelt he has set aside many new wildlife refuges and parks. But such actions do not add up to a sustainable society or a post-dualist civilization. Perhaps no state or its leader can act differently—but then perhaps the state is not where we should look for our next great transformation.

A state thinks like this: dam the Yangzi and send its hydropower and water north and south, east and west. Set aside big new spaces for the conservation of nature, like China's Great Panda National Park, which covers an area three times larger than Yellowstone. The state thinks in terms of constructing such massive, impressive monuments to its power. It aims at nothing less than bringing continents and oceans under its technological power. A state leader may talk, as Chairman Xi has done, about settling for "moderate prosperity" for all, a theme that President Roosevelt shared, but moderation is not how states behave. If the state continues to get bigger and stronger until it alone holds the power to tell citizens how much they should spend or acquire, or how many children they should have, then what hope is there for moderation? What will be the fate of ordinary people: their freedom, their autonomy, their capacity for innovation, their inner nature?

In 2018, after four decades of pushing the people this way and that, China's leaders abruptly decided to raise the number of babies allowed per family from two to three. Once again, the state was out to manage people and the earth. Parents were now urged to produce *more* children than before to ensure that the nation would continue to grow rich and powerful. Two years later, however, not more but fewer babies were being born each year—down to twelve million babies. That was too few, the state declared, but what then should the number be and who should decide? If the state alone has the power to determine human fertility, then is the state just another name for tyranny?

So far, the Chinese public's reaction to the three-child policy has been less defiant than indifferent. In public polls, couples are saying exactly what they are saying in other countries: stay out of our bedrooms. Allow us to govern ourselves. We don't want your mandates on these matters.

BUILDING THE ECOLOGICAL CIVILIZATION

A key conclusion in this planetary history is that no state can remain isolated behind its walls and boundaries. If Chinese officials believe that their ecological civilization can emerge without more openness to dissent, then they will fail in their project of leading a world transformation. All of us must become involved in determining the planet's carrying capacity. How can anyone—reactionaries or revolutionaries—bring a new transformation into being if we ignore the lesson of evolution that there is not and cannot be any plan? Or if we force women to have more children than they want? Or if we think of the planet as infrastructure? We must embrace one another as fellow citizens of earth, if we want to be ready for the next great transformation.

EPILOGUE
This Fertile Earth

How fortunate that we live on an intensely fertile planet, where all the right conditions have existed at the right time and place to produce a plenitude of oceans, continents, mountains, and valleys and to fill them with millions of species and their progeny, with human civilization, farms, and cities. But of course, we could not be here at all if the earth had not been so rife with life. No other planet so far discovered has been so organic, which is to say, so full of creatures that eat, reproduce, and invent. We live on the planet of potentiality. Its fruitfulness goes back billions of years, encouraging us to hope that it might go on forever. But already we are realizing through science that even such an amazing planet as ours has limits.

Even now, our planet's fertility cannot be killed off by anything we humans are likely to do. Even a nuclear war, or even the dreadful oxygen destroyer that killed the film monster Godzilla, could not end all life or stop all reproduction, although we do have technology that could set evolution back massively. Someday, to be sure, perhaps long after we humans are extinct, there will come a moment when the sun burns out. The sun is limited too, and the laws of entropy say that it will go dark someday. The sun has been blazing away for 4.6 billion years and, if we judge by similar sun-stars, ours is now half exhausted. It has only a couple of billion years left before it becomes a red giant and then blinks out.

Should we worry about that? No, for until that time the earth will continue to generate new life. The continents will continue to drift and the seas will continue to pound against the shores, snow and ice will accumulate and melt, climates will warm and cool, and species will evolve and go extinct.

This book has been about the extraordinary fertility of organic life on this small, inconspicuous planet, particularly the fertility of our own species and the hungers within that drive us to seek mates, reproduce, find food, and replenish the earth. Today many are worried about global warming, and reasonably so if one values our current civilization. But let us be rational in our fear. No matter how much CO_2 we emit to the planet's atmosphere, man-made warming will not end fertility. A warming climate will make the earth wetter, which will favor life. It is not Pollyannish to say that this living planet—our ecosphere—will endure for a long time to come.

We humans have had only a brief run so far, but during that short span we have invented what Karl Marx called "modes of production," several of them in fact. When we reached the limits of one mode, when it became unsustainable, a new one was created. This talent for innovation has happened on the broad scale only twice in history, but it is likely to happen again, perhaps soon. When it does, old modes will not completely vanish. Foraging and farming still exist today, though they have been pushed to the margins of the planet or drastically remade. The modern victor, industrial capitalism, will someday face extinction, perhaps losing out to the all-powerful state or to a new version of communism or to an ecological civilization.

Extinction is part of life. Perhaps 90 percent of all the life-forms that ever lived on earth have disappeared, though on average a species hangs on for a million years before going extinct. By comparison, human ways of life have been far less enduring, far less sustainable—but then we are not done trying.

To know why innovations fail or succeed, we need to expand our sense of history.[1] We need to study the history of human societies well before the modern era, before classical civilizations, before the rise and fall of hunters and gatherers. We need to become familiar too with all five of the planet's ice ages, the last of which, the Quaternary, lasted more than two million years.

As we discover how threatening those ages were for living creatures, let us also remember that during the last ice age humankind emerged and spread over the earth. A broader understanding of the past should reveal that humans and other species have been through many tough times, tougher than those we face now, and that we have survived, along with ten million other species. It is plain fact that fertility and innovation still exist. If we thought more deeply about that fact, how might we change our perceptions of the present or our expectations of the future?

The irrepressibility of life on our planet—including the irrepressible desire among humans to control their fertility—is the main lesson we should learn from history. Yet that lesson has been forgotten recently, as people worry that our best days are behind us, that our future looks bleak. Such pessimism is not supported by a deeper knowledge of the past. If we truly appreciate the tenacity of life and the power we have to restrain our own fertility, we should find hope. Whenever we are beset with fire, ice, hurricanes, snowfall, drought, famine, epidemics, or death we can be sure that life, human life included, will go on.

So far, however, humankind has been remarkable for its failure to find sustainability. Again and again, we have pushed earth's ecosystems to crash. We should not underestimate our capacity for doing that again and again, a capacity that has been deeply bred into our nature. Here is another core message of this book: we can survive indefinitely only by nurturing the life around us. For that we will need wits as well as hearts.

Innovation is a big part of human nature, passed on to us by life itself. If we continue to acquire knowledge of the planet and ourselves, learning how to manage better our reproduction, we can become much more sustainable. That humans might figure out how to manage their own fertility so successfully did not occur to pessimists such as Thomas Malthus. In later editions of his *Essay on Population,* Malthus finally allowed some possibility for controlling reproduction, but he never anticipated how far that control might go. He was blind to changes under way in his own day in agriculture and reproductive knowledge. Like his archenemy Karl Marx, Malthus did not foresee the appearance of a Margaret Sanger and her supporters, whose efforts are now enabling women everywhere to stay within the capacity of the earth and sustain life. No other species can innovate as we can, but then no other species has had to do so.

So, everything that lives must obey the earth's material limits and physical laws. Species that overrun those limits will vanish, but as wonderful innovators we are not fated to do that. By evolving naturally and culturally, we can avoid the fate of extinction.

The development of human fertility control has made our planet seem more exceptional than ever. Here is our sun circled by eight planets, from Mercury to Neptune, plus the dwarf planet Pluto, all beautiful in form and color, but only one of them, Earth, offers all the right conditions for life to flourish and for humankind to be fruitful or not, as we find necessary. Here is an oxygen-rich atmosphere, a moderate temperature range, a dazzling array of natural habitats where organisms have co-evolved, and an interdependent ecosphere that supports all the myriad creatures.[2] But aside from *sapiens*, where is there life that can manage its own reproduction?

Will we ever find another planet so amply blessed with fertility? So far, we have found no evidence even of simple bacteria, let alone species like us. If all the other suns in all the galaxies are circled by an average of one planet, there could be many trillion planets sprinkled across space—but only a minute fraction of them may offer all or most of the conditions for life as we know it. If we ever do find not a mere beginning of independent organic development but a planet rather like our own, where life is advanced, diversified, and adaptive, that place might be millions of light-years away and therefore beyond any practical relevance for ages to come. So far, however, even with powerful telescopes we have found no such place.[3]

The search for extraterrestrial life has barely begun, of course, and no one can predict its ultimate results. It appears that only the earth has produced a richness of organic life—evolution and reproduction on a grand scale—not a mere trace of bacteria but all the rest, and has done so, despite catastrophic interruptions, again and again. Why has matter become so fertile on this planet, and why has it been so sterile across the rest of space? Religionists may believe that there are transcendental spirits who have made earth a suitable home for their favored species and, for some unfathomable reason, have put us here to live. A humbler and more realistic conclusion is that everything materially necessary for life and human life just happened to come together on this rock and did not need any outside interference. The earth is by nature a fit environment. Here, the extraordinary happened again and again, until it became ordinary.

Every person on the planet should realize how incredibly rare it is for chemical elements like hydrogen, carbon, and oxygen to come alive as they did here some 3.5 billion years ago. The results include these astonishing outcomes: tiny crustaceans called krill serving as food for immense blue whales, praying mantises eating their mates after reproduction, lusty chimps seeking sex with other chimps, and acorn-producing oak trees providing habitat for birds, insects, raccoons, and wispy beards of moss. Competition, cooperation, symbiosis, food chains, and interdependency are all qualities we can find in the evolution of life—along with intelligence, beauty, and persistence. Today, taxonomists estimate there may be anywhere from three million to ten million species on earth, two thirds of them living on land, the other third in water, some born with eyes wide open to the wonder around them, some utterly sightless.

Who would want to damage or diminish this unique, precious spectacle? Yet, usually inadvertently, humans have done considerable damage. Over the past five centuries alone, we have caused nearly eight hundred species to go extinct (according to the International Union for the Conservation of Nature's Red List). That is not such a bad record if there are indeed ten million species left. So far, the loss of those species seems not to have materially affected us. Evolution will eventually replace all of them, regardless of what we humans do. A more sobering prospect opens if that loss of hundreds becomes the loss of a hundred thousand or a million or more species. But we are unlikely to let that happen.

A complete tally of environmental losses and gains during the planet's history would be too big a subject for any single book. To make a full account we would have to start before the Big Bang (circa 13.8 billion years ago), which sent matter and energy exploding across the heavens, colliding and interacting without purpose, plan, or design.

When photographed from the edge of the spreading cosmos, our earth looks like a tiny dot of no importance and no history worth noting, like a forlorn kid standing on an empty street corner. Our earth appears as a pale blue dot way out on the margins, inconspicuous and unpromising. Yet its unimpressive appearance has been very deceptive.

Around 3.7 billion years ago here on this planet, perhaps the first speck of life appeared in some undersea hotspot and, after a long preparation, new life crept forth onto the land. That moment must be the most interesting of all for us earthlings, far more interesting than the beginnings of plant and animal domestication or the discovery of Second Earth. Many other significant events have occurred. This book, however, has been selective and ignored most of that planetary history. Here the focus has been on the last two hundred thousand years, during which *Homo sapiens* emerged in Africa and spread outward to every continent except Antarctica.[4] We have pushed our fertility to new heights and exhibited a creativity that has never ceased or been superseded.

What we usually call history is, by contrast, a much diminished thing. Most historians, strangely, have shown little interest in the planet's fertility, let alone the why and wherefore of that gift. They have paid attention only to those few thousand years when humans became dominant over other forms of life and invented civilizations, languages, technologies, institutions, and different cultures out of the planet's fertility. That narrowing of history comes from believing that humans, and modern humans in particular, are alone worthy of attention. The only chapters of planetary history we want to know are those in which we were present. The rest of history we dismiss as "prehistory"—boring, primitive, and ignored, like a dusty attic devoid of interest.

Fortunately, natural historians like Charles Darwin have explored our attic, for which they deserve much credit. They have established that our kind emerged two hundred millennia ago and ever since have been responding to large and small environmental changes. Natural history has told us repeatedly that we humans are part of a much greater nature. Yet most historians ignore natural history, remaining self-absorbed and present-minded, paying little attention to how seas have formed or continents moved, or even how *sapiens* emerged as the offspring of hairless apes, foraging for a living for thousands and thousands of years.

A more inclusionary history is mainly what has been sought here. We need to think about the past as more than a saga of man making himself through innovations in cultural values, beliefs, and social ideals. We need to see humans as material creatures emerging from a deep material past, possessing a material nature of our own. Humans are more than their ideas; we are a species of animal filled with material desires, hungers, inclinations, and needs. The most important questions we have pursued here are these: How has our inherited nature shaped us over time? How has the earth created us and our desires? Which of our desires should now be leashed or checked, and who should do the checking? How might we become nurturers of this amazing planet?

Human fertility, as we learn to manage it better, will continue to be a powerful source of change. Trust in the earth's fertility and our own nature is the beginning of wisdom. We can be sure that many adaptations lie ahead, and some will come from ordinary folks like us, liable to make mistakes but also likely to do the best thing possible.

Notes

Introduction. Human Nature

1. Mencius is quoted in Judith Farquhar, *Appetites: Food and Sex in Post-Socialist China* (Durham, N.C.: Duke University Press, 2002), 1. For an alternative translation and background see *Mencius,* ed. and trans. Philip Ivanhoe (New York: Columbia University Press, 2011).

2. Edward O. Wilson has posited that it is human nature to love and protect other forms of life, in *Biophilia* (Cambridge: Harvard University Press, 1984).

3. Matt Ridley, *The Red Queen: Sex and the Evolution of Human Nature* (London: Penguin, 1993); and Jared Diamond, *Why Is Sex Fun? The Evolution of Human Sexuality* (New York: Basic, 1997).

4. "Autobiography," in *Darwin for Today,* ed. Stanley Edgar Hyman (New York: Viking, 1968), 388. Darwin's theory did not depend wholly on Malthus's influence; see Peter Vorzimmer, "Darwin, Malthus, and the Theory of Natural Selection," *Journal of the History of Ideas* 30 (October–December 1969): 527–542. The best overview of Darwin's life are the two volumes by Janet Browne, *Charles Darwin: A Biography* (Princeton: Princeton University Press, 1995 and 2002).

5. Both men had been students in the University of Cambridge, Malthus graduating from Jesus College, not far from Darwin's undergraduate dwelling, Christ's College. Smart, contentious, and conservative, Malthus left university to serve as an ordained clergyman in a Lincolnshire parish. Later he switched to a professorship in political economy at the East India Company College, but he was never free from religious-based thinking.

6. Gavin de Beer et al., eds., "Darwin's Notebooks on Transmutation of Species," part 6, *Bulletin of the British Museum (Natural History),* Historical Series 3 (March 1967): 152–163.

7. Darwin, *The Origin of Species and The Descent of Man* (New York: Modern Library, no date), 429. Darwin, a nineteenth-century liberal, was sure that the domestication of plants, animals, and humans had increased fertility for all, leading to social progress and civilization.

8. On Darwin's large family, see Browne, *Charles Darwin: A Biography*, vol. 1, 423–425, 433, 443, 474, 531, 535–537. The death of his eldest daughter, Anne, left him worried that his choice of a close relative for a wife had led to excessive inbreeding and illness. Browne also describes him as "agitated about the money needed to support a family" (426), yet unlike many others of his time he had ample means to do so.

9. For a provocative summary of the nature of human reproduction, see Edward O. Wilson, *On Human Nature* (Cambridge: Harvard University Press, 2004), chapter 6. For a critique of current thinking in humanities and social sciences, see Steven Pinker, *The Blank Slate: The Modern Denial of Human Nature* (New York: Penguin, 2016).

10. Jamshed R. Tata, "One Hundred Years of Hormones," *EMBO Reports* 6, no. 6 (June 2005): 490–496. See also E. J. W. Barrington, *Hormones and Evolution* (Princeton, N.J.: Van Norstrand, 1964); and Martie Haselton, *Hormonal: The Hidden Intelligence of Hormones* (Boston: Little, Brown, 2018), especially chapter 4, "The Evolution of Desire."

11. Bertram Murray, Jr., "On the Meaning of Density Dependence," *Oecologia* 53 (1982): 370–383.

12. See Timothy LeCain, *The Matter of History: How Things Create the Past* (New York: Cambridge University Press, 2017).

13. Clive Ponting's *A Green History of the World* (London: Sinclair-Stevenson, 1991) is organized around the same two major transformations, and so are Marxism and many other historical outlines. The fact that there have been sweeping material changes in human society is a given. Here the question is how we explain those changes.

14. Karl Polanyi, *The Great Transformation* (New York: Rinehart, 1944), 3.

15. *Karl Marx Frederick Engels: Collected Works*, vol. 5, *Marx and Engels: 1845–1847* (New York: International, 1976), 32.

Chapter 1. Out of Africa

1. Peter Cawood et al., "Secular Evolution of Continents and the Earth System," *Reviews of Geophysics* 60 (December 7, 2022). Cawood identifies seven discrete Earths, beginning with Proto-Earth (4.57 billion years ago) and ending with Contemporary Earth (from 0.8 billion years ago). His list does not include the Anthropocene, a popular label for recent times but contested by many scientists. In defense of that "epoch," see Will Steffen et al., "The Anthropocene: Conceptual and Historical Perspectives," *Philosophical Transactions, Series A* (2011): 842–867; opposing is Peter Brannen, "The Anthropocene Is a Joke," *Atlantic*, August 13, 2019, theatlantic.com/science/archive/2019/08/arrogance-anthropocene/595795/.

2. A classic in modern science is Wegener's *The Origins of Continents and Oceans* (originally, *Die Entstehung der Kontinente und Ozeane*, 1915).

3. According to the Chinese sage Laozi, a contemporary of Confucius, the earth originated thus: "The ten thousand creatures arise, but do not have a beginning. Creating but not possessing." *Dao De Jing*, chapter 2, trans. Bruce Linnell (Project Gutenberg, 2015), www.gutenberg.org/files/49965.

4. "The Chumash People," www.sbnature.org/collections-research/publications/14; Thomas Blackburn, *December's Child: A Book of Chumash Oral Narratives* (Berkeley: University of California Press, 1975).

5. John Reader, *Africa: Biography of a Continent* (New York: Vintage, 1997), 21–23, 499–501.

6. The difficulties in identifying the exact site of human emergence are discussed in Ann Gibbons, "Experts Question Study Claiming to Pinpoint Birthplace of All Humans," *Science: News*, October 28, 2019.

7. Robert Ardrey, *African Genesis: A Personal Investigation into the Animal Origins and Nature of Man* (New York: Atheneum, 1963), which purports to show that humans are descendants of "killer apes," an interpretation that subsequent research has questioned. See Dan Flores, *Wild New World: The Epic Story of Animals and People in America* (New York: W.W. Norton, 2022), especially chapter 2.

8. See David Quammen, *The Tangled Tree: A Radical New History of Life* (New York: Simon and Schuster, 2018).

9. The name *Homo sapiens sapiens* was coined by paleontologists and anthropologists to separate our kind from such near relatives as the Neanderthals and Denisovans.

10. Suzana Herculano-Houzelm writes, in the *Proceedings of the National Academy of Science* 109, supp. 1 (June 26, 2012): 10661–10668, that the human brain is "remarkable in its cognitive abilities and metabolism simply because of its extremely large number of neurons."

11. John L. Brooke, *Climate Change and the Course of Global History: A Rough Journey* (New York: Cambridge University Press, 2014), 55–108.

12. Thomas Hobbes, *Leviathan* (1651; New York: Cosimo, 2009), 72.

13. For an overview of meat eating in history, see Adrian Williams and Lisa Hill, "Meat and Nicotinamide: A Causal Role in Human Evolution, History, and Demographics," *International Journal of Tryptophan Research* 10 (May 2, 2017): 1–23.

14. Yong Ge et al., "Understanding the Overestimated Impact of the Toba Volcanic Super-eruption on Global Environments and Ancient Hominins," *Quaternary International* 559 (September 10, 2020): 24–33.

15. Ansley Coale, "The History of the Human Population," *Scientific American* 231, no. 3 (September 1974): 43. On the need for a longer time frame in demography, see Massimo Livi-Bacci, "What We Can and Cannot Learn from the History of World Population," *Population Studies* 69 (2015): S21–28.

16. Fekri Hassan and Randal Sengel, "On Mechanisms of Population Growth During the Neolithic," *Current Anthropology* 14 (December 1973): 538.

17. Michael Gurven and Raziel Davison, "Periodic Catastrophes over Human Evolutionary History Are Necessary to Explain the Forager Population Paradox," *Proceedings of the National Academy of Science* 11 (June 25, 2019): 12758. On the modern !Kung foragers' rate of growth, see Nancy Howell, *Demography of the Dobe !Kung* (New York: Academic Press, 1979).

18. Massimo Livi-Bacci estimates six million people in *A Concise History of World Population,* trans. Carl Ipsen (Cambridge, Mass.: Blackwell, 1992), while Colin McEvedy and Richard Jones, in *Atlas of World Population History* (New York: Facts on File, 1978), say four million. Mark Nathan Cohen, in *The Food Crisis in Prehistory* (New Haven: Yale University Press, 1977), suggests fifteen million.

19. S. Chao, "The Effect of Lactation on Ovulation and Fertility," *Clinics in Perinatology* 14 (March 1987): 39–50.

20. For a comprehensive overview, see Richard Lee and Richard Daly, eds., *Cambridge Encyclopedia of Hunters and Gatherers* (Cambridge: Cambridge University Press, 1999), "Introduction: Foragers and Others," 1–19.

21. Marshall Sahlins, *Stone Age Economics* (Chicago: Aldine-Atherton, 1972), 5, 6, 12.

22. Sahlins, *Stone Age Economics,* 32.

23. Stephen Pyne, *World Fire* (Seattle: University of Washington Press, 1997).

24. Robert T. Boyd's edited volume *Indians, Fire, and the Land in the Pacific Northwest* (Corvallis: Oregon State University Press, 1999) points to examples of increasing food supplies by intentional burning.

25. Paul Mellars, "Why Did Modern Human Populations Disperse from Africa ca. 60,000 Years Ago? A New Model," *Proceedings of the National Academy of Sciences* 103, no. 25 (June 20, 2006): 9381–9386. See also recent research summarized by Chris Stringer in "The Origin and Evolution of Homo Sapiens," *Philosophical Transactions: Biological Sciences* 371, no. 1698 (2016): 1–12.

26. Mark Elvin, *The Retreat of the Elephants: An Environmental History of China* (New Haven: Yale University Press, 2006).

27. Paul Martin and H. E. Wright, Jr., eds. *Pleistocene Extinctions* (New Haven: Yale University Press, 1967). David Reich, "One Hundred Thousand Adams and Eves," in Reich, *Who We Are and How We Got Here: Ancient DNA and the New Science of the American Past* (New York: Pantheon, 2018), Kindle ed., location 608–663. "African Multiregionalism: The New Story of Human Origins," *Atlantic,* www.theatlantic.com/science/archive/2018/07/the-new-story-of-humanitys-origins/564779/. Racial stereotypes obscure individual differences existing within Africa to focus on some homogeneous "African." See Vincent Sarich and Frank

Miele, *Race: The Realities of Human Differences* (Boulder, Colo.: Westview, 2004), and Nicholas Wade, *A Troublesome Inheritance: Genes, Race, and Human History* (New York: Penguin, 2014). The latter concludes that racial differences were in the beginning quite real but have become blurred over time until they no longer constitute scientific realities. See also Kevin de Queiroz, "Ernst Mayr and the Modern Concept of Species," *Proceedings of the National Academy of Sciences* 102, supp. 1 (June 2005): 6600–6607.

Chapter 2. The Agrarian Whip

1. The book of Genesis (chapters 1–3), written in Hebrew to explain the origins of the Jewish people, identifies the first humans and first farmers as Adam and Eve, who are portrayed as carnal and disobedient creatures. Although scholars disagree on when Genesis was written, a modern consensus says that the book dates to the sixth or fifth century BCE, long after farming had begun.

2. For an overview see Edward Melillo, *The Butterfly Effect: Insects and the Making of the Modern World* (New York: Alfred A. Knopf, 2020).

3. Smithsonian Institution, "Mutual Attraction: The Evolution of Agriculture in Ants," https://biogenomics.si.edu.

4. See E. O. Wilson and Bert Hollander, *The Ants* (Cambridge: Harvard University Press, 1990).

5. Edward O. Wilson, *The Social Conquest of Earth* (New York: Liveright, 2012), Kindle ed., location 109.

6. John L. Brooke, *Climate Change and the Course of Global History: A Rough Journey* (New York: Cambridge University Press, 2014), 121.

7. Peter Bellwood, *First Farmers* (Malden, Mass.: Blackwell, 2005), 54.

8. Bruce D. Smith, *The Emergence of Agriculture* (New York: Scientific American Library, 1995), 211.

9. Joy McCorriston and Frank Hole, "The Ecology of Seasonal Stress and the Origins of Agriculture in the Near East," *American Anthropologist*, n.s. 93 (March 1991): 46–69.

10. Bellwood, *First Farmers*, 7; Jared Diamond, *Guns, Germs, and Steel: The Fates of Human Societies* (New York: W.W. Norton, 1997), chapter 4.

11. Gideon Shelach, "The Earliest Neolithic Cultures of Northeast China," *Journal of World Prehistory* 14 (2000): 363–414; Li Liu et al., "Harvesting and Processing Wild Cereals in the Upper Paleolithic Yellow River Valley, China," *Antiquity* 92 (2018): 603–619. Both say that wild millet was domesticated sometime between nine thousand and fourteen thousand years ago. The first domestication of rice is even harder to pinpoint exactly; among Chinese scholars the date of origin is sometimes pushed back to 10,000 BP. See also Brian Lander,

The King's Harvest: A Political Ecology of China from the First Farmers to the First Empire (New Haven: Yale University Press, 2021).

12. See Ping-ti Ho, *The Cradle of the East: An Inquiry into the Indigenous Origins of Techniques and Ideas of Neolithic and Early Historic China, 5000–1000 B.C.* (Chicago: University of Chicago Press, 1975). Also see Zhang Chi and Hsiao-chun Hung, "The Emergence of Agriculture in Southern China," *Antiquity* 84 (March 2010): 11–25; Houyuan Lu et al., "Earliest Domestication of Common Millet (*Panicum miliaceum*) in East Asia Extended to 10,000 Years Ago," *Proceedings of the National Academy of Sciences* 106, no. 18 (May 5, 2009): 7367–7372; Robert B. Marks, *China: Its Environment and History* (Lanham, Md.: Rowman and Littlefield, 2012), 23–32.

13. For more details, see Bellwood, *First Farmers*, and Diamond, *Guns, Germs, and Steel*, passim.

14. Bruce Smith, "Origins of Agriculture in Eastern North America," *Science*, n.s. 246 (December 22, 1989): 1566–1571. The principal species selected were corn, beans, and squash, www.nal.usda.gov/collections/stories/three-sisters#. In *First Farmers*, Bellwood adds to those independent sites one more: the interior highlands of New Guinea, where taro, sugar cane, and banana were first domesticated.

15. On the dispersal of agriculture, see David Graeber and David Wengrow, *The Dawn of Everything: A New History of Humanity* (New York: Farrar, Straus and Giroux, 2021), 252–254. Unusually, they argue there were as many as fifteen to twenty independent centers of domestication.

16. Yuval Noah Harari, *Sapiens: A Brief History of Humankind* (New York: HarperCollins, 2015), Kindle ed., location 9–91.

17. Richard MacNeish, *Origins of Agriculture and Settled Life* (Norman: University of Oklahoma Press, 1992), 3.

18. Jack Harlan, "Indigenous African Agriculture," in *The Origins of Agriculture*, ed. C. Wesley Cowan and Patty Jo Watson (Washington: Smithsonian Institution, 1992), 59–70. See also Bellwood, *First Farmers*, 97–110; Diamond, *Guns, Germs, and Steel*, 384–400.

19. For an ecological analysis, see Mark Cohen, *The Food Crisis in Prehistory: Overpopulation and the Origins of Agriculture* (New Haven: Yale University Press, 1977), 97–111.

20. Joseph Ogutu, "Wildlife Migrations Are Collapsing in East Africa," *Open Access Government*, June 13, 2021, www.openaccessgovernment.org/wildlife-migrations/62746/.

21. Cohen, *The Food Crisis in Prehistory*, 40.

22. See Lewis R. Binford, "Post-Pleistocene Adaptations," in *New Perspectives in Archaeology*, ed. L. R. Binford and S. R. Binford (Chicago: Aldine, 1968), 313–341; and Kent Flannery, "The Origins of Agriculture," *Annual Review of Anthropology* 2 (1973): 271–310.

23. Cohen, *Food Crisis in Prehistory*, 41.

24. The practice of equilibrium-seeking among foragers is the theme in Roy Rappaport, *Pigs for the Ancestors*, rev. ed. (New Haven: Yale University Press, 1984), which focuses on the Tsembaga people of the New Guinea highlands.

25. Responding to critics who pointed out that the why of increasing population density remained unclear, Cohen admitted that much remains to be understood, but he concluded that "population density appears to be the central variable." Cohen, *Food Crisis in Prehistory*, 283.

26. Cohen, *Food Crisis in Prehistory*, 252–260.

27. Cohen, *Food Crisis in Prehistory*, 14.

28. Ester Boserup's most important work is *The Conditions of Agricultural Growth* (Chicago: Aldine, 1965); see also *Population and Technological Change* (Chicago: University of Chicago Press, 1981). For assessments of her career, see B. L. Turner II and Marina Fischer-Kowalski, "Ester Boserup: An Interdisciplinary Visionary Relevant for Sustainability," *Proceedings of the National Academy of Science* 107 (December 21, 2010): 21963–21965; and Jon Mathieu, "'Finding Out Is My Life': Conversations with Ester Boserup in the 1990s," *Human-Environment Interactions* 4 (2014): 13–22.

29. Boserup anticipated the cornucopian views of the late Julian Simon, *The Ultimate Resource* (Princeton: Princeton University Press, 1981), and Bjørn Lomborg, *The Skeptical Environmentalist* (originally published in Danish in 1998; revised edition, Cambridge: Cambridge University Press, 2001).

30. A significant challenge to the Boserupian view came from critically minded conservation biologists, including Paul Ehrlich, *The Population Bomb* (New York: Ballantine, 1968), and Rachel Carson, *Silent Spring* (Boston: Houghton Mifflin, 1962). The latter argued that agricultural intensification in the form of chemical pesticides threatened the life of the planet.

31. Mark N. Cohen, "Population Pressure and the Origins of Agriculture: An Archaeological Example from the Coast of Peru," in *Origins of Agriculture*, ed. Charles A. Reed (The Hague: Moulton, 1977), 137–177. See also Bennet Bronson, "The Earliest Farming: Demography as Cause and Consequence," 23–48, and Michael J. Harner, "Scarcity, the Factors of Production, and Social Evolution," 123–138, in *Origins of Agriculture;* and Marvin Harris and Eric Ross, *Death, Sex, and Fertility* (New York: Columbia University Press, 1987).

32. MacNeish, *Origins of Agriculture and Settled Life*, 3.

33. Graeme Barker, *The Agricultural Revolution in Prehistory* (Oxford: Oxford University Press, 2006), 1.

34. Hannah Ritchie and Max Roser, "Land Use," published online at *Our World in Data*, a project of Global Change Data Lab (September 2019), https://ourworldindata.org/land-use.

35. See J. Michael McCloskey and Heather Spalding, "A Reconnaissance-Level Inventory of the Amount of Wilderness Remaining in the World," *Ambio* 18 (1989): 221–227. The authors found that one third of the planet remained undeveloped land ("primarily shaped by the forces of nature"). They ignored wild lands that covered less than four hundred thousand hectares, which may explain why most of their wild lands lay in the polar regions, with only 20 percent in temperate zones.

36. James C. Scott, *Against the Grain: A Deep History of the Earliest States* (New Haven: Yale University Press, 2017), argues that the cultivation of grains was forced on early farmers by the state because grain is easy to measure and collect as revenue. See also Jared Diamond, "The Worst Mistake in the History of the Human Race," *Discover Magazine*, May 1987, 64–66.

37. Mark Nathan Cohen and George J. Armelagos, eds., *Paleopathology at the Origins of Agriculture* (Orlando, Fla.: Academic Press, 1984), especially chapters 2–5. See also Diamond, "The Worst Mistake in the History of the Human Race," 64–66.

38. On the fatal shift among farmers from perennial to annual plants, see Wes Jackson, *New Roots for Agriculture* (Lincoln: University of Nebraska Press, 1981); and Judith Soule and Jon Piper, *Farming in Nature's Image: An Ecological Approach to Agriculture* (Washington, D.C.: Island Press, 1991).

39. William McNeill, *Plagues and Peoples* (Garden City, N.Y.: Anchor Doubleday, 1976), 51–53.

40. Massimo Livi-Bacci, *A Concise History of World Population*, trans. Carl Ipsen (Cambridge, Mass.: Blackwell, 1992), 31.

41. The literature on plantations and slavery is immense, but there is no better place to start than Sidney Mintz's *Sweetness and Power* (New York: Viking, 1983).

42. "Works and Days," in *Hesiod*, ed. and trans. Glen Most, Loeb Classical Library (Cambridge: Harvard University Press, 2006), 121, 123, 125.

43. For a cultural materialist view that puts human desires back in the picture, see *Food and Evolution: Toward a Theory of Human Food Habits*, ed. Marvin Harris and Eric B. Ross (Philadelphia, Pa.: Temple University Press, 1989).

44. Steven Mintz, "Historical Context: Facts About the Slave Trade and Slavery," www.gilderlehrman.org/history-resources/teacher-resources/historical-context-facts-about-slave-trade-and-slavery. Also see the "Trans-Atlantic Slave Trade Database," ed. David Eltis and David Richardson, slavevoyages.org.

45. Benjamin Aldes Wurgaft, *Meat Planet: Artificial Flesh and the Future of Food* (Berkeley: University of California Press, 2020).

46. Charles Darwin's *On the Origin of Species* (1859) distinguishes two kinds of evolution: *artificial* (chapter 1, "Variation Under Domestication") and *natural* (chapter 2, "Variation Under

NOTES TO PAGES 75-83

Nature"). For further discussion, see David Rindos, *The Origins of Agriculture: An Evolutionary Perspective* (Orlando, Fla.: Academic Press, 1984); and Rindos, "Darwinism and Its Role in the Explanation of Domestication," in *Foraging and Farming: The Evolution of Plant Exploitation*, ed. David Harris and Gordon Hillman (London: Unwin Hyman, 1989), 27–41.

Chapter 3. Humpty Dumpty and the Fate of Power

1. See Joseph Tainter, *The Collapse of Complex Societies* (Cambridge: Cambridge University Press, 1988), 22–38.

2. This chapter owes much to the work of James C. Scott, particularly his *Against the Grain: A Deep History of the Earliest States* (New Haven: Yale University Press, 2017).

3. For a discussion of why organized societies become disorganized, see Jared Diamond, *Collapse: How Societies Choose to Fail or Succeed* (New York: Viking, 2005), prologue.

4. Robert L. Carneiro, "A Theory of the Origin of the State," *Science* 169 (August 21, 1970): 733.

5. Thorkild Jacobsen and Robert Adams, "Salt and Silt in Ancient Mesopotamian Agriculture," *Science* 128 (November 21, 1958): 1251–1258.

6. United Nations Convention to Combat Desertification, www.unccd.int/convention/overview.

7. On the view of China's history in Karl Wittfogel, *Oriental Despotism* (1957), see Donald Worster, *Rivers of Empire: Water, Aridity, and the Growth of the American West* (New York: Oxford University Press, 1985), 22–29.

8. For histories of flooding in China, see Ling Zhang, *The River, the Plain, and the State: An Environmental Drama in Northern Song China, 1048–1128* (New York: Cambridge University Press, 2016); Ruth Mostern, *The Yellow River: A Natural and Unnatural History* (New Haven: Yale University Press, 2021); and David Pietz, *The Yellow River: The Problem of Water in Modern China* (Cambridge: Harvard University Press, 2015).

9. Mark Elvin, "Three Thousand Years of Unsustainable Development," *East Asian History* 6 (December 1993): 7–46.

10. For an introduction see "Nile Basin Water Resources Atlas," https://atlas.nilebasin.org, especially chapter 5.

11. Robert Carneiro, "A Theory of the Origin of the State," *Science* 169 (August 21, 1970): 733–738. See also Carneiro, "The Circumscription Theory: A Clarification, Amplification, and Reformulation," *Social Evolution & History* 11 (September 2012): 5–29; and *The Muse of History and the Science of Culture* (New York: Kluwer Academic/Plenum, 2000), 156–158, 177–178, 185–186.

12. This reciprocity is underemphasized in James C. Scott, *Weapons of the Weak: Everyday Forms of Peasant Resistance* (New Haven: Yale University Press, 1987).

13. Mark W. Allen et al., "Resource Scarcity Drives Lethal Aggression Among Prehistoric Hunter-Gatherers in Central California," *Proceedings of the National Academy of Sciences* 113 (October 2016): 1212.

14. That interhuman violence is on the decline is the theme of Ian Morris, *War! What Is It Good For?* (2015), and Steven Pinker, *The Better Angels of Our Nature: Why Violence Has Declined* (2011). For another view, see Dean Falk and Charles Hildebolt, "Annual War Deaths in Small-Scale Versus State Societies Scale with Population Size Rather than Violence," *Current Anthropology* 58, no. 6 (December 2017): 805.

15. Garrett Hardin reconciled this apparent conflict between state power and local assertion with the simple phrase "mutual coercion, mutually agreed upon by the majority of the people affected." See his essay "The Tragedy of the Commons," *Science* 162 (December 13, 1968): 1247.

16. D. Bruce Dickson, "Circumscription by Anthropogenic Environmental Destruction: An Expansion of Carneiro's (1970) Theory of the Origin of the State," *American Antiquity* 52 (October 1987): 709–716.

17. Carneiro, "A Theory of the Origin of the State," 735–736.

18. For an overview of pre-Columbian settlements in Brazil, see Justin Buccifero, "Neither Counterfeit nor Paradise," *Economic Anthropology* 3, no. 1 (January 2016): 12–30. On the Incans, see Jeremy Mumford, *Vertical Empire* (Durham, N.C.: Duke University Press, 2012); and Gordon McEwan, *The Incas: New Perspectives* (New York: W.W. Norton, 2008).

19. Henri J. M. Claessen, "On Early States—Structure, Development, and Fall," *Social Evolution & History* 9 (March 2010): 14. See also "Was the State Inevitable?," *Social Evolution & History* 1 (July 2002): 101–117; and *The Early State: A Structural Approach,* ed. Henri J. M. Claessen and Peter Skalnik (The Hague: Mouton, 1978), 533–596.

20. The phrase is from William Ophuls, *Immoderate Greatness: Why Civilizations Fail* (Scotts Valley, Calif.: CreateSpace, 2012). The wag's quote is from Peter Davidson, *Atlas of Empires: The World's Great Powers from Ancient Times to Today* (Mount Joy, Pa.: Companion-House, 2018), 7.

21. See Edward Gibbon, *The History of the Decline and Fall of the Roman Empire* (originally published in six volumes in London by W. Strahan and T. Cadell, 1776–1789). Gibbon's classic has long been admired for its elegant prose, sense of irony, and animus against organized religion, but it is also woefully short of ecological understanding.

22. Tim Flannery, *Europe: A Natural History* (New York: Atlantic Monthly Press, 2018), Kindle ed., locations 1189, 1215–1219, 1606.

23. Scientists have discovered dramatic fluctuations in sea level around Mallorca, ranging from over six meters to five meters below current level. See https://news.climate.columbia.edu/2021/01/21/reconstructing-6-5-million-years-western-mediterranean-sea-levels.

24. J. Donald Hughes, *Pan's Travail: Environmental Problems of the Ancient Greeks and Romans* (Baltimore: Johns Hopkins University Press, 1994), 14.

25. See Jose Torrent, "Mediterranean Soils," in *Encyclopedia of Soils in the Environment*, vol. 2, ed. Daniel Hillel (Oxford: Elsevier Academic Press, 2005), 418–427; Randall Schaetzl and Sharon Anderson, "Terra Rossa Soils of the Mediterranean," in their study *Soils: Genesis and Geomorphology* (Cambridge: Cambridge University Press, 2005), 201.

26. Hughes, *Pan's Travail*, 130–148.

27. For the environmental history of the Mediterranean, see David Attenborough, *The First Eden* (Boston: Little, Brown, 1987); A. T. Grove and Oliver Rackham, *The Nature of Mediterranean Europe* (New Haven: Yale University Press, 2003); Peregrine Horden and Nicholas Purcell, *The Corrupting Sea* (Hoboken, N.J.: Wiley-Blackwell, 2000); J. R. McNeill, *Mountains of the Mediterranean World* (New York: Cambridge University Press, 1992); Fernand Braudel, *The Mediterranean and the Mediterranean World in the Age of Philip II*, trans. Siân Reynolds (Berkeley: University of California Press, 1996).

28. While the triad NKP elements are vital for soil fertility, carbon is also important. See H. Tiessen et al., "The Role of Soil Organic Matter in Sustaining Soil Fertility," *Nature* 371 (October 27, 1994): 785.

29. Vladimir Simkhovitch, "Rome's Fall Reconsidered," *Political Science Quarterly* 31 (June 1916): 209. Simkhovitch was an émigré from Russia who taught economics at Columbia University.

30. Simkhovitch, "Rome's Fall Reconsidered," 209.

31. On Roman soil exhaustion, see Hughes, *Pan's Travail*, 138–139, and McNeill, *Mountains of the Mediterranean World*, 311–325.

32. Marc Bloch, *Feudal Society*, trans. L. A. Manyon (Chicago: University of Chicago Press), 1961.

33. Simkhovitch writes that even in Cato's day (234–149 BCE), agriculture had already declined over most of Italy. Cato's *Husbandry*, "the earliest Roman agricultural book that has come down to us, practically disregards the cultivation of grain crops. His attention is devoted to the cultivation of the vine and olive" ("Rome's Fall Reconsidered," 212). On the long history of the latifundia, see Simkhovitch, 203–205.

34. Edward Melillo, "The First Green Revolution: Debt Peonage and the Making of the Nitrogen Fertilizer Trade, 1840–1930," *American Historical Review* 117 (October 2012): xiv–xvii.

35. This common view among Romans is documented in Peter Garnsey, *Famine and Food Supply in the Graeco-Roman World* (Cambridge: Cambridge University Press, 1989), 255.

36. John Perlin, *A Forest Journey: The Role of Wood in the Development of Civilization* (Cambridge: Harvard University Press, 1993), 128.

37. John L. Brooke, *Climate Change and the Course of Global History: A Rough Journey* (New York: Cambridge University Press, 2014), 339–347.

38. Kyle Harper, *The Fate of Rome: Climate, Disease, and the End of an Empire* (Princeton: Princeton University Press, 2017), 15, 159–198.

39. Sing Chew, *World Ecological Degradation* (Walnut Creek, Calif.: Altamira Press, 2001), 86.

40. John L. Brooke, "Malthus and the North Atlantic Oscillation," *Journal of Interdisciplinary History* 46 (Spring 2016): 569. See also R. J. Littman and M. L. Littman, "Galen and the Antonine Plague," *American Journal of Philology* 94 (Autumn 1973): 243–255.

41. Harper, *Fate of Rome*, 31.

42. Harper, *Fate of Rome*, 76–78.

43. Harper, *Fate of Rome*, 35.

44. Harper, *Fate of Rome*, 80.

45. Smallpox appeared in early Nile farm settlements and spread as far away as India via merchants and traders. Stefan Riedel, "Edward Jenner and the History of Smallpox and Vaccination," *Proceedings of the Baylor University Medical Center* 18 (January 2005): 21.

46. Cicero, *De Natura Deorum*, trans. H. Rackham, Loeb Classical Library (Cambridge: Harvard University Press, 1933), II, 271. "Second" nature is supposed to replace "first" nature, but then why not a third, fourth, or fifth nature?

47. Kathryn Glattera and Paul Finkelman, "History of the Plague: An Ancient Pandemic for the Age of COVID-19," *American Journal of Medicine* 134 (February 2021): 176–181.

Chapter 4. The Discovery of Second Earth

1. For a highly Eurocentric account, see Karl Polanyi, *The Great Transformation* (New York: Rinehart, 1944).

2. Richard Dawkins, *The Selfish Gene* (New York: Oxford University Press, 1976), 203–215. The first printing of texts began in China around 700 CE, relying on carved wood blocks with images that were pressed on silk or paper. The Koreans invented movable type printing in the fourteenth century, about sixty years earlier than Gutenberg. See Lucien Febvre and Henri-Jean Martin, *The Coming of the Book* (New York: Verso, 1997), 75–76.

3. J. N. Biraben, "Essai sur l'évolution du nombre des hommes," *Population* 34 (1979): 15. Europe's population began growing faster than anywhere else, although it had the smallest land base. See also Colin McEvedy and Richard Jones in *Atlas of World Population History* (New York: Facts on File, 1978).

4. Biraben, "Essai sur l'évolution du nombre des hommes," and McEvedy and Jones, *Atlas of World Population History.*

NOTES TO PAGES 116-126

5. McEvedy and Jones, *Atlas of World Population History,* 349. See also Massimo Livi-Bacci, *A Concise History of World Population,* trans. Carl Ipsen (Cambridge, Mass.: Blackwell, 1992); and Organization for Economic Co-operation and Development, "Appendix B: World Population, GDP and GDP Per Capita Before 1820," in *The World Economy,* vol. 1, *A Millennial Perspective,* and vol. 2, *Historical Statistics* (Paris: OECD Publishing, 2006). For the population rebound in Europe after the Black Death, see James Belich, *The World the Plague Made: The Black Death and the Rise of Europe* (Princeton: Princeton University Press, 2022); Bruce Campbell, *The Great Transition: Climate, Disease, and Society in the Late-Medieval World* (Cambridge: Cambridge University Press, 2016).

6. Pre-modern deforestation had an important impact on the planet's climate, long before the burning of coal or oil. See Warren Ruddiman, *Plows, Plagues, and Petroleum: How Humans Took Control of Climate* (Princeton: Princeton University Press, 2005), part 3. For other overviews, see I. G. Simmons, *An Environmental History of Great Britain* (Edinburgh: Edinburgh University Press, 2001), 92–100; and B. A. Holderness, *Pre-Industrial England* (London: Dent, 1976).

7. Maria Valbuena-Carabaña et al., "Historical and Recent Changes in the Spanish Forests," *Review of Palaeobotany and Palynology* 162, no. 3 (October 2010): 492–506. This special issue is devoted to Iberian vegetational change. For contributing factors see Joseph O'Callaghan, *Reconquest and Crusade in Medieval Spain* (Philadelphia: University of Pennsylvania Press, 2004).

8. Anthony Wrigley, *Continuity, Chance, and Change: The Character of the Industrial Revolution in England* (Cambridge: Cambridge University Press, 1988), 5–6.

9. By the 1520s Germany's Anabaptists were worrying about the Apocalypse and Martin Luther was reading the book of Revelation, indicating the unease and pessimism that counterpointed the Age of Discovery. See Winfried Vogel, "The Eschatological Theory of Martin Luther," *Andrews University Seminary Studies* 45 (Summer 1987): 183–199.

10. Poul Holm et al., "The North Atlantic Fish Revolution (ca. AD 1500)," *Quaternary Research* 108 (2019): 92–106.

11. Columbus's origins have become controversial, with some holding that he came from Genoa, others that he was a Sephardic Jew from Portugal. Here he will be simply Christopher Columbus of disputed birthplace.

12. "Toscanelli's Letter to Canon Martins" (1474), *Journals and Other Documents on the Life and Voyages of Christopher Columbus,* ed. Samuel Eliot Morison (New York: Horizon Press, 1963), 13–14. Columbus received a personal note of encouragement from Toscanelli, which clinched his ambition to cross the Atlantic Ocean.

13. Zheng He (1371–1433/35) was born in China's Yunnan Province. Though he was castrated and enslaved in his youth, he grew up a protégé of Chinese leaders and learned the arts

NOTES TO PAGES 127-135

of war, diplomacy, and navigation. His state-funded expeditions followed old trade routes and tribute gathering along the South Asian coast. Zheng and his contemporaries, although highly skilled in deep-sea voyaging and mapmaking, ignored the Pacific Ocean. See Robert Marks, *The Origins of the Modern World*, 4th ed. (Lanham, Md.: Rowman and Littlefield, 2020), 44; Gang Deng, *Chinese Maritime Activities and Development, c. 2100 BC–1900 AD* (Westport, Conn.: Greenwood, 1997); and Louise Levathes, *When China Ruled the Seas: The Treasure Fleet of the Dragon Throne, 1405–1433* (New York: Simon and Schuster, 1994).

14. See Dava Sobel, *Longitude: The True Story of a Lone Genius Who Solved the Greatest Scientific Problem of His Time* (New York: Walker, 1995).

15. See Samuel Eliot Morison, *Admiral of the Ocean Sea* (Boston: Little, Brown, 1942); Gianni Granzotto, *Christopher Columbus* (Garden City, N.Y.: Doubleday, 1985); William D. Phillips, Jr., and Carla Phillips, *The Worlds of Christopher Columbus* (Cambridge: Cambridge University Press, 1992); and Felipe Fernández-Armesto, *1492: The Year the World Began* (New York: HarperCollins, 2009).

16. In 1507 a map by Martin Waldseemüller first identified the new lands as "America," thus memorializing Amerigo Vespucci, an Italian merchant-explorer (1451–1512) who was the first to realize that the lands Columbus discovered were in fact a pair of continents. Viewed as a unified landmass, North and South America covered forty million square kilometers, making them larger than Africa but smaller than Eurasia.

17. Antonio Pigafetta, *Magellan's Voyage*, 2 vols. (New Haven: Yale University Press, 1969); John Delaney, *Strait Through: Magellan to Cook and the Pacific* (Princeton: Princeton University Library, 2010); and Joyce Chaplin, *Round About the Earth: Circumnavigation from Magellan to Orbit* (New York: Simon and Schuster, 2013).

18. A world map showing the Americas appeared in China in 1602, introduced by the Italian priest Matteo Ricci (1552–1610).

19. Francis Drake, *The World Encompassed* (London: Nicholas Bourne, 1628), 12. This publication was compiled from Drake's travel notes (1577–1580) and included a map of the voyages he made. The spelling has been modernized.

20. See Kenneth Andrews, *Drake's Voyages* (New York: Scribner, 1967); Henry Kelsey, *Sir Francis Drake* (New Haven: Yale University Press, 2000); and Laurence Bergreen, *In Search of a Kingdom* (New York: Custom House, 2021).

21. Massimo Livi-Bacci, *The Population of Europe: A History*, trans. Carl Ipsen (Malden, Mass.: Blackwell, 2000), 6–7.

22. See Alfred Crosby, *Ecological Imperialism*, 2nd ed. (New York: Cambridge University Press, 2004); and Dan Flores, *Wild New World: The Epic Story of Animals and People in America* (New York: W.W. Norton, 2022).

23. Livi-Bacci, *A Concise History of World Population*, 69.

24. For a summary and evaluation of Gregory King's data, see W. G. Hoskins, *The Making of the English Landscape* (London: Hodder and Stoughton, 1988), 117–118.

25. On the enclosures, see Hoskins, *The Making of the English Landscape*, 121–169.

26. Flores, *Wild New World*, 89; Wilbur R. Jacobs, "The Tip of an Iceberg: Pre-Columbian Indian Demography and Some Important Implications for Revisionism," in Jacobs, *The Fatal Confrontation* (Albuquerque: University of New Mexico Press, 1996).

27. The reality turned out to be quite different, as Africans suffered malnutrition and infections working as slaves on West Indian plantations. See Kenneth Kiple, *The Caribbean Slave* (New York: Cambridge University Press, 1984).

28. See Crosby, *Ecological Imperialism;* Charles Mann, *1491: New Revelations of the Americas Before Columbus* (New York: Alfred Knopf, 2005); and *1493: Uncovering the New World Columbus Created* (New York: Alfred A. Knopf, 2011).

Chapter 5. Dreams of Infinite Wealth

1. Karl Marx and Friedrich Engels, *The Communist Manifesto*, ed. Samuel Beer (1848; New York: Appleton, Century, Crofts, 1955). Written by Marx with help from Engels, in an elegant business building facing the Grand Place in Brussels, Belgium, the pamphlet appeared in print just a few weeks before a radical insurrection broke out in Paris, leading many to fear that a revolution was erupting across Europe.

2. Robert L. Heilbroner traces the thoughts of those who turned the "drive for wealth" into abstract philosophy in *The Worldly Philosophers* (New York: Simon and Schuster, 1953), 16. See also Fernand Braudel, *The Perspective of the World*, vol. 3, *Civilization and Capitalism* (New York: Harper and Row, 1979), and Karl Polanyi, *The Great Transformation* (New York: Rinehart, 1944).

3. The founders of communism were being self-descriptive when they wrote, "In place of the old wants, satisfied by the production of the country, we find new wants, requiring for their satisfaction the products of distant lands and climes." Marx and Engels, *The Communist Manifesto*, 16.

4. *Karl Marx Frederick Engels: Collected Works*, vol. 5 (New York: International, 1976), 28–29n. In the next chapter I address the one exception to Marx's disinterest in ecology, evolution, and environmental science—his brief discussion of Justus Liebig's work on soil depletion. A provocative but unpersuasive counterview is provided by Kohei Saito, *Karl Marx's Ecosocialism: Capital, Nature, and the Unfinished Critique of Political Economy* (New York: Monthly Review Press, 2017).

5. Quoted in Janet Browne, *Charles Darwin: The Power of Place* (Princeton: Princeton University Press, 2002), 188.

6. See Browne, *Charles Darwin*. The upwardly mobile Marx family moved through a sequence of residences, starting in working-class Chelsea and then relocating to Soho, Leicester Square, Kentish Town, and finally Maitland Park—each move marking an improvement in their living standards.

7. Brinley Thomas, "Escaping from Constraints: The Industrial Revolution in a Malthusian Context," in *Population and Economy*, ed. Robert Rotberg and Theodore Rabb (London: Cambridge University Press, 1986), 169–193.

8. R. D. Lee and R. S. Schofield, "British Population in the Eighteenth Century," in *The Economic History of Britain Since 1700*, vol. 1, ed. Roderick Floud and Donald McCloskey (Cambridge: Cambridge University Press, 1981), 17–22.

9. As Marx put it in a little-noticed passage, the industrial capitalist mode of production "only makes its appearance with the increase of population"; *Karl Marx Frederick Engels: Collected Works*, vol. 5, 32.

10. As late as 1868, imported food amounted to no more than 20 percent of the British diet; today, it has risen to nearly 50 percent.

11. Thomas, "Escaping from Constraints," 184; and B. R. Mitchell and Phyllis Deane, *Abstract of British Historical Statistics* (New York: Cambridge University Press, 1962), 94.

12. Richard Wilkinson, *Poverty and Progress: An Ecological Perspective on Economic Development* (New York: Praeger, 1973), 126.

13. See Donald Worster, *Shrinking the Earth: The Rise and Decline of American Abundance* (New York: Oxford University Press, 2016), 51–53. There I discuss *The Coal Question* (1865), a book written by the Victorian economist William Stanley Jevons, who warned that Britain's coal supply was exhaustible and that it would someday limit the country's economic growth, not fuel it. On the various energy revolutions, see Vaclav Smil, *Energy Transitions* (Santa Barbara, Calif.: Praeger, 2010).

14. Thomas, "Escaping from Constraints," 169.

15. Adam Smith, *An Inquiry into the Nature and Causes of the Wealth of Nations*, 5th ed. (New York: Modern Library, 1937), 590.

16. Guillaume-Thomas Raynal, *Histoire philosophique et politique, des Éstablissmens & du commerce des Européens dans les deux Indies* (Amsterdam: n.p., 1770), 1. The translation from French is my own.

17. Raynal, *Histoire philosophique et politique*, 1.

18. What was once called "natural history" is the subject of Michael Dove's *Hearsay Is Not Excluded: A History of Natural History* (New Haven: Yale University Press, 2024).

19. Entry 172672 in the *Oxford English Dictionary*, https://www-oed-com.

20. David Wootton, *The Invention of Science: A New History of the Scientific Revolution* (New York: HarperCollins, 2015), Kindle ed., location 333.

21. Critiques of Bacon's utilitarian science can be found in William Leiss, *The Domination of Nature* (Boston: Beacon, 1974); Carolyn Merchant, *The Death of Nature* (New York: Harper and Row, 1980); and Donald Worster, *Nature's Economy*, 2nd ed. (New York: Cambridge University Press, 1994), 30–31.

22. The translation from Latin comes from Mattia Gianlucca Worster.

23. Bacon, *Novum Organum,* Book I, aphorism 3.

24. Engels quoted in Ian Angus, "How Darwin Influenced Marx and Engels," *Tribune Magazine,* April 19, 2022, https://tribunemag.co.uk/2022/04/darwin-evolution-natural-selection-karl-marx-friedrich-engels-on-the-origin-of-species-capital.

Chapter 6. The Good Muck

1. This chapter originated as a plenary address to a conference on "Resourceful Things: An Interdisciplinary Symposium on Resource Exploration and Exploitation in China," April 20–22, 2016, which was organized at Harvard University by Ling Zhang. I wish to thank her and Peter C. Perdue, James Scott, Robert Marks, Bin Wong, and others for their comments and suggestions. I am also indebted to my colleagues at Renmin University of China for further help—especially to Xia Mingfeng, Hou Shen, and Chen Hao. And also to Cao Mu for expert advice and Joshua Nygren and Zheng Kunyan for research assistance. Thanks to the Rachel Carson Center, which published an earlier version in its *Perspectives* series.

2. Rose George, *The Big Necessity: The Unmentionable World of Human Waste and Why It Matters* (New York: Metropolitan, 2008), 109.

3. Especially popular among China's affluent classes is Toto's top of the line model, the Neorest 550H Dual Flush Toilet, which retails at about 35,000 yuan (U.S. $5,000) and, according to its advertising, offers "ecology-minded luxury" in its "technologically advanced Washlet, Tornado siphon jet flushing system, remote control, heated seat and CeFiONtect glaze, an extraordinarily smooth, ion-barrier surface to help keep the bowl cleaner longer."

4. A single gram of feces can contain "10 million viruses, 1 million bacteria, 1,000 parasite cysts, and 100 worm eggs," writes Rose George in *The Big Necessity,* 1. For the most part those organisms are harmless to humans, and they are sometimes necessary for our bodies to function, but, George adds, "plenty are malign."

5. According to the book *Qimin Yaoshu* (published circa 544 CE; reprint, Beijing: Science Publisher, 1958), written by the early agronomist Sixie Jia, a wide diversity of animal wastes, including silkworm droppings, were used by early Chinese farmers, though he does not say exactly when that began or how large the quantities were. Anonymous inventors made fertilizer by collecting straw and other residues after harvesting, spreading the straw on a flat surface, and making oxen walk over it. Other methods included boiling horse, ox, sheep, pig, and deer bones with snow melt and adding the juice of monkshood.

6. Some early economists in the West wanted to create a circular, perpetual economy based on excrement, but they were wildly impractical. See Dana Simmons, "Waste Not, Want Not: Excrement and Economy in Nineteenth-Century France," *Representations* 96 (Fall 2006): 73–98.

7. Franklin H. King's *Farmers of Forty Centuries: Or Permanent Agriculture in China, Korea, and Japan* was first published in 1911 in Madison, Wisconsin, by King's widow and was then republished by the Organic Gardening Press (Emmaus, Pa.), which is the edition cited here. A Chinese translation by Cheng Cunwang and Shi Yan was published by Beijing's Oriental Press in 2011.

8. Kenneth Pomeranz, *The Great Divergence: China, Europe, and the Making of the Modern World Economy* (Princeton: Princeton University Press, 2000), compares Jiangnan favorably to the West; see 31–68.

9. Franklin King to Carrie King, March 10, 1909, Franklin King Papers, Wisconsin State Historical Society, box 2, folder 2, page 142. Mostly his letters home focus on the travel arrangements King had to make, the costs of his travel, and reports on his health (he suffered from rheumatism).

10. Pearl Buck, whose famous title inspired the more sardonic one of this chapter, is worthy of more attention by historians. Born Pearl Sydenstriker in 1892, she was the daughter of American missionaries who took her to Anhui and Jiangsu provinces, where she spent more than three decades. Eventually she married the Nanjing-based agricultural economist John Lossing Buck, but in 1934 she left her husband for the United States. In 1938 she was awarded the Nobel Prize in Literature.

11. Randall E. Stross, *The Stubborn Earth: American Agriculturalists on Chinese Soil, 1898–1937* (Berkeley: University of California Press, 1986), 8.

12. Stross, *The Stubborn Earth*, 22.

13. King, *Farmers of Forty Centuries*, 239, 240.

14. Liu Ts'ui-jung et al., *Asian Population History* (Oxford: Oxford University Press, 2001).

15. Since King's day the arable land/people ratio in both China and the United States has declined precipitously, as land has been converted to housing and industrial development. According to the World Bank (worldbank.org), China's arable land fell from 0.16 hectares per person in 1961 to 0.08 in 2013, while the United States experienced a similar decline from 0.98 hectares per capita to 0.48. See Vaclav Smil, "Who Will Feed China?," *China Quarterly* 143 (September 1995): 801–813.

16. According to King (*Farmers of Forty Centuries*, 214), corn yields averaged 420–480 catties per mu in Shangdong province. Converting the traditional measurement of catties to kilograms and mu to hectares, those farmers were getting 6,750 kilograms of food production

per hectare. American farmers, in contrast, from 1860 to 1940 harvested on average only 1,630 kilograms per hectare. See A. E. Tiefenthaler, I. L. Goldman, and W. F. Tracy, "Vegetable and Corn Yields in the U.S., 1900–Present," *HortScience* 38 (October 2003): 1080.

17. King, *Farmers of Forty Centuries*, 147.

18. Mark Elvin, *The Pattern of the Chinese Past* (Palo Alto: Stanford University Press, 1973), 309, 312, 314.

19. King, *Farmers of Forty Centuries*, 241.

20. Justus Liebig (1803–1873) was a German chemist who made significant contributions to organic chemistry. In 1840 he published *Chemistry in Its Applications to Agriculture and Physiology*, which led him to develop and promote the use of "chemical manures" to enhance crop production. For his life and ideas, see Margaret W. Rossiter, *The Emergence of Agricultural Science: Justus Liebig and the Americans, 1840–1880* (New Haven: Yale University Press, 1975).

21. King, *Farmers of Forty Centuries*, 173.

22. King, *Farmers of Forty Centuries*, 179.

23. On the history of the flood-prone Yellow River, see chapter 3, note 8.

24. Franklin King to Carrie King, March 4, 1909, Franklin King Papers, box 2, folder 2, page 125.

25. See Donald Worster, *Nature's Economy: A History of Ecological Ideas*, 2nd ed. (New York: Cambridge University Press, 1994), chapter 12; and Worster, *Dust Bowl: The Southern Plains in the 1930s* (New York: Oxford University Press, 1979 and 2004).

26. Charles Darwin's last published work was about farming and the role of earthworms in the soil ecosystem: *The Formation of Vegetable Mould, Through the Action of Worms* (1881), which introduced an ecological perspective that anticipated the concept of the "ecosystem."

27. Gabrielle wrote in a letter to Albert in 1905, "The plant knows no division of science—in growing and carrying out its functions it uses all." Quoted by Louise E. Howard in *Albert Howard in India* (London: Faber and Faber, 1953), 15.

28. Albert Howard's *An Agricultural Testament* was first published in England in 1940 and then republished by Oxford University Press in 1943. Today it is accessible at the website www.journeyforever.org/farm library, which is the source cited here. See also his *Soil and Health: A Study of Organic Agriculture* (Lexington: University Press of Kentucky, 1947); and Philip Conford, *The Origins of the Organic Movement* (Edinburgh: Floris, 2001).

29. Howard, *Agricultural Testament*, 3.

30. Howard, *Agricultural Testament*, introduction.

31. Howard, *Agricultural Testament*, preface.

32. An ambitious recent work on the commodification of cotton is Sven Beckert, *An Empire of Cotton: A Global History* (New York: Alfred Knopf, 2014).

33. Howard, *Agricultural Testament*, 15.

34. A popular myth in China is that the country emerged either about five thousand years ago under the legendary Yellow Emperor Huang Di or during the Xia dynasty, a mythic state according to some scholars. Written records began only three or four thousand years ago. How then did King arrive at his estimate of forty centuries (or four thousand years) of Chinese farming?

35. Wang Lihua, "'Turning Waste into Treasure': An Overview to Waste Utilization in Chinese Agricultural History," unpublished essay furnished to the author. See also Hu Houxuan, "Reexamination of Fertilizer in Yin Dynasty Farming," *Social Science Front Monthly* (1981): 102–109; and Yu Xingwu, "Farmland Reclamation of the Shang Dynasty, in the Perspective of Shang Calligraphy of Inscriptions on Bones," *Archaeology* (1972): 40–45.

36. For an amusing overview of pigs in Chinese history, see C. W. Hayford's blog article, "Pigs, Shit, and Chinese History, Or Happy Year of the Pig," January 28, 2007, www.froginawell.net/china/2007/01.

37. William Shurtleff and Akiko Aoyagi, "History of Soybean Crushing: Soy Oil and Soybean Meal," *History of Soybeans and Soyfoods*, www.soyinfocenter.com/HSS/soybean_crushing1.php.

38. Li Bozhong, "Analysis of the Amount of Jiangnan Fertilizer Demands in the Ming and Qing Dynasties: The First Discussion of the Fertilizer Problem of Ming and Qing Dynasties," *Qing History Journal* (1999): 30–38, 108. Mark Elvin has argued that an earlier agricultural revolution occurred in China between the eighth and twelfth centuries, based on "the mastery of wet-field rice cultivation, which allowed a great southward migration"; Elvin, *The Pattern of the Chinese Past*, 113, 118–120.

39. For an overview of what the author calls "agrarian urbanization," see Xue Yong, "'Treasure Nightsoil As If It Were Gold': Economic and Ecological Links Between Urban and Rural Areas in Late Imperial Jiangnan," *Late Imperial China* 26 (June 2005): 41–71.

40. Xue Yong, "'Treasure Nightsoil As If It Were Gold,'" 60–61. The imperial official report he cites can be found in *Qinding shoushi tongkao* (1737), vol. 35, 7–8.

41. Data are from Liang Fangzhong, *The Statistics of the Household and Population, Farmland and Land Tax in Ancient China* (Beijing: Zhonghua Book Company, 2008), 430–437, 446–447, 450–451; Cao Shuji, *The History of China's Population*, vol. 4, *Ming Dynasty* (Shanghai: Fudan University Press, 2000), 137–138; and vol. 5, *Qing Dynasty* (Shanghai: Fudan University Press, 2001), 72–77, 85–86, 105–107.

42. Karl Marx, *Capital: A Critique of Political Economy* (reprint, New York: Modern Library, 1906), 554–555. See also John Bellamy Foster, "Marx's Theory of Metabolic Rift: Classical Foundations for Environmental Sociology," *American Journal of Sociology* 105 (September 1999): 366–405.

43. See Li Bozhong, "Analysis of the Amount of Fertilizer Jiangnan Region Demands in Ming and Qing Dynasties," in which he illustrates the excremental economy by an old story, *Digging New Holes: The Miser Became a Rich Man,* written by the Master of the Zhuoran Pavilion.

44. Franklin King Papers, Box 2, folder 2, page 40.

45. Cao Mu, "The Public Lavatory of Tianjin: A Change of Urban Faeces Disposal in the Process of Modernization," *Global Environment* 9 (2016): 196–218.

46. Cao's source for these new regulations is "Renovating the City's Public Lavatory, 1937," Archive of Tianjin, J0001-3-000624.

47. Mark Elvin, *The Retreat of the Elephants: An Environmental History of China* (New Haven: Yale University Press, 2004), 9–85.

48. Dwight H. Perkins, *Agricultural Development in China, 1368–1968* (Chicago: Aldine, 1969), 10. See also Philip C. C. Huang, *The Peasant Economy and Social Change in North China* (Stanford: Stanford University Press, 1985).

49. Judith Banister, "A Brief History of China's Population," in *The Population of Modern China,* ed. Dudley L. Poston, Jr., and David Yaukey (New York: Plenum, 1992), 51.

50. Howard, *Agricultural Testament,* 14.

51. The best account is Vaclav Smil, *Enriching the Earth: Fritz Haber, Carl Bosch, and the Transformation of World Food Production* (Cambridge: MIT Press, 2004). See also Smil, "Nitrogen Cycle and World Food Production," *World Agriculture* 2 (2011): 9–10; and Smil, "Detonator of the Population Explosion," *Nature* 400 (1999): 415.

52. Zhun Yu et al., "Historical Nitrogen Fertilizer Use in China from 1952 to 2018," *Earth Systems Science Data,* doi.org/10.5194/essd-14-5179-2022; and Kai Zhang, "The Evolution and Development of Chinese Agricultural Fertilization in the Last Hundred Years," *Agricultural History of China* 3 (2000): 107–113.

53. Dan Charles, "Our Fertilized World," *National Geographic* 223 (May 2013): 94–110. See Food and Agriculture Organization of the United Nations, "Current World Fertilizer Trends and Outlook to 2016," ftp://ftp.fao.org/ag/agp/docs/cwft016.pdf.

54. Zhen Yu et al., "Historical Nitrogen Fertilizer Use in China from 1952 to 2018," *Earth Systems Science Data,* November 23, 2022, https://doi.org/10.5194/essd-14-5179-2022.

55. E. C. Ellis and S. M. Wang, "Sustainable Traditional Agriculture in the Tai Lake Region of China," *Agriculture Ecosystems & Environment* 61 (1997): 177–193.

Chapter 7. The Empty Cradle of Hope

1. Sandburg's poem *The People, Yes* was first published by Harcourt, Brace in 1936.

2. Sandburg, *The People, Yes* (reprint, New York: Harcourt, Brace, Jovanovich, 1980), 285.

3. At the beginning of the twentieth century average fertility rates in the United States were as low as 3.83 (fewer than four children per woman), whereas they had been as high

as 8.0 or more during the early years of the nation. Fertility rates pertain only to women, whereas birthrates are a percentage of the whole population, men and children included. During the 1930s U.S. fertility rates dropped, but by 1958 they were up to 3.6 children per woman, before falling again. See Jean-Claude Chesnais, *The Demographic Transition* (Oxford: Clarendon Press, 1992), 543.

4. Even as more and more came to the United States, immigrant women quickly followed native women in this trend. Aaron O'Neill, "Total Fertility Rate of the United States, 1800–2020," Statistica.com.

5. See Richard Grove, *Green Imperialism: Colonial Expansion, Tropical Island Edens and the Origins of Environmentalism, 1600–1860* (New York: Cambridge University Press, 1995). There is no single comprehensive history of American conservation, but for its origins, see Richard Judd, *The Untilled Garden: Natural History and the Origins of American Conservation, 1730–1850* (New York: Cambridge University Press, 2009). Also see Samuel Hays, *Conservation and The Gospel of Efficiency: The Progressive Conservation Movement, 1890–1920* (Pittsburgh: University of Pittsburgh Press, 1959), and *Beauty, Health, Permanence: Environmental Politics in the United States, 1955–1985* (New York: Cambridge University Press, 1989); and Roderick Nash, *Wilderness and the American Mind*, 4th ed. (New Haven: Yale University Press, 2001). However, because these works focus on ideas, culture, and politics, they do not explore the evolutionary link between environmental conservation and material change.

6. Donald Worster, *Shrinking the Earth: The Rise and Decline of American Abundance* (New York: Oxford University Press, 2016), part 1.

7. Evidence for birth control, including abortion, has been found in Egypt and Mesopotamia as far back as 1850 BCE. Ancient scrolls recommended the use of honey, acacia leaves, and lint to block sperm from entering the womb. See Vern L. Bullough, *Encyclopedia of Birth Control* (Santa Barbara, Calif.: ABC-CLIO, 2010).

8. On landscape change in New England, see Carolyn Merchant, *Ecological Revolutions: Nature, Gender, and Science in New England* (Chapel Hill: University of North Carolina Press, 1989); Theodore Steinberg, *Nature Incorporated: Industrialization and the Waters of New England* (New York: Cambridge University Press, 1991); Brian Donahue, *The Great Meadow: Farmers and the Land in Colonial Concord* (New Haven: Yale University Press, 2004); and William Cronon, *Changes in the Land: Indians, Colonialists, and the Ecology of New England* (New York: Hill and Wang, 1983). Also see Thomas Cole's famous painting *The View from Mount Holyoke—The Oxbow* (1836), which depicts a western Massachusetts countryside that has been heavily deforested, a vision of impending disaster.

9. Stephen J. W. Tabor, "The Late Charles Knowlton," *Boston Medical and Surgical Journal* 45 (September 1851): 109–111.

10. Karl Ernst von Baer, a German-Baltic nobleman and embryologist, reported in 1827 that he was the first person to verify the human female egg. See Jane Oppenheimer, "Baer, Karl Ernst von," *Dictionary of Scientific Biography* (New York: Charles Scribner's Sons, 1970), 385–389.

11. Massachusetts was among the last states to legalize birth control, due to pressure from the Catholic Church. Linda Gordon, *The Moral Property of Women: A History of Birth Control Politics in America* (Chicago: University of Illinois Press, 2002), 299.

12. Charles Bradlaugh (1833–1891) was a Liberal member of Parliament, an atheist, and a disciple of Thomas Malthus; Annie Besant (1847–1933) was a socialist, theosophist, and women's rights activist.

13. Knowlton, *The Fruits of Philosophy,* ed. Charles Bradlaugh and Annie Besant (reprint, San Francisco: Readers Library, 1891), 8–9, available online at https://archive.org. The British editors changed Knowlton's subtitle to *A Treatise on the Population Question.*

14. Ellen Carol DuBois, *Feminism and Suffrage: The Emergence of an Independent Woman's Movement in America, 1848–1869* (Ithaca: Cornell University Press, 1978); Eleanor Flexner, *Century of Struggle* (Cambridge: Belknap Press of Harvard University, 1959).

15. On the recent convergence of feminism and ecology, see Charlene Spretnak, "Ecofeminism: Our Roots and Flowering," in *Reweaving the World,* ed. Irene Diamond and Gloria Orenstein (San Francisco: Sierra Club, 1990), 3–14, and the many works of the environmental historian Carolyn Merchant, whose influence appears throughout this book.

16. Sripati Chandrasekhar, *"A Dirty Filthy Book": The Writings of Charles Knowlton and Annie Besant on Reproductive Physiology and Birth Control and an Account of the Bradlaugh-Besant Trial* (Berkeley: University of California Press, 1981), 23.

17. Chandrasekhar, *"A Dirty Filthy Book,"* 46.

18. For further reading about the control of reproduction in the United States, see Peter Engelman, *A History of the Birth Control Movement in America* (Santa Barbara, Calif.: Praeger, 2011); Elaine Tyler May, *America and the Pill* (New York: Basic, 2010); Andrea Tone, *Devices and Desires* (New York: Hill and Wang, 2001); James Reed, *From Private Vice to Public Virtue* (New York: Basic, 1978); and John Noonan, Jr., *Contraception* (Cambridge: Harvard University Press, 1965).

19. Knowlton, *The Fruits of Philosophy,* chapter 3, gutenberg.org. The doctor wanted to show "how desirable it is, both in a political and a social point of view, for mankind to be able to limit at will the number of their offspring, without sacrificing the pleasure that attends the gratification of the reproductive instinct."

20. Francis Galton (1822–1911), one of Britain's leading scientists, was eager to improve human intelligence through the practice of selective breeding. His embrace of eugenics

would make him a target for many critics, including Matthew Connelly in *Fatal Misconception: The Struggle to Control World Population* (Cambridge: Harvard University Press, 2006).

21. Allison Bashford, *Global Population* (New York: Columbia University Press, 2014), 2, 3, 12, 81–99, 211. For an on-the-scene report, see C. F. Close, "The World Population Conference of 1927," *Geographical Journal* 70 (November 1927): 470–472.

22. Margaret Sanger's life has been told by Jean Baker, *Margaret Sanger* (New York: Hill and Wang, 2011); Ellen Chesler, *Woman of Valor: Margaret Sanger and the Birth Control Movement* (New York: Simon and Schuster, 2007); and David Kennedy, *Birth Control in America* (New Haven: Yale University Press, 1970).

23. Margaret Sanger, *The Autobiography of Margaret Sanger* (Minneola, N.Y.: Dover, 1971), 344. Sanger was to some extent ill-informed about China, for its citizens had practiced birth control for centuries, featuring traditional herbal remedies.

24. See Armond Fields, *Katharine Dexter McCormick: Pioneer for Women's Rights* (Westport, Conn.: Praeger, 2003).

25. On Pincus and Chang, see Jonathan Eig, *The Birth of the Pill* (New York: W.W. Norton, 2014), 21–28, 62–89. Pincus's own writings include *The Control of Fertility* (New York: Academic Press, 1965) and *The Eggs of Mammals* (New York: Macmillan, 1936). On Chang's career, see Kimberly A. Buettner, "Min Chueh Chang (1908–1991)," *Embryo Project Encyclopedia*, http://embryo.asu.edu/handle/10776/1667.

26. See Margaret Marsh and Wanda Ronner, *The Fertility Doctor: John Rock and the Reproductive Revolution* (Baltimore: Johns Hopkins University Press, 2008).

27. Albert Q. Maisel, *The Hormone Quest* (New York: Random House, 1965).

28. The first modern oral contraceptive contained 100–175 micrograms of estrogen and 10 milligrams of progestin. After some alarming results, chemists settled on a much lower level of estrogen and progestin.

29. Carl Djerassi, *The Pill, Pigmy Chimps, and Degas' Horse: The Autobiography of Carl Djerassi* (New York: Basic, 1992), 118. See also Lara Marks, *Sexual Chemistry: A History of the Contraceptive Pill* (New Haven: Yale University Press, 2001); and Planned Parenthood, "The Birth Control Pill: A History," www.plannedparenthood.org/files/1514/3518/7100/Pill_History.

30. Betty Friedan, *The Feminine Mystique* (New York: W.W. Norton, 1963), 3, 167, 465. She did mention the abortifacient RU486, which she predicted "will soon make the whole issue of abortion obsolete" (502–503).

31. See Greer, *The Female Eunuch* (1971; New York: HarperCollins, 1991), 57. Barbara Seaman's *The Doctors' Case Against the Pill* (1969) inspired U.S. Senate hearings on the oral contraceptive. See Bill Christofferson, *The Man from Clear Lake: Earth Day Founder Senator Gaylord Nelson* (Madison: University of Wisconsin Press, 2004), 260–262.

32. Cited in Djerassi, *The Pill*, 126.

33. Rainey Horwitz, "The Dalkon Shield," *Embryo Project Encyclopedia* (2018), https://hdl.handle.net/10776/13043.

34. United Nations, Population Division, "Contraceptive Use by Method," 2019.

35. Today in the sub-Saharan region, a year's supply of birth control pills can cost hundreds of dollars a year, which could exceed the annual budget of some families.

36. On the environmental costs and pressures from human numbers, see John Bongaarts, "Population Growth and Global Warming," *Population and Development Review* 18 (June 1992): 299–319; Thomas Dietz and Eugene Rosa, "Effects of Population and Affluence on CO_2," *Proceedings of the National Academy of Sciences* 94 (1997): 175–179; David Pimentel and Marcia Pimentel, "Global Environmental Resources Versus World Population Growth," *Ecological Economics* 59 (2006): 195–198; Chu Cyrus, "Biodiversity Decline and Population Externalities," *Journal of Population Economics* 21 (2008): 173–181. See also Lester Brown, Gary Gardner, and Brian Helweil, *Beyond Malthus: Nineteen Dimensions of the Population Challenge* (New York: W.W. Norton, 1999); and Bill McKibben, *Maybe One: A Personal and Environmental Argument for Single-Child Families* (New York: Simon and Schuster, 1998).

37. "Current World Population," *Worldometer,* Worldometers.info/world-population.

38. Derick Moore, "U.S. Population Estimated at 335,893,238 on Jan. 1, 2024," December 28, 2023, United States Census Bureau, www.census.gov/library/stories/2023/12/happy-new-year-2024.html.

39. See U.S. Central Intelligence Agency, "Country Comparison: Total Fertility Rate," *The World Factbook,* www.cia.gov/the-world-factbook.

40. U.S. Central Intelligence Agency, "Country Comparison: Total Fertility Rate."

41. Wolfgang Lutz and Erich Striessnig, "Population: The Long View," *Population Studies* 69 (2015): S69–S76; Stuart Basten, Wolfgang Lutz, and Sergei Scherbov, "Very Long-Range Global Population Scenarios to 2300 and the Implications of Sustained Low Fertility," *Demographic Research* 28 (May 2013): 1145–1166. See also Stein Emil Vollset et al., "Fertility, Mortality, Migration, and Population Scenarios for 195 Countries and Territories from 2017 to 2100," *Lancet* 396 (October 2020): 1285–1306.

42. See, for example, Phillip Longman, *The Empty Cradle: How Falling Birthrates Threaten World Prosperity and What to Do About It* (New York: Basic, 2004); Paul Morland, *The Human Tide: How Population Shaped the Modern World* (New York: Public Affairs, 2019); and Jennifer Sciubba, *8 Billion and Counting: How Sex, Death, and Migration Shape Our World* (New York: W.W. Norton, 2022).

43. For discussion of changing sexual and reproductive behavior, see Alan Weisman, *Countdown: Our Last, Best Hope for a Future on Earth?* (New York: Little, Brown, 2014). On

carrying capacity, see Joel E. Cohen, *How Many of Us Can the Earth Support?* (New York: W.W. Norton, 1996). Shrewdly, Cohen refuses to give a firm answer.

44. The new nature conservation called "rewilding" seeks to reintroduce ancient and sometimes extinct species to Europe and allow them to reestablish themselves. See the website *Rewilding Europe,* www.rewildingeurope.com, for information on current projects and goals.

45. On the environmental consequences of modern agriculture, see Vandana Shiva, *The Violence of the Green Revolution* (Lexington: University Press of Kentucky, 2016). Also see John H. Perkins, *Geopolitics and the Green Revolution* (New York: Oxford University Press, 1997).

46. Paul Ehrlich, *The Population Bomb* (New York: Ballantine, 1968). See also "Paul Ehrlich on The Population Bomb, 50 Years Later," May 3, 2018, www.climateone.org. According to Ehrlich, over the preceding half century some two hundred million to five hundred million people had "starved to death or died of nutrition-related illness," and things would get even worse. By 2018 about 1.8 billion people were either starving to death or suffering from malnutrition.

47. French scientists wanted to know why fertility had begun falling so early in France and whether that decline could be arrested and the French restored to glory. The historian Ferdinand Braudel answered that "the liberation of [men] from the teachings, the restrictions, and the yoke of the Catholic Church" was responsible; cited in Guillaume Blanc, "The Cultural Origins of the Demographic Transition in France" (2024), https/documents. manchester. ac.uk/display.

48. For a good overview of the theory see John Caldwell, "Toward a Restatement of Demographic Transition Theory," *Population and Development Review* 2 (1976): 321–366; and Frank Notestein, "Economic Problems of Population Change," in *The Evolution of Population Theory,* ed. Johannes Overbeek (Westport, Conn.: Greenwood Press, 1977), 139–152.

49. Controversy over the relation of economic growth to population levels continues, but clearly the level of wealth is not the most reliable indicator of fertility. What matters are the reproductive behaviors among women. See Carl Haub, "The U.S. Recession and the Birth Rate," *Population Research Bureau Report,* https://pbr.org, July 8, 2009.

50. Kingsley Davis, "The World Demographic Transition," *Annals of the American Academy of Political and Social Science* 237 (January 1945): 11. We should base theories on more than one nation's experience. The population of the United States reached 150 million in 1950 and more than doubled in size by 2000. It is now projected to reach 400 million by 2058; Jonathan Vespa et al., "Demographic Turning Points for the United States" (February

2020), www.census.gov/publications. Where is any "world demographic transition" in those numbers?

51. An example of unscientific analysis is a study that reported an increase in the literacy rate of South Asian females from 46 percent in 2000 to 57 percent in 2010, which caused a substantial drop in the fertility rate; Saba M. Sheikh and Tom Loney, "Is Educating Girls the Best Investment for South Asia?," *Public Health* 6 (2018): 172. The facts here do not address what makes fertility drop. Women should be asked about their motivations at the end of their fertile years, not at the beginning. Here feminist assumptions about the importance of liberating girls (which this author shares) may have distorted research into fertility rates.

52. Sandburg, *The People, Yes*, 253–254.

Chapter 8. Building the Ecological Civilization

1. Judith Shapiro, *Mao's War on Nature* (New York: Cambridge University Press, 2001). See also Shapiro, *China's Environmental Challenges*, 3rd ed. (Cambridge: Polity, 2024).

2. "China Population 1950–2024," www.macrotrends.net/global-metrics/countries/CHN/china/population.

3. Long before Thomas Malthus ran afoul of Karl Marx and his followers, China produced its own "Malthusian" prophet, Hong Liangji (1746–1809), a philosophical statesman who was banished by the emperor for his essay "On Governance and Well-being of the Empire" (Zhi Ping Pian), which warned that population growth would one day destroy China.

4. Michael Schoenhals, "Mao Zedong: Speeches at the 1957 'Moscow Conference,'" *Journal of Communist Studies* (1986): 109–126.

5. Richard Jackson, "Ma Yinchu: From Yale to Architect of Chinese Population Policy," *American Journal of Chinese Studies* 19 (April 2012): 47–54; Edgar Snow, "Population Control in China," in *The Population Crisis*, ed. Larry Ng (Bloomington: Indiana University Press, 1965), 102.

6. Daniel Goodkind, "The Astonishing Population Averted by China's Birth Restrictions," *Demography* 54 (2017): 1375.

7. The Brundtland report became the book *Our Common Future: From One Earth to One World*, Report of the World Commission on Environment and Development (New York: Oxford University Press for the United Nations, 1987).

8. *Our Common Future*, 6.

9. On imaginaries, see Sheila Jasonoff and Sang-Hyun Kim, eds., *Dreamscapes of Modernity: Sociotechnical Imaginaries and the Fabrication of Power* (Chicago: University of Chicago Press, 2015). For changing constructs in ecology, see Donald Worster, "The Ecology of Order

and Chaos," in Worster, *The Wealth of Nature: Environmental History and the Ecological Imagination* (New York: Oxford University Press, 1994), 156–170.

10. See Ma Tianjie, "Pan Yue's Vision of Green China," *Dialogue Earth,* March 8, 2016, https://dialogue.earth/en/pollution/8695-pan-yue-s-vision-of-green-china/. See also Mary Evelyn Tucker, "Pan Yue's Vision for Ecological Civilization," December 8, 2008, https://sites.duke.edu/jamesmiller; and Jonathan Watts, "China's Green Champion Sidelined," *Guardian,* March 12, 2009.

11. Wang Lihua, "Chinese Environmental History Research Provides Lessons for the Construction of Ecological Civilization," *Chinese Social Science Today,* http://ex.cssn.cn/zx/bwyc/201908/t20190813_4956425.shtml.

12. For a recent translation see *Zhuangzi: Basic Writings,* trans. Burton Watson (New York: Columbia University Press, 2003).

13. See Martin Schönfeld and Xia Chen, "Daoism and the Prospect of an Ecological Civilization," *Religions* 10 (November 2019): 630; Lloyd Doyle, "Toward an Ecological Civilization: Perspectives from Daoism," *Journal of Daoist Studies* 14 (2021): 221–228; and James Miller, *China's Green Religion: Daoism and the Quest for a Sustainable Future* (New York: Columbia University Press, 2020).

14. Xi Jinping, "Usher in a New Era of Ecological Progress," in Xi, *On Governance* (Beijing: Foreign Language Press, 2014), vol. 1, 231.

15. Xi Jinping, "Secure a Decisive Victory in Building a Moderately Prosperous Society in All Respects and Strive for the Great Success of Socialism with Chinese Characteristics for a New Era," address delivered at the Nineteenth National Congress of the Communist Party of China, October 18, 2017, Chinadaily.com.cn.

16. See Judith Shapiro and Yifei Li, *China Goes Green: Coercive Environmentalism for a Troubled Planet* (Cambridge: Polity, 2020); and Judith Shapiro, *China's Environmental Challenges,* 2nd ed. (Cambridge: Polity, 2015).

17. Steve Harrell, *An Ecological History of China* (Seattle: University of Washington Press, 2023).

18. Iring Fetscher, *Überlebensbedingungen der Menschheit* [Conditions for the Survival of Humanity], 3rd ed. (Berlin: Dietz Verlag, 1991), 7. On Haeckel, see Donald Worster, *Nature's Economy: A History of Ecological Ideas,* 2nd ed. (New York: Cambridge University Press, 1994), 192.

19. Other prominent advocates include the American theologian John Cobb and the Australian philosopher Arran Gare, whose book *The Philosophical Foundations of Ecological Civilization* appeared in 2017. Cobb promotes the ideas of Alfred North Whitehead, while Gare looks to Germany's Friedrich Schelling and postmodernist critics of science. See also

Eileen Crist, *Abundant Earth: Toward an Ecological Civilization* (Chicago: University of Chicago Press, 2019).

20. Rachel Carson, *Silent Spring* (Boston: Houghton Mifflin, 1962), frontispiece; Aldo Leopold, "The Land Ethic," in his *Sand County Almanac* (New York: Oxford University Press, 1949), 201–226.

21. Leopold, *Sand County Almanac*, 203, 204.

22. Leopold, *Sand County Almanac*, 204.

23. Leopold, *Sand County Almanac*, 205.

24. Fetscher, *Überlebensbedingungen der Menschkeit*, 7. See also Theodore Roszak, *The Making of a Counterculture: Reflections on the Technocratic Society and Its Useful Opposition* (New York: Doubleday, 1969).

25. Robert Heilbroner, *An Inquiry into the Human Prospect: Looked at Again for the 1990s* (New York: W.W. Norton, 1991), 30, 132–133. The first edition was published in 1974.

26. Hans Jonas, *The Phenomenon of Life* (New York: Harper and Row, 1966), 26, 282–284.

27. Hans Jonas, *The Imperative of Responsibility: In Search of an Ethics for the Technological Age* (Chicago: University of Chicago Press, 1984), 4. See also Theresa Morris, *Hans Jonas's Ethic of Responsibility: From Ontology to Ecology* (Albany: State University of New York Press, 2013).

28. Jonas, *The Imperative of Responsibility*, 7.

29. Jonas, *The Imperative of Responsibility*, 8, 138.

30. Aaron O'Neill, "Countries with the Largest Gross Domestic Product," September 19, 2024, www.Statista.com/statistics/268173/countries-with-the-largest-gross-domestic-product-gdp/.

Epilogue. This Fertile Earth

1. Environmental historians have done much to expand our sense of the past. In addition to H. G. Wells's pioneering opus *The Outline of History* (London: George Newnes, 1920), see David Christian, *Maps of Time* (Berkeley: University of California Press, 2004); Peter Frankopan, *The Earth Transformed* (New York: Knopf, 2023); Daniel Headrick, *Humans Versus Nature* (New York: Oxford University Press, 2020); J. R. McNeill and William H. McNeill, *The Human Web* (New York: W.W. Norton, 2003); William McNeill et al., *World Environmental History* (Great Barrington, Mass.: Berkshire, 2012); Anthony Penna, *The Human Footprint* (Chichester, U.K.: Wiley-Blackwell, 2010); Clive Ponting, *A New Green History of the World* (New York: Vintage, 2007); Sunil Amrith, *The Burning Earth* (New York: W.W. Norton, 2024); and B. L. Turner et al., eds., *The Earth as Transformed by Human Action* (New York: Cambridge University Press, 1990).

2. See Lawrence J. Henderson, *The Fitness of the Environment* (New York: Macmillan, 1913), an old but still essential book. Henderson, a biochemist at Harvard, applied Darwinian biology to the whole cosmos, but I am content to stay with this planet.

3. See "The Search for Life," https://exoplanets.nasa.gov/search-for-life/can-we-find-life, and Neil deGrasse Tyson, *StarTalk* (Washington, D.C.: National Geographic, 2019).

4. A new and improved natural history can help us know the planet before humans appeared. See the writings of Andrew Knoll, David Beerling, Robert Hazen, Lewis Dartnell, Tim Flannery, Richard Fortey, Richard Dawkins, and Henry Gee. For the rise of a more scientific history of the planet, see Donald Worster, *Shrinking the Earth: The Rise and Decline of American Abundance* (New York: Oxford University Press, 2016), chapter 9, and Paul Warde, Libby Robin, and Sverker Sörlin, *The Environment: A History of the Idea* (Baltimore: Johns Hopkins University Press, 2018).

Acknowledgments

My greatest debt is to Hou Shen, once my student and colleague, now a distinguished senior professor at Peking University and translator of an earlier edition of this book into Mandarin. She is a gifted writer, translator, lecturer, and scholar of great insight. I also want to thank everyone at Renmin University of China, starting with Sun Jiazhou and Huang Xingtao, my deans in the School of History, and including all my colleagues in the department of world history. Also, thanks to the Fund for Building World-Class Universities and Disciplines of Renmin University of China, and to my students and student teaching assistants at that school, including Daqian Lan, Kunyan Zhang, Weilan Ge, Wenzheng Fang, and Xiao Yi.

A long list of other personal friends and former students in China and elsewhere have contributed to my re-education. In China they include Hou Wenhui, Xia Mingfang, Mei Xueqin, Chen Hao, Wang Lihua, Fu Chengshuang, Cao Mu, Gao Guorong, Fei Sheng, Jinghao Sun, and Wu Lingjing. For help in publishing the Chinese edition of this book I thank Hong Ke, a bold thinker and a true lover of books. Not least I thank Jean Thomson Black and others at the Yale University Press who have guided this English-language version into print. I thank also my literary agent, Don Fehr, who has helped me navigate the always shifting book publishing marketplace.

Other debts are obvious in my endnotes, but I want to single out several longtime friends whose advice I cannot credit enough: Adam Rome, Daniel Rodgers, Mark Harvey, John McNeill, Carolyn Merchant, William Cronon,

ACKNOWLEDGMENTS

Dan Flores, Sara Dant, and the late Alfred Crosby. For all those who have aided me, and they are legion, I am immensely grateful.

But in the end, it was growing up on America's western deserts and plains that led me somehow to think on a big scale and imagine a new planetary history. Becoming more aware of the earth and its ecology, I have also come to know and accept my own weaknesses and limits. As any pioneer knows, what counts most is not the harvest one reaps but the seeds one sows.

Index

abortion, 218, 219, 288 n.7
acacia, 19
Adams, Robert, 77
Aden, Gulf of, 34
Africa, 18–19, 28, 32, 93, 100, 228–229; agriculture in, 55–57; emigration from, 26–27, 30, 31, 32–34; Great Rift Valley, 19–20, 21, 29, 48; human origins in, 17–18, 19
agrarianism, 120, 146
agriculture, 41–73; agribusiness, 62–63, 137, 186; by ants, 41–46; dependence on, 63–64; domestication and, 54–55, 63, 64, 68–69; ecological, 190, 191, 199–200; Green Revolution and, 233; human development of, 45, 46–53, 57–58, 65–68; malnutrition and, 65, 66; organic, 183, 205–206; population growth and development of, 57–61
agronomy, 234
air pollution, 103, 153
Akkadian Empire, 76
Alaric, 108
Alexandria, 103
Amazonia, 84, 85–86
Americas, 37–38, 52, 64. *See also* Second Earth
amino acids, 66

Ancón coast, 59
annual plants, 66–67
anteaters (Vermilingua), 43
Anthony, Susan B., 217
Anthropocene, 268 n.1
anti-dualism, 249
Antioch, 103
Antonine Plague, 104
ants, 7; farming by, 41–46
aphids, 42, 46, 55
Arabian Plate, 19
Arendt, Hannah, 254, 255
Argentina, 135
Armada de Molucca, 129
Armelagos, George, 65
artificial selection, 72–73, 220
Attenborough, David, 162
Augustus, Caesar, 95, 105
Australia, 34, 135, 137, 152, 162. *See also* Second Earth
Australopithecus africanus, 20, 21
avocados, 84

baboons, 19
Babylonian Empire, 76
Bacon, Francis, 159–160
Baer, Karl Ernst von, 289 n.10
Bailey, Liberty Hyde, 175

INDEX

bananas, 63, 272 n.14
Bangladesh, 227
Banister, Judith, 201–202
Bantu people, 56
baobab, 19
Barker, Graeme, 61
barley, 49, 55, 63, 64
BASF chemical company, 203
beans, 64, 272 n. 14
Beijing, China, 198
Bellwood, Peter, 46, 50, 52, 272 n.14
Beringia, 37
Berkshire Hills (Massachusetts), 214
Besant, Annie, 216–217, 219, 289 n.12
Bible: Adam and Eve story, 11, 17, 271 n.1; Proverbs, 42
Binford, Lewis R., 58
Biraben, Jean-Noël, 115
birth control, 105–106, 212–213, 215, 217–219, 234, 263, 288 n.7; in China, 242–244, 258. *See also* contraceptives
Bok choy, 205
bonobos, 19
Book of Mencius, 1
Bosch, Carl, 203
Boserup, Ester, 60–61, 80, 100, 151
Bradlaugh, Charles, 216–217, 219, 289 n.12
brain, human, 21–22, 27
Braudel, Ferdinand, 292 n.47
Brazil, 71, 84, 227
breastfeeding, 27
Britain, 52, 71, 111, 116–118, 131, 135, 149–154, 161–162; enclosures, 136, 193; fertility in, 8, 150–151; food importation in, 151–153; habitat shrinkage in, 118; innovation in, 151; population of, 117, 120–121, 133–134, 149–150, 154; science in, 158–160
Brooke, John, 22, 46, 104; *Climate Change and the Course of Global History,* 45

brown soils, 96
Brundtland, Grø Harlem, 237, 245
bubonic plague, 109, 111, 116
Buck, Pearl, 284 n.10; *The Good Earth,* 174
Buck, Philip Losing, 175
buffalo, African, 19

Cabot, John, 131
Caligula (Roman emperor), 91
Cambridge Group for the History of Population and Social Structure, 149, 150
Canada, 136, 162
Canton, China, 111, 171
Cao Mu, 197, 198
capitalism, industrial, 12–13, 113, 143, 144–147, 153, 231, 239; discovery of Second Earth and, 131, 146, 155–156; state-controlled, 241, 252
Caribbean Sea, 127–128
Carneiro, Robert, 75–76, 81–82, 84–85, 86
Carson, Rachel, 237, 254
Carthage, 94, 103
Cato: *Husbandry,* 277 n.33
Cawood, Peter, 268 n.1
Chandrasekhar, Sripati, 218
Chang, Min Chueh (Zhang Mingjue), 222, 223, 224
Charles, Dan, 204
cheetahs, 19
Chernozem soils, 96
chickens, 104, 135
Chillón River, 59
chimpanzees, 19
China, 35, 64, 148, 199–208, 239, 257, 278 n.2; agricultural practices in, 171–176, 177–178, 188; Belt and Road Initiative, 251; birth control in, 242–244, 258; chemical fertilizer used in, 202, 203–205, 206; development of agriculture in,

INDEX

50–52, 188; epidemics in, 111; evolution of state in, 79–81; infanticide in, 221; one-child policy, 242–243, 244; population of, 86, 176, 192, 201–202, 227, 228, 241–243, 258; use of human bodily waste, 164–165, 166, 167–168, 187–198, 205; Warring States period, 248; Xinhai Revolution, 86, 172. *See also* ecological civilization
cholera, 168
Christianity, 108
Chumash people, 17
Cicero, Marcus Tullius, 110, 111–112
circumscription, theory of, 84–86
Claessen, Henri J. M., 87–88
Claudius II (Roman emperor), 108
climate change, 45–46, 51, 102, 227
coal, 153–154
Coale, Ansley, 25
Cobb, John, 294 n.19
coffee, 139
Cohen, Mark Nathan, 58–60, 61; *The Food Crisis in Prehistory*, 57–58, 273 n.25
Colombo, Cristoforo (Christopher Columbus), 124–128, 140
communism, 142–143, 147, 148
competition, 83
composting, 170
condoms, 226
Confucianism, 2
Confucius, 249
Congo, Democratic Republic of the, 29, 227–228
conservationism, 176, 213, 292 n.44
Constantine (Roman emperor), 109
Constantinople, 109, 124
continental drift, 15–16
contraceptives, 224–227; oral, 222–225, 226–227, 290 n.28; types of, 219, 226. *See also* birth control

Cook, James, 131
corn, 64, 66, 272 n.14
cornucopian economics, 61
cotton, 139, 153, 186
cows, 55, 63, 104, 135
coyotes, 233
Cretaceous epoch, 46
Crosby, Alfred, 139
cultural evolution, 114
cultural values, 9
Cyprian's Plague, 104, 107–108

Dalkon shield, 225–226
Dao De Qing, 249
Daoism, 249
Dart, Raymond, 20
Darwin, Charles, 3, 11, 17, 158, 162, 182, 185, 266, 267 nn.5 and 7; and artificial selection, 72, 220; *The Descent of Man*, 3, 8, 9–10, 148; on earthworms and soil formation, 182, 285 n.26; influence of Malthus on, 4–5, 6–10; Marx and, 144, 147–148; offspring of, 8, 150, 268 n.8; *On the Origin of Species*, 3, 72, 147–148
Darwin, Emma Wedgewood, 8
Davis, Kingsley, 236
Dawkins, Richard, 114
deer, 233
deforestation, 118, 119
demographic transition theory, 235–236
Demuth, Helene, 150
Denby, Charles, 174–175
Deng Xiaoping, 241, 242, 243
Denmark, 231
density dependence, 10
deoxyribonucleic acid (DNA), 11–12, 139–140
desertification, 78–79
Diamond, Jared, 50, 52
diarrhea, 106, 168

301

INDEX

disease, 67, 104, 106–107, 120, 138–139, 168. *See also* epidemics
Djerassi, Carl, 224
dogs, 55, 64; wild, 19
Domesday Book, 118
domestication of other species, 54–55, 63, 64, 68–69
Drake, Francis, 130–133, 138, 140
dualism, man-nature, 144–145, 147–148, 247–248, 251–252
ducks, 135
dysentery, 106, 132, 168

Earth Day, 213
ecological civilization, 239, 240, 245–246, 248, 249–252, 253
ecology, 182, 246, 253
Ecumene, 125
Egypt, 19, 81, 101, 105, 106, 162, 227, 288 n.7
Ehrlich, Paul, 292 n.46
elands, 19
elephants, 35
Elizabeth I (queen of England), 131, 133
Elvin, Mark, 81, 178
empires, 76–77, 113. *See also* Roman Empire; states
Engels, Friedrich, 144, 148, 149, 161
England. *See* Britain
Enovid, 224, 225, 227
entropy, 170
environmental degradation, 57
environmentalism, 235
environmental limits, 119, 147, 160–161, 166, 170, 208, 213, 263
epidemics, 67, 97, 104, 106–109; bubonic plague, 109, 111, 116; smallpox, 106–107
erosion, 79, 80, 99, 180–181
estrogen, 224, 290 n.28

Ethiopia, 19, 227
eugenics, 220
Euphrates River, 47, 76
Eurasia, 35–36, 115
Europe, 52, 93, 119
eusociality, 43–44
evolution, 7, 9, 11, 144–145, 185
evolutionary biology, 161, 182
extinction, 16, 260, 261, 264–265

Fairchild, David, 175–176, 179
famine, 120, 152
farming. *See* agriculture
Fertile Crescent, 35, 47, 48, 49, 52
fertility, 64, 262, 287 n.3; breastfeeding and, 27; decreasing rates of, 150–151, 210–214, 236; density dependence and, 10; female control over, 212, 214, 216, 217–219, 235; foraging and, 25–26, 27; modification of, 212; of planet, 260; resources and, 5–7; soil, 183
fertilizer, chemical, 164–165, 202, 203–205, 206
Fetscher, Iring, 253, 255
fire, 31
Flannery, Kent, 58
Flores, Dan, 137
food: desire for, 1, 3, 95–96; importation of, 95, 97, 101, 151–153; supply of, 48, 147, 201
foraging, 12, 19, 23, 27–31, 56, 68; fertility and, 25–26, 27; transition to agriculture, 45, 46–53, 57–58, 65–68
Formicidae family, 41
Foster, John Bellamy, 193
France, 96, 101, 292 n.47
Frankfurt Institute for Social Research, 253
Franklin, Benjamin, 7, 235
Friedan, Betty, 225

INDEX

Galton, Francis, 220, 289 n.20
Gambia, 162
Gaozi, 1, 2, 3, 11
Gare, Arran, 294 n.19
Genoa, Italy, 124
George, Rose, 164, 283 n.4
Gerbilliscus kempi, 107
Germany, 96, 101, 203
geronticide, 30, 67
Ghana, 229
Gibbon, Edward, 90
giraffes, 19
goats, 55, 63, 64
Goodall, Jane, 162
Goodkind, Daniel, 244
goosefoot (*Chenopodium*), 52
gorillas, 19
Gosnold, Bartholomew, 131
grains, 64–65, 66
Graunt, John, 235
Great Plains, 96
Greenland, 121
Green Revolution, 233
Greer, Germaine, 225
Griswold v. Connecticut (1965), 224
Grove, Richard, 213
guinea pigs, 64
Gutenberg, Johannes, 114

Haber, Fritz, 203
Hadrian (Roman emperor), 90
Haeckel, Ernst, 253
Han dynasty, 79–80, 189
Hangzhou, China, 192
Harari, Yuval Noah, 54–55
Hardin, Garrett, 276 n.15
Harper, Kyle: *The Fate of Rome,* 104–105, 106, 108
Hawai'i, 38

Hazda people, 29
Heidegger, Martin, 254
Heilbroner, Robert, 142, 255
Herculano-Houzelm, Suzana, 269 n.10
Hesiod, 70–71
high equilibrium trap, 178, 201
hippopotamus, 19
Ho, Ping-ti (Bingdi He), 50
Hobbs, Thomas, 22–23
Hole, Frank, 49
Holocene epoch, 36, 45, 46
Homer, 92
hominins, 20–21
Homo erectus, 21, 31
Homo ergaster, 21, 31
Homo habilis, 21
Homo heidelbergensis, 21
Homo neanderthalensis, 21, 35
Homo sapiens, 21
Homo sapiens sapiens, 21, 22, 23, 24–25
Hong Kong, 111, 171
Hong Liangji, 293 n.3
Horkheimer, Max, 253–254
horses, 63, 104, 135
Howard, Albert, 182–187, 206–207
Howard Matthaei, Gabrielle, 182, 183, 285 n.27
Howard Matthaei, Louise, 183
Huang Di, 286 n.34
Hughes, Donald, 93
Hu Jintao, 249
human nature, 1–14, 145, 146, 200
"Humpty Dumpty," 74
humus, 183
hutongs, 164
hyenas, 19
Hymenoptera order, 41

303

INDEX

Iberian peninsula, 90, 95, 113, 118–119, 120, 121, 126, 134, 135
ice ages, 35, 123, 133, 261–262
Iceland, 38, 121
impalas, 19
Incan empire, 84–85
India, 52, 111, 162, 182, 186; population of, 201, 227
Indonesia, 34, 52, 227
Indore, India, 182
Industrial Revolution, 154
infanticide, 30, 67, 219, 221
infrastructure, 250, 252
innovation, 31–32, 34, 115–116, 151, 232, 261, 262
International Institute for Applied Systems, 229–230; *Journal of the Royal Statistical Society,* 230
involution, 207
Iran, 243
Iraq, 77
Ireland, 121, 134, 149, 152
iron ore, 152
Israel, 19
Italy, 94, 124, 135, 233

Jacobs, Wilbur, 137
Jacobsen, Thorkild, 77
Jamaica, 38
Japan, 52, 171, 172, 227, 228, 231, 243–244
Jevons, William Stanley, 282 n.13
Jiangnan, China, 171, 190, 191, 194, 196, 199
Jonas, Hans, 254, 255–57
Jordan River, 47, 49
Justinianic Plagues, 104, 109

Kalahari Desert, 26
Kenya, 57, 229
Khrushchev, Nikita S., 242

King, Carrie, 171, 173
King, Franklin H., 171–174, 175–179, 180–181, 190, 191, 195–196, 206–207; *Farmers of Forty Centuries,* 171, 176, 178, 179, 180, 186, 188, 284 n.16
King, Gregory, 135–136
Kinshasa, Democratic Republic of the Congo, 29
Knapp, Seaman, 175
Knowlton, Charles: and guide to birth control, 214–219, 289 n.19
Korea, 52, 172, 228, 243, 244, 278 n.2
kudus, 19
!Kung, 26

Lagos, Nigeria, 29
land: burning of, 31; under agriculture, 62–64, 135–137
land ethic, 254–255
Laozi, 269 n.3
latifundia, 100
lead pollution, 103
leopards, 19
Leopold, Aldo, 254–255
Li Bozhong, 190–191, 194, 199
Libya, 229
Liebig, Justus, 179, 181, 285 n.20
lions, 19
Lisbon, Portugal, 125
Livi-Bacci, Massimo, 134
llamas, 64
loess, 50–51, 79
lomas, 59
Lucretius Carus: *De Rerum Natura,* 98
Lutz, Wolfgang, 229

MacNeish, Richard, 61
Magellan, Ferdinand, 129–130, 140
Magellan Strait, 129
maize, 55, 63, 64, 66, 124

INDEX

malaria, 106, 138
malnutrition, 65
Malthus, Thomas, 5, 60, 215, 216, 235, 267 n.5; Darwin and, 4–5, 6–10; *Essay on Population,* 4, 262
mammoths, 35
manioc (cassava), 63, 64
Mao Zedong, 166, 238, 240, 241, 242, 243
maps, 125–126, 128, 129, 280 nn.16 and 18
Marcus Aurelius, 106
Marcuse, Herbert, 254
Marsh, George Perkins, 213
Marx, Karl, 13, 144–149, 150, 161, 238, 261, 282 n.9; *Capital,* 149, 193–194; *Communist Manifesto,* 142–143, 155, 156, 161, 281 nn.1 and 3
Mauritius, 229
Ma Yinchu, 242, 243
McCormick, Katharine, 222, 224
McCorriston, Joy, 49
Mediterranean Sea, 91–94, 96
Mellars, Paul, 34
memes, 114
Mencius, 1, 2, 3
Meng Haoran, 248
Mesopotamian Empire, 76–78, 288 n.7
metabolic rift, 193, 196
Mexico, 52, 136, 227
Meyer, Frank, 175
Middle East, 64
migration, 32–40, 118, 121, 134, 214; from Africa, 26–27, 30, 31, 32–34; to Americas, 37–38, 52, 134–135; of animals, 37, 38–39
millet, 55, 64, 188; wild, 51, 271 n.11
Ming dynasty, 190, 191, 193, 201
Mississippi Valley, 52
modernization theory, 235–236
Mongolia, 111
moral standard, 2, 3, 133

muck, 164. *See also* waste, human bodily
multilectics, 148

Nanjing, China, 192, 204
Native Americans, 64, 137–138
Natufian people, 49–50
natural selection, 72
nature, 264–266; human control over, 110–111, 145, 250, 251–252, 255; as supreme farmer, 183–185
Needham, Joseph, 173
Nero (Roman emperor), 91
Newfoundland, 121, 162
New Guinea, 272 n.14
New York City, 162
New Zealand, 38, 135, 137, 162
Niger, 229
Nigeria, 29, 162, 227, 228
night soil. *See* waste, human bodily
Nile River, 52, 56, 81, 100
Notestein, Frank, 235
Nubian Plate, 19

Odoacer, 102
Ogutu, Joseph, 57
olives, 64
Opium Wars, 172
origin stories, 16–17
Oryza sativa, 81
Ottoman Empire, 124
Our World in Data, 64
Ouyang Xiu, 248
Oxford English Dictionary, 158

Pacific oyster, 7
pacifist movement, 220–221
Pakistan, 227
Paleocene epoch, 46
Palestine, 19
pandemics, 97

INDEX

Pangea, 15, 16, 18, 41, 92
Panthalassa, 16
Pan Yue, 246–248, 249, 251–252
Pearl, Raymond, 221
peas, 64
perennial plants, 66–67
Pergamum, 103
Perkins, Dwight, 201
Perlin, John, 102
Permian-Triassic Extinction event, 16
Peru, 52, 59, 84–85
Philippines, 52, 227
pigs, 63, 64, 104, 135, 196
Pincus, Gregory, 222–223, 224
Pinker, Steve, 2
plagues. *See* epidemics
plants: annuals and perennials, 66–67; invasive, 139
plate tectonics, 15–16, 19, 36
Pleistocene epoch, 23–24, 32, 33, 45, 46
Pliny the Elder, 94
podzolic soils, 96
Polanyi, Karl, 13
pollution, 103, 153, 165, 168, 227
Ponting, Clive, 268 n.13
population, 138, 176–177, 258; agriculture and, 57–61, 67; of Britain, 117, 120–121, 133–134, 149–150, 154; of China, 86, 176, 192, 201–202, 227, 228, 241–243, 258; decrease of, 116, 118, 210, 230–232, 234; growth of, 34, 46–47, 54, 59, 60, 67, 85, 87, 111, 114–116, 120–121, 123, 139, 149–150, 154, 192, 201–202, 212, 221, 227–229, 241; of India, 201, 227; initial human, 25–26; of Roman Empire, 103, 105–106
Portugal, 118, 125, 129
potatoes, 55, 63, 64, 84, 124; and Irish famine, 152
printing, 114, 278 n.2

progestin, 224, 290 n.28
Ptolemy, Claudius, 125
pumas, 233
pumpkins, 64
Pusa, India, 182

Qin dynasty, 79, 188
Qingdao, China, 171–172
Qing dynasty, 188, 190, 191, 193, 195
Quaternary ice age, 261
quinoa, 84

Raleigh, Walter, 131
Raynal, Guillaume-Thomas, 156–157
religion, 88, 108
reproduction, 209–210; desire for children, 1, 3, 11–12. *See also* fertility
rewilding, 292 n.44
rhinoceros, 19, 22
Ricci, Matteo, 280 n.18
rice, 55, 56, 63, 64, 66, 81, 139, 178, 188; wild, 51, 55, 271 n.11
rice paddies, 81
Richard III (king of England), 74
Rock, John, 223, 224
Roman Climate Optimum (RCO), 102
Roman Empire, 74, 89–91, 94–112; disease in, 97, 104, 106; fall of, 91, 95–97, 101, 102–103, 109; food production in, 97–101; growth of, 94–95; population of, 103, 105–106; size of, 90; soil degradation in, 96–97
Romania, 101
Romulus Augustus, 102
Roosevelt, Theodore, 257, 258
Russia, 99, 148, 227

Sabrosa, Portugal, 129
Sahlins, Marshall, 28, 29, 30, 47, 65
Sahul subcontinent, 34

INDEX

salinization, 77–78, 96
Sandburg, Carl, 210–212, 237
Sanger, Margaret, 221–222, 237, 263
Sargon the Great, 76–77
Schweitzer, Albert, 254
Science for the People, 225
scientific revolution, 157–160
Scotland, 134, 149, 158
Scott, James C., 65
Second Earth, 121–124, 129, 139–41, 146, 149, 155–157, 159
Septimius Severus (Roman emperor), 101
sexual desire, 1, 11, 13, 50, 53–54, 59
sexual selection, and "secondary" sexual characteristics, 10
Shakespeare, William, 117
Shang dynasty, 79, 189
Shanghai, China, 171, 198, 230
Shapiro, Judith, 240
sheep, 55, 63, 64, 104, 135, 196
Shelley, Percy Bysshe, 75
shengtai wenming. *See* ecological civilization
Sicily, 94
siltation, 78, 80, 96
Simkhovitch, Vladimir, 97, 98, 100, 277 n.33
Singapore, 228, 243
Sixie Jia, 283 n.5
slavery, 99; abolition of, 217; of aphids, by ants, 42, 46; domestication of plants and animals and, 68–69, 71–72; human, 69–72, 138–139
smallpox, 106–107
Smith, Adam: *The Wealth of Nations*, 155–156
Smith, Bruce, 47–48
Snow, Edgar, 242
social coercion, 99. *See also* slavery

soil additives, 189, 190, 283 n.5; chemical fertilizer, 164–165, 202, 203–205, 206; human bodily waste, 164, 169–170, 173, 178, 179–180, 187–198, 205
soils, 102, 181; brown, 96; Chernozem, 96; degradation of, 77–79, 96–97, 98, 120; depletion of, 96, 97, 98–99, 120, 187; erosion of, 79, 80, 99, 180–181; loess, 50–51, 79; podzolic, 96; quality of, 183; terra rosa, 94, 96
Somalian Plate, 19
Song dynasty, 80, 190, 248
sorghum, 56, 63
South Africa, 162, 229
South Korea, 228, 243, 244
soybeans, 63, 64
Spain, 85, 118, 125, 127, 129, 130
squash (*Cucurbita*), 52, 64, 272 n.14
states, 74–112, 258; definition of, 76; growth of, 87–89; as protectors, 82–84, 88–89; reasons for, 82–84; vulnerabilities of, 74–75. *See also* Roman Empire
sterilization, 226
Sudan, 19, 162
sugar beet, 63
sugar cane, 63, 139, 272 n.14
Sumatra, 24
Sumer, 76
sunflowers (*Helianthus*), 52
Sun Yat-Sen, 172
Su Shi, 248
sustainability, 59, 183–184, 244, 262
sustainable development, 162, 244–245
Suzhou, China, 192, 195, 198
sweet potato, 63
Switzerland, 233

Tai Lake, 205
Taiwan, 111
Tan brothers, 190–191

INDEX

Tang dynasty, 248
Tanzania, 19
taro, 272 no.14
tea, 153
terra rossa, 94, 96
Tethys Ocean, 92–93
Thomas, Brinley, 149, 151, 154
Thoreau, Henry David, 213
Tianjin, China, 172, 197–198
tigers, 22, 35
Tigris River, 47, 76
timber, 102, 152
Toba volcano, 24
tomatoes, 64, 84, 124
tools, 32, 49
Toscanelli, Paolo dal Pozzo, 126, 127
tuberculosis, 106
Tunisia, 94, 229
Turner, J. M. W., 162
typhoid, 106
typhus, 168

Uganda, 162
Ukraine, 96
United Nations, 78–79; Conference on the Human Environment, 244; Food and Agriculture Organization, 60; *Our Common Future*, 245; Population Division, 229
United States, 136, 152, 162, 176–177, 227

Vespucci, Amerigo, 280 n.16
Vietnam, 228, 243
Vikings, 121, 125
violence, 83
Visigoths, 108
Voltaire, 158–159

Waldseemüller, Martin, 280 n.16
Wang Lihua, 189, 248
Wang Wei, 248
waste, human bodily, 164–171; composition of, 168, 179; as fertilizer, 164, 169–170, 173, 178, 179–180, 187–198, 205; as pollutant, 168–169, 203; trade in, 191–193, 194–198; use in China, 164–165, 166, 167–168, 187–198, 205
Wegener, Alfred, 16
Wei River, 50
Westphalen, Jenny von, 150
wheat, 49, 55, 63, 64, 66, 78, 152, 153, 178, 188; Roman Empire and, 94, 95, 96, 97, 100–101
wildebeests, 19
wilderness, 64
Wilkinson, Richard, 152
William of Ockham, 47
Wilson, Edward O., 43
wolves, 233
women, 236–267; and control over fertility, 212, 214, 216, 217–219, 235
women's rights movement, 217, 221
wood, 102, 152
wool, 152
Wootton, David, 159
Worcester Foundation for Experimental Biology, 223
Wordsworth, William, 162
World Bank, 284 n.15
Worldometer Population Clock, 227
World Population Conference (WPC), 221
Wrigley, Anthony, 119–120

Xia dynasty, 79, 286 n.34
Xi Jinping, 241, 250–251, 252, 257, 258

yams, 56
Yangzi River, 50, 51, 80, 171, 192
yellow fever, 138

INDEX

Yellow River, 50, 51, 79, 80, 180
Yersinia pestis, 109
Yokohama, Japan, 171
Younger Dryas cold period, 46
Yu the Great, 79

zebras, 19
Zheng He, 126, 279 n.13
Zhou dynasty, 79, 189
Zhou Enlai, 242, 243
Zhuangzi (Zhuang Zhou), 248–249